BLESSED FOOTSTEPS

To: Mrs. Vicki

Thank you so much for having me at the bookstore. I am so grateful and humbly thankful for all your support. It truly means a lot to me.

All the best,

JR Holden

D1454027

BLESSED FOOTSTEPS

Memoirs of J.R. Holden

JON-ROBERT HOLDEN

Printed in the United States of America

ISBN-13: 9780615372877

Library of Congress Control Number: 2010934913

To my loving daughter, my princess, you're daddy's world, your dreams are my dreams, you're the miracle of life that love has made and God has blessed me with. I love you.

Preface

THE GAME OF basketball was invented in 1891 by Dr. James Naismith, in Springfield, Massachusetts. Dr. Naismith later moved to Kansas and it was there that John McLendon became a student of the game. And even though McLendon wasn't allowed to play basketball (because he was African-American), Coach Naismith took an interest in him and taught him the intricacies of the game.

Later, Coach McLendon would be the one to teach me and others this game, now known around the world. And as one of the first African-American coaches in the south (University of South Carolina under Coach Frank McGuire in 1973), I have seen a lot of things change in the game—some good and some bad. Coach McLendon always talked to us about the "Globalization of Basketball" but in the 1940s–1950s we couldn't really comprehend what he was saying. He would always say that one day we would see American kids playing basketball in Europe, Asia, and all over the world; and those youngsters would be getting scholarships to our universities and playing in the NBA. Today it is apparent that Coach McLendon's vision is alive and well in the spirit and play of athletes like J.R. Holden. He was one of the rare ones—a pioneer.

I met J.R. through his brother Darius and after researching his accomplishments I thought to myself, "John McLendon, here is your man right here!" Coach McLendon used to say that the ball is mightier than the gun, and J.R. can do more with that basketball than any politician or

CIA agent could to bridge cultures from around the world. He is and should be recognized as an ambassador of the game!

To J.R. Holden

I wish to express my appreciation to you for helping to globalize the great game of basketball. Every time an American player applies his craft in another country, it helps make the world smaller, bringing nations, cultures, and humanity closer. The complete globalization of the game has always been my hope. You have helped pave the way for other young Americans.

God Bless
Coach Ben Jobe

Foreword

When a child is born, you hope he will be healthy, happy, and a good citizen of the community. My son has grown to be a good citizen of the world.

I love him and I'm proud of him and all that he has accomplished.

It's a Boy!!!

In the late 1960s, I had thoughts about being a dad, and not knowing exactly what it meant, but like many men, I wanted a son. At the hospital I remember the joy, the fear, and the expectations. Marvin, my brother-in-law, said my son had blue eyes. That was Marvin—cracking jokes to lighten the mood. My answer to that joke was, I don't care what eyes he has, he's mine—no matter what he looks like. My friend John brought a bottle of Chivas Regal to the waiting room to celebrate my son's birth. We prayed for his health, and just as important, for the health of my wife. It was a good day; it was a very good day!

Ephesians 6:4 Fathers, do not exasperate your children; instead, bring them up in the training and instruction of the Lord.

Boop's life in sports began at the age of 6, in the footsteps of his older brother, Warren, playing midget football. He loved running the drills and practicing with the team. But what stood out was how good he was at motivating the team. At the age of 8, my son earned a starting spot playing on the Allies—a team with 9- and 10-year-old players. I remember a playoff game on a rainy, cold November morning in McKeesport, Pennsylvania. The field was wet and our star running back fumbled the ball late in a 7–6 game; it looked like a sure loss for us at that point. Onto the field went the defense for one more possible chance to save the game, but the star running back and best defensive linebacker was pouting because of his fumble. That's when my son, the smallest kid on the field, grabbed his face mask and encouraged him to step up, quit crying, and win the game. Well, we won the game by a forced fumble. Without question, the win was nice, but I was elated and proud to see my son's early leadership skills.

After football he played baseball for a couple of years. Boop was never going to choose baseball as a career; I believe he may have played just to make his dad happy, and by age 13 he found his true love, basketball. Baseball became a distant memory.

As a 9th grade starting point guard on both the junior varsity and varsity basketball teams at Wilkinsburg High School, my son learned a tough lesson. He lost to older, bigger, and faster kids. He never liked losing, so he learned to play smarter and harder and be more disciplined at his craft. By the 10th grade, Boop had transferred to Linsly High School in Wheeling, West Virginia, about 80 miles south of Pittsburgh. At Linsly, he continued to learn that hard work pays off. In his senior year, they won the Private School League championship.

Proverbs 22:6 Train a child in the way he should go, and when he is old he will not turn from it.

While attending Bucknell University, my son had the opportunity to show off his growing talent against some of the best; he helped put Bucknell University on the NCAA map (A Patriot League team beating an SEC team—Alabama). I traveled to almost every game—home and away—during his junior and senior years because I wanted him to know that he had his biggest supporter in the crowd at every game. Sometimes I would have to sneak away from work early in the company van to see my son play. Not wanting to take away from his focus on the game,

I would try and sit way up in the stands in hopes of going unnoticed, but before long, his teammates would be pointing me out, letting Boop know that I was there. To me, it didn't matter if the game was 20 minutes away or a 12-hour flight away; I simply wanted my son to know that no matter the outcome—I was going to be there for him—with him. A father's love for his son many times can't be explained, so I tried to show him that what he wanted, I wanted. And his basketball journey was just another adventure we would share together as this gave him an avenue to explore a pro career.

> *1 Thessalonians 2:11-12 For you know that we dealt with each of you as a father deals with his own children, encouraging, comforting and urging you to live lives worthy of God, who calls you into his kingdom and glory.*

From the great loss at the Final Four in Moscow, to the great victory in Prague, I have marveled at my son's talent, his drive, and mastery of the game he loves. This path he has chosen has led him to become one of the best overall guards in Europe—each challenge greater than the one before it. I have watched him grow into manhood and remembered the baby boy we brought home. I wish I could start this journey all over again. Not to change anything, but relive it; enjoy it and marvel in it once again. I have always loved him. What he has accomplished brings me so much joy because it's what he wanted to do.

> *Malachi 2:15 Has not [the LORD] made them one? In flesh and spirit they are his. And why one? Because he was seeking godly offspring.*

My one word of advice is to enjoy the ride of life. Kids are all different and if you get a chance to call one yours, remember this—what they become is in part dependent on what they see and learn—even from you.

Robert L. Holden

1 | **Getting Here**

It was a hot summer day. As I took my seat on the aircraft, I began to anticipate our next destination. The flight wasn't going to be long, so as soon as I strapped myself in, I closed my eyes and drifted into deep thought about the tough opposition that had brought us to this point.

My first thought was of the intense competition my comrades and I had just faced. They were considered to be the greatest spectacle the world had seen. They were viewed as giants and known simply as the "Redeem Team." They were a group of elites assembled to erase all doubt that they were superior at their craft. As the floor general, I was expected to take my team into battle and give some form of hope that we could stand our ground against such an amazing force. Through life's many battles, I learned not to fear competition, and I had prepared myself to be in the best shape humanly possible. Facing these so-called giants was just another obstacle for me—another hurdle I needed to get over to reach my destination—to be considered one of the best at what I do. In spite of my personal outlook on this group of elites, I could see the fear in the eyes of some of my team. Some, I could tell were in awe at the mere presence of such phenomenal opposition; but the mere thought of clashing with these elites excited me to a point that I could hear my heart racing. I wanted to make my presence felt from the beginning—and so I did.

While anticipating the start of this contest, my mind would often drift to the biblical story of how the boy, David, defeated the giant Goliath. I asked myself—would it be written that I could possibly achieve as colossal a victory as David? Would my name be placed in history as the one who took down the unstoppable and done the unthinkable? Could we REALLY do this? COULD WE? No, we couldn't! The giants defeated us—but it wasn't an easy task for them—because we refused to go down without a fight. We, as a unit, found no victory; there was no real comfort in my knowing that I had made a valiant effort to overthrow the unbeatable. I found no relief in losing a tough battle but knew that I had but a short time to dwell on defeat. Lurking in the midst was another fierce competitor—one that wasn't as powerful as our previous adversary, but just as potent. Our next game was against China's finest. We were to take our competitive edge on their soil. Fueled by the spoils handed to us previously, we were determined not to suffer another defeat. We battled privately, where no wandering eyes could witness our victory or vanquish. We readily defeated our opponents, but it was a battle all the same. I could see the positive effects of going against a force as powerful as the "Redeem Team," and how it had strengthened our outfit. I felt as though we were ready to accomplish the goals waiting to be achieved by us.

My recollection of these events was abruptly interrupted—I noticed that it was time to exit the aircraft. As the doors to the plane opened, an extreme heat greeted me—a hot and muggy heat—one that can only be experienced in the southernmost parts of the United States at the height of summer—the type of heat and humidity that takes your breath away. After gathering my belongings (and breath), I was shocked by what looked to be a sea of people. They were all dressed in uniforms of light blue tops—directing, escorting, assisting, and guiding any and everyone who didn't have on the same color uniform. I was amazed at the scale of this organized chaos. The amount of energy and level of excitement with which these people assisted us was nothing I had seen before. Everyone seemed to have a position and a role to play, and they were playing it with precision.

Once we had our luggage we then traveled to what looked to be some type of checkpoint. We all had to get clearance and accreditations to travel further. It was a very thorough procedure and once we all had been cleared, we were put on another bus to take us to our final destination. We had not traveled far before we arrived at some towering brick structures. There had to be at least 150 of these buildings. One of the first things that caught my attention were the flags—flags of every imaginable color. Each of these flags represented 1 of the 203 countries present. I suddenly saw my flag, but I only noticed one of them. My eyes began to search feverishly for the other flag. I then asked why there wasn't a flag representing my birthplace? Since the beginning of my travels abroad, seeing the USA flag or meeting people from my birthplace always made me feel safer. It was as if I had a little piece of home with me no matter where I was. So not seeing the USA flag startled me and left me wondering why it wasn't represented. And even though initially I wasn't provided an explanation, I later found out that it wasn't there for safety reasons. No other explanation was provided, and I was left feeling very disappointed. In any case, the flags signified where everyone was staying. So, for the protection and safety of my U.S. family, their dwelling place had to be kept somewhat private. This left me with a funny feeling inside, but, I was here to do a job!

Upon arrival at the building where we were to stay, I was ushered inside and quickly shown our sleeping quarters. Prior to our arrival, I learned that I would be sharing my room with someone else, and I could choose my roommate. I chose a guy by the name of Victor and he was of mixed descent—half African and half Russian. Victor spoke English quite well, and I was very comfortable sharing a room with him. Our living arrangement was designed efficiently; there were 20 of us confined to one floor. When I opened the door to my room, I saw twin beds, a cupboard that we were to share, a window, and a bathroom that would be used by me as well as 3 others. This was no luxury hotel by any stretch of the imagination, but it would suffice. I had seen and experienced much worse.

As I began to look around the colorless room, I experienced a moment of confusion—WHERE was I? WHAT was I doing here? And finally, HOW did I get here? I lay down on my bed hoping for a moment of clarity, when I heard commotion in the distance. I walked to the window and looked out over the expanse below. I saw a vast landscape occupied by a massive amount of people. People of all races, colors, ethnicities, sizes, and shapes were walking around feverishly, as if they had somewhere important to be. It was at that point I remembered my purpose for being here. I was in Beijing, China—at the 2008 Summer Olympics. I was here to lead my team, the Russian Men's National Basketball Team, to win a medal in Men's Basketball in front of the entire world! I was a proud black AMERICAN who had received RUSSIAN citizenship a few years before with the belief and trust that one day I would be here representing my other country in the Beijing Olympics!

So how did my life's travels bring me to Beijing, China? Well to get here, one has to start at the beginning. I was born on August 10, 1976, and weighed in at 7 pounds 15 ounces. I was born in St. Francis Hospital in Pittsburgh, Pennsylvania, to proud parents Regelia and Robert Holden. My mom says that my name, Jon-Robert, came from my older brother, Warren, and my father. My dad wanted me to be a "junior" but my mom wanted my brother and me to be close as we had different fathers. Warren's middle name is Jon and because my dad's first name is Robert, my dad decided to take my brother's middle name and his first name and make them my first name. Thus, Jon-Robert was born! I don't have a middle name, even though most people think my first name is Jon and my middle name is Robert. This is not the case.

My birth name had little bearing on me growing up and that was mainly because everyone in the neighborhood knew and called me by my nickname—"Booper." No one even knew what my real name was. I guess because I came out of the womb with everyone calling me "Booper"; it just stuck! I got my nickname while my mom was pregnant. My twin cousins, Marcia and Margarite, are responsible for it.

The day before my mom went into the hospital to have me, the twins asked if they could give me a nickname. They wrote down a few names that they liked and put them in a bag. At the hospital, all the family and closest friends added their nickname ideas to the bag as well. Anyway, in the morning, one of the twins picked a name out of the bag and it was one of their names, "Booper." She put the name back in the bag and that afternoon the other twin picked a name out of the bag. Lo and behold, it was the same name. So, Booper was the nickname of choice. Obviously, this pleased Marcia and Margarite to no end. In fact, to this day, they still remind me of this story AND—the nickname has stuck with me!

So there I was, brought into this world by two loving parents, an older brother to protect me, and soon followed by a younger sister for me to protect as well. I guess you can say I was dealt the upper hand in life—being born into such a loving family.

In my early years, I don't remember much, but I do recall spending a lot of time with my father. I was without a doubt, a daddy's boy. I was connected to my dad's hip. I was his little man. My dad would play cards with his friends, drink, and just enjoy a Saturday night with his buddies. I would be right in his lap. He would watch a Pittsburgh Steelers' football game on a Sunday afternoon and I would be right beside him. I never left my father's side as a young buck. I did everything he did. I wanted to be just like him. I guess it was destined because I am a lot like him to this day.

My parents were separated by the time I was 7 years old, but their separation never had a negative effect on me. My father made sure of that. Even though he didn't live with us, he was around all the time. He was there whenever the family needed him. My dad is a great father and provider—everything a son could ask for. I don't know how he was as a husband to my mom, but as a father, he was second to none.

My dad was the quiet, reserved, and introverted one; my mom was the exact opposite—always the life of the party. She was upbeat, energetic, and full of life and love. She has always pushed me to try new things, to never quit anything that I started, and as cliché as it may sound, to always be the best I can be. She would attend everything I participated in. She would show up at my elementary school waving and shouting, saying how proud she was of me, even if I just received the smallest award. It could be perfect attendance in kindergarten, and my mom would celebrate like I had just won the Nobel prize. She adored all of her children and even showed a great deal of love to other people's children as well.

My mom would show this to me in a big way when she would take in my best friend and allow him to become a part of our family when his family situation fell apart. She has always had a big heart—full of life and love; she is the same upbeat, kindhearted person to this day.

My sister Robyn and I were like Frick and Frack growing up. Robyn is two years younger than I am and we have a tight relationship—to this day.

I always played sports and she was always a cheerleader, so we were always in close proximity. I remember one day when I was 9 or 10 years old, Robyn and I were racing down the street. She was fast like me, so I had to really run to beat her. Anyway, while running, Robyn tripped and fell hard to the pavement. She skinned up her knees and face a little bit. I was afraid that she was seriously hurt. I was scared. I picked her up as she cried and I started to cry with her. I wasn't hurt, but she was, so I figured we should both cry. She was my sister and also my best friend—and that is what best friends do, cry for each other. She got up and we walked home—both of us in tears. This was just one of many moments and times that we were like one. We were as thick as thieves. Our relationship has always been that way and remains the same. Our love and bond are just that strong.

My brother, Warren, was the eldest child. He was 7 years older than I, so I couldn't really hang out with him or his friends until I got older. I remember him trying to show me different things when I was 10 or 11 years old. He would show me how to fight, how to play sports, and most importantly, how to beat my friends at Nintendo video games.

I'm talking about a time when video games were made for kids! You didn't need an associate's degree to play the games. And as kids, we didn't care how real the players looked. Your goal, if you were playing football, was to get Bo Jackson or Walter Payton to the top of the screen—and it was TOUCHDOWN! We really only played sports games on Nintendo. We had two favorite games: Double Dribble, a basketball game, and Tecmo Bowl, a football game. Warren would kick my butt in the video games and frustrate me. He would keep beating me until I would almost be in tears. Even at 10 years old, I hated to lose and would try and learn the strategies he used to make the plays I needed to use in order to win the game. In retrospect, my "demoralization" helped me dominate my friends in the same games. I would use Warren's team and try to do all the things he did to me, to my friends. My friends and I would play video games for hours. Then I would wait for Warren to get home so I could try and beat him. Most nights he would laugh and say he wasn't going to play me. Then other times he would say, "You gotta do the dishes if

I win, wash my car if I win, or make me a sandwich if I win this game," I didn't care what I had to do if I lost, I just wanted the opportunity to play and beat him.

He would beat me every time—until it happened—the day that all younger brothers dream of. I still remember how crazy I became the first time I beat him in Tecmo Bowl. I can remember it like it was yesterday.

We were playing; he was the San Francisco 49ers and I was the Chicago Bears. I was playing tough, but he was winning, so he was just being his normal cool self. Then the phone rang. Uh oh, could this be the help I needed, a little distraction? He started talking on the phone and slowly but surely I started to take control of the game. He was paying attention but not 100 percent. I started yelling every time my team made a play. I grew excited and I felt the tide turning for my team. He started to get a little agitated but he stayed on the phone, playing it cool. At age 17, guys have to be cool when talking to girls on the phone, so obviously Warren had to keep his composure. At age 10, I wasn't cool yet or really into girls so to me this was like a gift from the video gods!

All of a sudden, he was off the phone and into the game. He was on edge and it was starting to look like I was going to pull off the upset. He made a stupid mistake trying to make a big play really fast. I then had total control of my destiny, defeating him for the first time. I jumped up and down and yelled. I pointed my finger at myself saying, "Who's the man, who's the man?" Warren was pissed off, I could tell, but I didn't care. With about 20 seconds left in the game he clicked the game off—or as we say in the hood, if you stop the game before the clock says 0:00, tap out! I started running full speed up the steps, screaming. I could tell my sister and mom that I beat Warren in Tecmo Bowl. I acted like I had just won the NFL Super Bowl. I jumped on my bed. My mom looked at me like I was crazy—smiling and telling me to calm down. My sister looked at me like, "Who cares?" I was the happiest little dude in the world that night. I finally had beaten my hero, my teacher—my big brother.

I grew up in Wilkinsburg, a borough on the east side of Pittsburgh, Pennsylvania. I loved my home town. My family and I lived on Franklin Avenue—a fun street to live on for an active kid. It had 2 sides. You had the end that was more geared to kids playing and having a good time—just everyday blue-collar working class families trying to make ends meet. Fortunately for me, we lived on this end of the street. The bottom end of Franklin Avenue wasn't the same. There was a lot more crime, drugs, and other stuff like that. I didn't bother with all that for many reasons—I was a sportsman, and most of the kids who sold drugs or who were into that kind of thing liked me and encouraged me to stay away from that kind of stuff. They wanted me to make it out of the neighborhood. I was the smart, athletic kid who most everybody kind of liked. I was rather quiet like my Pops, but I did like being around the other kids. I loved playing sports, hide-and-seek with the girls, or just sitting in someone's house on the block playing Nintendo. Like any kid, I had a few altercations and run-ins with kids who didn't like me, for whatever reason. I simply chalked these squabbles up to kids being kids. When I look back on it now, as a man, I realize that I'm blessed to have made it out of there and to have had the success that I have.

Back when I was growing up, hearing the sound of gunfire and see-ing drug deals go down, I didn't realize how difficult it was for a lot of people to get out of the "hood" and away from that lifestyle. A lot of the things that I was subjected to every day, I deemed as normal—what most children experienced growing up. For instance, I didn't realize at the time that all kids (regardless of how far away from school you lived) didn't walk to school. There wasn't a bus system in Wilkinsburg, so to get to school, you either walked or hitched a ride. Walking didn't come without its own set of dangers.

My parents tell the story of a young girl who lived on our street who was kidnapped while walking to school. The incident took place when I was just an infant. The girl was around my older brother's age. The elementary school she attended wasn't 5 minutes from her house. Unfortunately, she never made it to school that day and was never found. I sometimes ponder what if? What if that would have been me or my sister walking home or walking to school and never made it? How then would my story read—or would I even have a story to tell?

I also remember playing basketball at my school playground and everyone having to lie down on the pavement quickly when we heard gunfire. All of our bodies had to hit the pavement swiftly because we had no idea where the gunshots were coming from. Even worse, it was a normal occurrence to see a fight break out and someone get severely beaten. What wasn't normal was our reaction to the fights; we would just walk away. Unless the fight involved one of your close friends and/or family members, you didn't jump in or get involved to help the injured party. You just stayed out of it and pretended like you didn't see anything.

This mentality kept the neighborhood kids safe as we learned from the environment we lived in. We learned to be street-smart (to always be aware of our surroundings); to never show fear; to be cautious, to act like we belonged; and to know who to interact with—dealings with the wrong person could get you in to some serious trouble. I experienced genuine love in our neighborhood and I could be true to myself. I could hang out with the nerds and the hustlers. All in all, my neighborhood showed me the good and bad that came with trying to live the best life you can.

As a kid growing up near Pittsburgh during the late 1970s you pretty much had to be a sports lover. The Steelers were winning Super Bowls and the Pirates were winning World Series. I guess you could say the city was full of itself and sports talk was the buzz all over the city. I caught that buzz at a very early age and kept it through much of my childhood. During that time, most kids either played football or baseball. I had an older brother who was active in sports and anything he did I wanted to do as well. I was raised by parents who always showed support for anything their children were involved in—I was ALWAYS around some sports event. My passion for sports developed at an extremely early age. I grew up being a three-sports person: football, baseball, and later on basketball.

I was playing Pee Wee/Midget football when I was 3 years old. I would go to every practice my brother had and just sit on the bench. Warren was 9 years old at the time, and I just wanted to be there to watch him. My dad realized I loved football so much that he decided to buy me my first football uniform. It was a Pittsburgh Steelers uniform with the #32. That jersey number belonged to my favorite player at the time—the legendary Franco Harris. When I was 5, I still wasn't old enough to play, but I reported to the field faithfully each day. So, the team presented me with an official Wilkinsburg uniform and sort of made me the mascot.

In fact, my family has a photograph of me running for an extra point as a 5-year-old, in one football game. I was so excited!

Early on, most of Warren's teammates' parents thought I was destined to be a football success. They would come up to my mom and dad and say, "He is going to be a star one day; he loves the game so much." My parents would just laugh. All they wanted was for me to participate in activities and be active. All I knew at the time was that I wanted to follow my brother around and do whatever he was doing. He was my big brother and I just wanted to be like him. If he had a game at the field, you could expect that our whole family would be there to support him. That was just how our family did things. Then, when I turned 6 years old and was finally old enough to actually play on one of the football teams, something really ironic happened—I refused to play. I didn't tell my mom or dad why, but I told them I wanted to take the year off. To this day, they don't know why I didn't play that year, and the funny thing is, I don't know either.

The next year, my father worked as an assistant coaching for the older kids and wanted me to join his team. I was hesitant at first because he told me I probably wouldn't play. As a kid, I thought that kind of sucked. On the flip side, I could play football for the All-Americans (an age group one level up from where I should be playing). In my eyes, they were the big boys. That made me feel even more special as a young player, so I told my dad that I was OK with moving up a level and didn't care if I played that much. A crazy thing happened that season—I ended up starting every game as a 7-year-old.

My dad did everything he could to help each kid reach his potential playing football for us. For instance, one boy named Franklin wasn't very fortunate financially, but he had a lot of talent. He was also a naturally big kid, not overweight, but chiseled. Anyway, he needed help making the weight limit. Players had to maintain an ideal weight in order to play in the game. Franklin wasn't fat, but being a naturally big kid, he had to lose a few pounds to play in the game every week. Because he couldn't really eat healthy due to his circumstances, my dad decided to step in and help him make the weight limit.

As a young black kid in the inner city, you ate what your mom cooked. You didn't eat salads and fruit if she didn't fix that or have it in the house.

Not knowing if this were true in Franklin's case, my dad brought him fruit and salads every day. We would take him home after football practice, and I would run with him around a basketball court near his house for 30 to 45 minutes while he wore a garbage bag under his clothes to help him lose weight. Needless to say, Franklin made it under the weight limit all year. It wasn't easy, but he just needed someone to encourage him, to really care about him, and to push him a little bit. Franklin helped us to be a great team.

Years later when I ran into Franklin as a college football player, he told me how much that time my dad and I spent with him meant to him. He said he became a better person and football player because of it. That experience showed him that it took discipline and hard work to be successful, and he wasn't afraid to be successful. Many NFL scouts said that he had NFL potential, but he never got the chance. Franklin was killed in a drive-by shooting, I believe, outside of his mom's house. He was an innocent bystander. It hurt my dad and me when we heard the news. He was a good kid in college, trying to do the right thing. My heart still goes out to his family.

Pee Wee football in Pittsburgh also afforded me the opportunity to play against and see future NFL players during their early years. I played against NFL player Mike Logan who played for West Mifflin at the time. NFL Future Hall of Famer Curtis Martin played for McKeesport when he was 12 or 13 years old. Current Steeler Charlie Batch and a few other NFL players also played in the league. The talent in Pittsburgh was the real deal. There were also many special players I got to see play at a young age who never played in the NFL. The talent and competition made me tough and pushed me to try and reach my full potential.

Whenever football season ended, it was time for baseball. I started playing "tee-ball" at the age of 6. Again, I found myself playing baseball because Warren played. I thought baseball was easier to play because there was no real contact. Don't misunderstand me, it takes real skills to play baseball; it just wasn't as physical as football. The one thing I couldn't do very well was hit the ball. Hitting was my weakness. On the other hand, I could catch the ball with the best of them. From an early age, because of my speed and eye–hand coordination, I always played the skilled and key positions. I was a catcher, short stop, second baseman, and center fielder. I enjoyed playing baseball, but I really didn't love it the way I did football.

As I got older, I started to follow professional players I wanted to emulate. My favorite was short stop, Ozzie "The Wizard" Smith. He was incredible, and I practiced every day trying to do what he did on the field. He made plays that were extremely difficult, look easy, and he was so smooth. That was my man, and I would work hard believing that when the games started and I was playing short stop, I was him, not "Booper." In spite of this, the older I got, the less I loved playing baseball. I just didn't have a passion for the game. By age 14, I was simply playing baseball because I thought my dad wanted me to. Once I got his blessing to stop, baseball was finished for me.

11 | A Passion Is Born

As a child, I had some interest in basketball, but it was nothing serious. We had a hoop on our garage where Warren used to play some ball. Of course, that enticed me to shoot hoops as well. However, he never would let me play with him, but when he was gone, I would go out there and play by myself. Sometimes my mom would force Warren to let me get some shots up, in between the games he played with his friends. I just wanted to be out there because he was out there. With kids my age, sometimes I would go to the Johnston Elementary School playground at the end of my street to play some ball. I thought I was pretty decent in basketball because most of my friends couldn't beat me. Plus, the older kids always picked me first from my age group when they wanted youngsters to play with them. I liked basketball, but I always considered football my sport. Basketball was more like a hobby to me, until I ran into a kid named Glen.

I was around 11 or 12 years old and on my way to play basketball with a few friends from my neighborhood, when I saw a boy around my age delivering newspapers. I can't remember how we engaged in conversation, but I believe it was just the normal interaction when you see a kid your age, you say, "What's up?" I believe he asked me where was I going to play ball. He said his name was Glen. He might come play ball later with my friends and me, but first he had to do his paper route. I said, "OK," and that maybe I would see him later. I never thought I would see the kid again. I knew all the kids my age in Wilkinsburg, but I didn't know him. I assumed he must have just moved to the neighborhood.

A few hours later Glen popped up at the fence of the playground and watched my friends and I play ball. We were playing a game called 33. It's a game where everyone plays for themselves, and the first person to get 33 on the nose wins the game. Some cities call it 21, but we played 33. Anyway, he asked if he could join us, and of course we all said, "Yep, sure." To my amazement, once he started playing, I noticed right away that he was really, really good. I sensed he was better than all of us. I didn't really like that because I was known as the best young player at the Johnston court. He didn't win the game but that was only because he started the game late. It was evident that he was the best player. I won the game, and after the game we all decided to play some 2 on 2. A little afraid of losing my juice as the best player, I chose him to be on my team—my two friends really didn't want to play with him so they agreed. Glen and I beat them easily a few games and that was it. He had to go.

I had no clue at the time that we would remain life-long friends—like brothers. I also had no idea that his name wasn't Glen. His real name was Darius Duval Newsome. I wouldn't find that out until the summer ended and we would start school together. On that first day when the teacher called out for Darius Newsome, I would realize that my new friend Glen was actually named Darius. Darius would later tell me that he attended a camp one summer and a counselor told him he looked like a "Glen," so he decided to use that name instead. No one agreed with the counselor so the name Glen was thrown out and we decided to address him by his true first name, Darius—and do so to this day.

My interest in basketball would continue to grow over the next couple of years, especially as I began playing summer basketball on the Hill. The Hill District is where the best players from all over Pittsburgh came to play in the summer in what is called the Ozanam Summer Basketball League. The first game of the Ozanam Summer Basketball League begins at noon and is for kids aged 12 and under. The last game of the day is at 9 P.M. and is for kids aged 13–18.

My first experience playing on the Hill came when I was 12 years old playing for a coach named John Byrd. He saw me play in the Borough next to Wilkinsburg called Homewood. I am not sure why I was in Homewood playing basketball but it was a coincidence that would

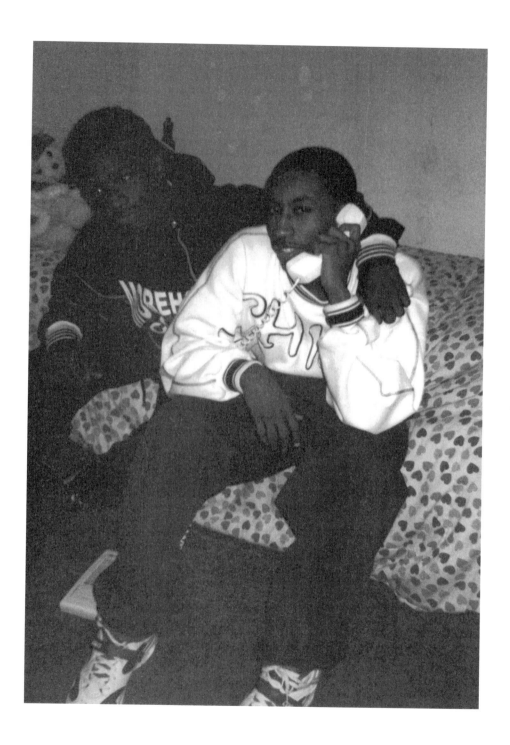

It was a brisk autumn morning—a Saturday to be exact. It wasn't really cold but it was just one of those days that I didn't feel like delivering papers. I would've much rather been playing basketball or just dribbling a basketball.

On this particular day after finishing my route, I stood at the fence of Johnston Elementary School watching 3 kids play basketball. I itched to join their game. I was new to the neighborhood and did not know them, so I was hesitant, even a little afraid to jump into their game of "33." As I watched at the fence, this kid name Quadar saw me and invited me over. Excited about playing, I played it cool and said, "Yeah, I would like to play." I noticed that I could do things with the ball that they weren't accustomed to. I was a fierce competitor, which I think brought out the competitor in all of them.

Before the game was finished, they wanted to play 2-on-2. They were not going to lose a game of "33" to a dude they didn't know, who didn't sound like them, named Glen. It didn't matter to me, because I was just as good or better at basketball.

One kid was a little better than the others. His name was Booper. He was quiet, but you could tell he was respected and "the man" at this particular playground. He had a decent straight dribble, and a sidewinding jump shot that was money. When asked who he wanted on his team first, he picked me. We went on to win and dominate the games very easily. The games would have been better if Booper and I had been on opposite teams. I asked him a few years later why he picked me to be on his team. He laughed and said he wasn't trying to lose to a dude who had just finished delivering newspapers. From that first day of playing basketball together, a friendship was born.

change my life as a basketball player. Coach Byrd was a good man. After seeing me play, he instantly put me on his 14-year-old-and-under team. He must have loved kids or really wanted to win games because our team was from all over the city. He would drive for at least 2 hours to pick up and drop off all the players on his team. In retrospect, I say he loved kids because at the time, I was an average player. I wasn't the type of player who was going to help him win many games on my talent alone. He must have seen a lot of potential in me, because he allowed me to play several minutes in every game. The players on my team were good, but playing at Ozanam afforded me the opportunity to see how great other players my age were throughout Pittsburgh.

That summer I got to see 2 of Pittsburgh's finest young ballplayers, Mike Berelli and Terrance Parham. They were playing for a team called the Hoyas, later known as the Future Stars. Mike and Terrance were so talented that they were going to Russia to play basketball. The 1st time I saw the two of them play I was amazed! They were incredible and they were my age. Right then at the age of 12, I realized that basketball was fun, but I'd better stick with football. I had always been pretty good and well known in football, but in basketball—I was not even a blip on the radar in Pittsburgh.

By this time, I was attending Wilkinsburg High School and in Wilkinsburg, the high school started in the 7th grade. That meant I was 12 years old and able to see and bump elbows with other students who were 5 and 6 years older than I was. In school, I ran mostly with Darius, but I also had my football buddies to hang out with. Darius and I were in honors classes together and back then, it was cool to be smart. A lot of the "cool" kids, the cute girls that dudes wanted, and the athletic attractive guys that the girls wanted, were all in honors classes together. This took a lot of pressure off of me to hide my intelligence around my peers. Actually, I embraced my smarts, and competed with other students to do well in class. It was a healthy competition where we all wanted to do the best we could to get good grades. The kids I hung out with had a lot of love and respect for each other, and like most kids between the ages of 12 and 14, we argued, talked about each other, and even sometimes came close to fighting. The comfort level we had developed sometimes provided the opportunity for some friendly ripping to take place. I really wasn't a huge fan of ripping.

Fortunately for me, Darius was the class clown and saved me from most of the rip sessions. Ripping is nothing more than jokes, sometimes the truth, but told in a funny way where one person talks about another in order to get people to laugh. Sometimes it gets personal and a fight may break out, but most times it's just kids getting on each other to make people laugh. Darius, being my friend and all, wouldn't let anyone talk about me without him getting on them. I was a short kid with glasses and a hook head. My classmates would draw a picture of my hook head and pass the paper around the class. Although it was funny, I hated this, and Darius knew it. When the picture would start to circulate around the class, Darius would laugh and then start firing (ripping) on everyone who passed the picture. He was a good friend. We grew closer and I developed a greater interest in the things my new best friend liked as well.

It was during this time I met a classmate whom I really liked. I never thought in a million years she would like me back though. When I was around her I would try my best to hide how much I liked her. She was in most of my classes, so I was able to interact with her on a daily basis. Her name was Kenya Felton, a brown-skinned, slim, smart girl—a flat-out cutie! I knew that a lot of the older guys were chasing after her, and back then, if the older guys liked a girl, my chances of getting her were probably slim to none. But through our everyday interaction in class, we eventually exchanged phone numbers and I would call her from time to time after school. I remember calling her one day and talking for hours on the phone. At one point, I ran out of stuff to say, but Kenya being such a sweetheart and knowing I didn't want to get off the phone with her, kept the conversation going. She knew I was nervous and didn't have any game with women. I was your normal 12-year-old kid with little to no experience with females. Yet, Kenya would help change that with communication. She taught me that I should always be myself—that staying true to myself was enough for a girl to like me. I didn't have to lie or do something that wasn't me in order to impress a girl. If she really liked me, she would like me for who I truly was. And although it never went past a friendly kiss, Kenya gave me the confidence to simply be me when it came to interacting with females.

At the age of 12 or 13, I was playing on the oldest team of Pee Wee football, and like years past, I was on a very good team. The Wilkinsburg High School team was a little upset with me because I could have played high school ball that season or I could have at least played junior varsity football. However, I knew I wasn't quite physically ready yet to perform at that level and be successful. So, I chose to play my final year of Pee Wee football.

It was during that final season that a private school from West Virginia, Linsly, began to recruit me along with a teammate of mine. They were looking at having us come to their school to play football and get a quality education. The year before, they had recruited 2 older teenagers from Pittsburgh. I wasn't sure how things went for them in West Virginia, but I did know they both came back home after just 1 year. They both decided they would rather play for a powerhouse Pittsburgh city school named Perry Traditional, known for producing solid college football and basketball players. Now, my mom could have cared less about Perry and their sports program. She wanted to know more about Linsly and the opportunity they were offering me. My father was pretty impartial on how he felt, so he left it to my mom to make the crucial decision about where I would be attending high school in the future. Me, I didn't care about Linsly or anything they had to offer. I wanted to stay home and continue to go to school with my friends at Wilkinsburg.

After the Linsly recruiters had a few conversations with my mom, I was on my way to Wheeling, West Virginia, to visit Linsly School. All I could think was, "Where in the world is Wheeling, West Virginia?" As a kid from the inner city, I couldn't think of one reason why I needed to go to high school in West Virginia. On the ride to Linsly, I could tell my mother was excited about the possibilities this school could provide, but all I kept thinking was—"West Virginia? Seriously, we're going to West Virginia?" Although it was only an hour and change outside of Pittsburgh, it felt like a world away.

Riding in my mom's car down the highway, I saw nothing but woods and a lot of green grass. It wasn't like we didn't have trees and grass in

Pittsburgh but these were trees in West Virginia. And on that day, I wasn't excited about anything that was going to separate me from my friends back home. The more we drove down I-70 West, the more alone I began to feel. The one good thing was that they were recruiting my friend and star teammate from Pee Wee football, Aarron Moore, as well. So there we were; my mother, Aarron, his father, and I all packed in my mom's Corsica on our way to Wheeling, West Virginia. No one in the car that day really knew what to expect, but 2 of the 4 people involved in the ride were at least optimistic about what Linsly had to offer and it wasn't Aarron and me.

Arriving at the Linsly campus, I felt as if I had walked on to the set of a movie. I saw all these kids dressed in the same uniform—walking around, talking, and smiling. I was amazed that there was actually a place where all the kids dressed in the same attire. To me, that was just crazy! I mean, why would I want to wear the same clothes as everyone else? There was no individuality there. No style! I was ready to place my vote right then and there on whether Linsly School was the place for me. I looked around thinking, "There's no way I'm going to school here! This place is corny and whack!" And if I needed any more of a reason to get in the car and head home, I didn't see any black students. I only remember seeing one black student the whole time I was there. He was a football star named Shiraz. I thought to myself, "I know he is lonely. If I feel alone and out of place with my mother here by my side—he must be REALLY lonely!" Clearly this was not the place for me, and there was no way I was going to school there.

As part of our visit, Aarron and I had to take a standardized test. This test would determine if we qualified academically to get in to the school and also the grade we would enter, if accepted. A few hours after we had finished the test, it was time to continue our tour and meet a few people. As we walked around campus, I noticed how clean it was. I was impressed that there was no writing on the lockers or walls. This was nothing like my school back home. We met and talked to the dean of the school and a few coaches and teachers. After these boring conversations in which they talked to our parents more than to us, it was time to hit the road. We couldn't afford to stay at a hotel and I was glad about that because I was ready to go home. It was an attractive facility and everyone at the school was very nice, but it just seemed too serious and business-like for me. I hoped that my mom would agree with me—this was not the high school for me.

In spite of what I felt, on the ride home, I found out she was very open-minded about Linsly. She was extremely positive about the visit that day. I remember Aarron's dad saying some positive things about the school as well, but he was concerned about the lack of ethnicity. My mom was shaking her head up and down as he spoke, so I was hoping, "No Linsly for me." I would be happy about that! I didn't want to leave all my friends and attend this all-white school in West Virginia.

As life would have it, I was accepted. However, they told my mother they wanted me to repeat the 9th grade. My mom gave them an emphatic NO and said, "thanks, but no thanks." She told them that I either needed to stay on course and be placed in the 10th grade the following school year, or I wouldn't be attending Linsly. I was laughing to myself because first, I knew I purposely didn't do my best on the test they had given me and second, I could've cared less if Linsly wanted me because in my mind, I wasn't going to that school anyway.

By 1990, my interest in basketball had grown immensely and I was hoping to play for the varsity team as a freshman for Wilkinsburg High School. There were try-outs and Coach Edward Fleming was taking a look at a few freshmen. He wanted to see if they were good enough to play varsity basketball. Fortunately for me, I was one of those freshmen. Back then, it was more like open gym (where everyone just plays pick-up basketball, street ball, 5-on-5 for the most part), not actual try-outs. We knew Coach Fleming would be watching, so it was kind of like try-outs without the added pressure, I guess. Throughout the try-outs I played solid basketball. However, I believe that I had made a few plays that stood out from the other freshman. Nevertheless, I didn't know what Coach Fleming would think about me or my play. I would find out soon.

A few days after the open gym workouts, Coach Fleming came up to me and another freshman named Steve Johnson and said we would play with the varsity team that season. I was ecstatic. I didn't scream or act crazily, although I wanted to; I knew my best friend Darius and a few other freshmen wanted the spot. I felt bad for Darius because I knew he was probably the better player at the time. I could shoot the ball better than he could, but he was the better point guard. It was hard to know that I had made the team, but my best friend who pushed me to play basketball didn't.

Once Darius found out that I had made the team, he showed me genuine love. He was so excited and enthused—it was as if he had made the roster instead of me. He told me he would help me work on my ball handling, and do anything he could to help me improve my game and play well that season. His kindness and helpfulness were that of a true friend—a young man beyond his years! Darius put me at ease about being overjoyed at making the varsity team. I accomplished something that I had no idea I had the talent or ability to do. What made it even more special was that I had my best friend by my side supporting me, and that made the world of difference to me.

That freshman season may have been the most important season of my basketball career. For the first time, I was on a losing basketball team, and I was one of the worst point guards in our entire league. I was a starter for Wilkinsburg High School, but I wouldn't have started for any other team in our conference. My attributes were simple: I could dribble the ball over half court, I could play fairly good defense, and I could make open shots. Then again, for Wilkinsburg to compete at winning anything, I wasn't nearly at the level of the other top-rated point guards on the other teams. My lack of talent and ability was exposed by a few top point guards at the varsity level. The one positive from all of this was that Coach Fleming kept pushing me to get better. He would work with me before and after practice. He would always encourage me, and he never gave up on me. He saw something in me that a lot of others didn't, including me. He made me believe that I had the potential to be very good, but I had to work my butt off to reach it. I wasn't that elite athlete, but I could be a good player if I pushed myself when no one was looking or applauding me. He made me believe in myself as a player, and I am forever grateful for that. We ended the season with a record of 3–21 that year, one of the worst seasons in Wilkinsburg High School basketball history. It was, nevertheless, my first step toward a successful future playing basketball.

After basketball season was over, I played baseball for the high school team. That turned out to be a joke. We barely had enough players to make a team and it really didn't matter much to me or anyone else at the high school. My interest was waning in baseball anyway, so this joke of a team enabled me to keep continuously working on my basketball skills. Coach Fleming really wanted me to develop as a player and he thought that going to camp would help my growth. So, he started working on getting me into Metro Index Summer Basketball Camp in California, Pennsylvania. In spite of everything Coach Fleming was doing for me, my mom was still talking to Linsly about me attending their school the next year. In fact, she was basically dotting I's and crossing T's for me to attend there. By the end of my 9th-grade school year, I knew I was going to Linsly.

I hated the thought of leaving Wilkinsburg, but what hurt most was that I would have to tell Coach Fleming that I wouldn't be playing for him next year. He had invested so much time and energy in me that I thought I could never tell him about my departure. I would constantly talk with Darius about my dilemma and he said I needed to tell Coach as soon as possible. Darius strongly insisted that Coach would understand my situation and be supportive. For the next few weeks, all I could think about were ways NOT to attend Linsly. Every excuse I thought of was either rejected or denied by my parents.

My mom knew what was best for me, but at the time, I couldn't see it for myself. When I finally got up the nerve to tell Coach Fleming about me transferring schools there was about a week left in the school year. When I told him that I would be leaving Wilkinsburg for a private school in West Virginia, I had my head down and I knew I was barely audible. I expected him to express how disappointed he was in me, but to my surprise, he said "That is great news!" and that I should definitely take advantage of such a great opportunity. Coach also told me to never forget where I came from. He told me to continue to work hard, and that I was going to be a varsity star one day. He then asked if I was still going to attend the summer basketball camp. I told him that I probably wouldn't, because I didn't have the money to pay for it. He just smiled and told me something that completely blew me away. He said that it would be an honor for him to pay for me to go to camp! I was speechless. I walked into his office thinking he was going to be angry with me and now this! I was so happy and relieved that he understood my situation, that for a brief second, I felt it was OK for me to attend Linsly. Coach seemed happier when he heard that I was leaving, than when I was there working with him trying to get better as a basketball player. I learned at that moment that adults knew more than us kids. Coach knew my mom was making the right decision. I had a lot of respect for him. Coach Fleming invested in a young man when he didn't have to. When he saw a better opportunity for that same young man that he believed in, he embraced it and wanted that young man to accomplish great things. Coach Edward Fleming was a phenomenal man, and I would really like to thank him for taking an interest in me, for being so understanding, and for showing me so much genuine love.

That summer I started my first year playing basketball for a coach named Roger Simmons. Everyone simply called him Raj. He was the coach of a group of kids called the Future Stars. The Future Stars were supposedly the best basketball players from all over the city of Pittsburgh, playing together on the same team, in different age groups. It was like an AAU (Amateur Athletic Union) team without the money and sponsors. Every good player or player who thought he was good wanted to play for Raj. I had met Raj through Darius—at a Wilkinsburg High School game during my freshman year. I knew from Darius that Raj was more than a coach for most of the players; he was like a father figure and what he said was golden. He didn't permit his players to swear or use the N-word—anything derogatory that didn't sit well with Raj was not done around him. He was building young black men's self-esteem. Raj cared about his people, especially young African-American men. He took care of those that weren't expected to be successful and gave all young people a sense of hope. The bottom line was that Raj simply cared, and that summer I did everything he asked me to.

That summer at Ozanam I played for Raj's 14-and-under Future Star team. I knew that most of Raj's teams won so I assumed Raj would be all about winning. This was far from the truth. Raj wanted to win, but not at the expense of building quality relationships with his players and his players with each other. Also, he wanted every player to develop—to get better at his craft.

Raj would have us meet on Saturday and Sunday mornings and we would run hills, run drills, and sometimes he and his assistant, Coach D (Darwin Lane) would beat us up in 1-on-1 or 2-on-2 games. Other times, we would simply sit and talk about life and growing up as young men in Pittsburgh.

We won the 14-and-under championship at Ozanam that summer—my first-ever basketball championship! It felt good to be a part of a winning basketball team, especially after going 3–21 at Wilkinsburg that school year. I loved playing on the Hill, in the Ozanam Summer League. My parents, on the other hand, weren't very fond of the Hill District. They didn't like me playing ball in such a rough environment so far away from home. To complicate matters, they really didn't know or trust Raj. Early on, it was more my mom than my dad who didn't take to Raj. I think this was because he was as outspoken and persistent about what he believed in as she was. My mom wasn't too worried about my affiliation with Raj though, because she knew in August, I was headed to Linsly.

I made the most out of that summer both on and off the court as my friendship with Darius continued to blossom. We started working out together and we would play 1-on-1 games against each other in order to improve our skills. One day, while at a park called Whitney Field, we were playing 1-on-1 full court. At the time, there was no doubt that Darius was a better ballplayer than I was, but I was the ultimate competitor. We were playing a series; the best 2 out of 3. We had split the first 2 games, and were in a dogfight to determine the winner of the 3rd and final game. He led most of the game, but I managed to come back and tie the score. Knowing that I was getting tired, and he started to pick up steam and was definitely going to win, so I faked an injury.

I can't even remember the entire lie I told him, but I said something about a mole on my stomach giving me problems breathing. I had to stop playing. Darius, being a genuine friend, was very concerned and didn't care much about winning the game. He said, "No problem, let's stop."

I thought, "Thank goodness, I did not want to lose." So, we got on our bicycles and rode home. Before I knew it, I was pedaling as fast as I could. Why? I am not sure, maybe it was because I had just escaped losing a series, but, I think, it was just to beat Darius to the house! I laugh at it now, because to this day, he has never beaten me in a series of 1-on-1. I hated losing—even as a kid, I did whatever it took to win. It didn't matter if it was something serious like a sporting event, or something silly like being the first to reach the house on a bike. Losing was not a word in my vocabulary!

By the time August rolled around, Darius was basically living with my mom, sister, and me. He had a complicated family situation that I didn't quite understand at that time. It didn't matter to me because he was my friend. All I needed to know was that my best friend was OK. By the time he moved in with my family, it was time for me to move out. I left for Linsly in early August.

I received a full scholarship to play football at Linsly. I didn't quite know what to expect, but I guess my expectation was that I would go down there and be a star. I obviously had no idea what I was getting myself into. When the time came for me to put on that equipment and go out there for our first practice, I was shocked at how big and fast most of the players at my position were. I started to second guess right then and there whether coming to Linsly was a good choice. I took for granted that I would be a star in football, no matter where I played. Now, I was with the big boys and it looked like I might not even play. Aarron Moore, my friend from back home, had accepted his scholarship for football as well. He wasn't going to be a starter as a sophomore either. This was not what we expected when we decided to attend Linsly. However, things would get better for Aarron. He was a very good player and he would eventually earn minutes on the varsity that season. I was happy for him and proud to be his friend from home. Me, I just played junior varsity. When the varsity played, all I did was stand on the sideline in my uniform and watch.

As football season was tough on me, I was really excited when basketball season rolled around that year. I knew that I would probably start for Linsly, not known for their basketball team. I figured that I had started as a freshman at Wilkinsburg, so starting here was a given. To my surprise, Coach Ray Smith didn't start me as a sophomore. He decided that it would be best for the team if I came off the bench. I was pissed, and I didn't accept not being a starter. I handled the situation all wrong.

I acted like I was entitled to the starting position, when in fact I had to earn it. What I did in the summer time and the work I put in back home didn't hold any weight here. I had to earn my keep. So, my plan was to work my butt off to be a better player.

Instead of working on my game to get better to help the team, I worked endlessly on my game to be the star of the team. It was an extremely selfish plan. But my pride was hurt, and I wanted to show Coach Smith I was going to be the best player ever to play at Linsly. I refused to accept that those white players were better than the city and street kids that I competed against back home. In retrospect, that was a very close-minded point of view, but at that time, that was what I thought. Although players at Linsly weren't as talented as the Future Star teams that I had played for in the summer, this was not a summer league. The time had come for me to learn how to integrate my game and my skills with the team system Coach Smith wanted. It was a learning process and I wanted to play, so I had no choice but to accept it.

It was a miserable season for me. Our team was average, and although the guy in front of me was a solid player, I felt I had more upside and skills. The starter was a good passer and a team guy; Coach Smith saw me as more of a me-guy. It wasn't easy accepting this, but it helped me to mature as a person and as a student of the game of basketball. This lesson learned proved to be another step toward a successful future with a game I was falling in love with.

During my 10th-grade year I fell in love with a new breed of ballers, a new team that most young black city kids loved, the Fab 5 from the University of Michigan. They burst onto the scene in college basketball and made me realize that age didn't matter—skill did. They were supremely confident and had a swagger that I tried to emulate. They were 5 freshmen who took the college world by storm: Jimmy King, Ray Jackson, Juwan Howard, Chris Webber, and my favorite, Jalen Rose. Jalen was a city kid from Detroit who had the swagger and confidence that only special players had. I wanted to be special, so I took in his every move, his walk, the way he talked, as well as the way he led his team. On the court, I just wanted to emulate everything he did. I wanted to have that type of impact playing basketball. I wanted to be like Jalen Rose. In spite of him having way more game than I, I just felt like I could reach that pinnacle (NCAA Division 1 Basketball) by watching and doing what he did. He was everything I wasn't, and maybe that was why I loved his game so much. He talked trash and I didn't; he was a vocal leader and I wasn't; he had swag and big confidence and I didn't; he was 6' 8" and I was scraping 5' 10". He was just the man to me—a leader—he was that guy that people hated, but loved in the same breath. Jalen was that dude!

After a below-average football, basketball, and baseball season, I looked forward to the summer. So, as the school year ended, all I did was work on my basketball skills. I knew that I would be going home soon and I had to be ready to compete with all my friends who I knew were working on their basketball skills as well. More important, I knew Darius would be better and as competitive best friends, I had to stay on top of my game.

At school I would stay in the gym for 3 or 4 hours just shooting and working on my skills. I even played 1-on-1 against imaginary NBA players. I would be in there all by myself, making shots against all the great players at the time, including Tim Hardaway, Kenny Anderson, Isaiah Thomas, and Magic Johnson. Everyone always preached practice, practice, practice, so that's what I did. I wanted to get better, but I also knew that I had to get better if I wanted to continue to play and start for Raj and his Future Stars teams in the summer. That was added motivation for me. That gave me the extra incentive to keep working as much and as hard as I could. Somehow being in the gym playing basketball in West Virginia made me feel connected to my friends back home and I loved that. I knew they were home playing ball too, and the game was our connection. By the time school ended, I was excited and ready to get home so I could play ball with friends and for my favorite coach, Raj.

As for my school experience at Linsly that year, it was—OK. The students were all nice and accepting of the new kids from Pittsburgh. The academics were not as hard as they had made it sound to my mom. Maybe it was my decision to fully apply myself. Or, maybe it was the teachers actually taking the time to teach me how to study. Either way, I was learning and doing well in school. One of the things I had to do as a first-year student was go to the library every day for study hall for 2 hours from 7:30 P.M.–9:30 P.M. I hated going at first, but all first-year students were required to attend study hall for the first 2 semesters. Eventually, study hall was not an issue at all and became routine. However, "lights out" at 11:00 P.M was a little more difficult rule for me to follow. They tried to control every little aspect of my life and that had me hating the rules. I was a young city kid who just wanted his freedom to act like a grown man. So, my instinct was to become rebellious and try to buck the system.

After a few months, everything they wanted from me became second nature. I learned that in the end they had their reasons for making us do the things they did. I still use a lot of the same good habits that Linsly instilled in me. I learned to take the proper time to do my work—to be neat and to be organized. I learned that order and doing things the right way made my life easier in the long run. For example, if an assignment was supposed to take me 3 hours to complete and ended up taking me 3 hours and 30 minutes to complete—if I took my time and did it correctly, it would not come back to haunt or hurt me later. In hindsight, I am so thankful for Linsly and the type of structure and guidance the school provided, because looking back on it, I realize that it made me a better student and person.

Although I had a solid first year, there was one thing that bothered me and made me uncomfortable there—my race. As a black student, I felt like I stood out like a sore thumb. There weren't many of us. No more than 5 or 6 black students out of a student body of 300 or so. We were all on scholarships and as I remember, we all played sports. I felt like it was, "Know your place. You're here for a reason." Although that was never said to me directly, that was how it felt. Maybe some of that was in my own mind, because of my discomfort with being around so many white people for the first time in my life. Like I said before, no one ever actually said those words to me, but I could feel an undercurrent. Still, almost all the students and faculty were very receptive to me. I know they wanted me to feel like any other student. However, many times their exaggerated kindnesses didn't seem genuine and made me feel even more like a fish out of water.

That summer was very important to my mental and physical growth as a basketball player. I played for Raj's 16-and-under team, and was given a chance to start and really develop my swagger as a player. Raj had two 16-and-under teams that summer, the A team and the B team; I was on the B team. He had the guys that he thought were the "best of the best" at 16 years old and younger on the A team, and the rest of us were on the B team.

As a member of the B team, I worked hard every day—whether it was dribbling on my porch at midnight or watching old college hoop games that Darius and I had recorded in years past. Either way, my mind was on basketball 24 hours a day. I had to do whatever it took to get better as a player. I wasn't pushing myself to be a pro or even an elite college player at that time. I was simply trying to be considered one of the top players playing for Raj. Raj didn't have two teams to slight any of his players. His plan was to try to give us all a chance to play more minutes and get more game experience. So all in all, we got the best of both worlds! We got to play for Raj and were given the opportunity to compete against each other. This allowed us to see who among us was truly the "best of the best" on the court—and not just on paper.

To my delight, Darius and I were on the same team that summer. It gave us both a chance to grow as players and as friends—both on and off the court. On the court was very easy for us. Darius was becoming a very good point guard and a true leader. He could handle the ball better than anyone I knew. We had played so much together over past summers that he knew where I liked the ball, where I could score, and so on and so forth. That made for a great backcourt. We were both finally being recognized as good players, and that recognition by our peers, teammates, and others made us feel good. What's more, sharing the spotlight with my best friend (who felt more like my brother) just made the accomplishments that much sweeter. There was never any jealousy or anything between us. I was good at what I did on the court, and he was good at what he did. The best part about it was that I wasn't as good at what he did and vice-versa. It just made things smooth. Our partnership and brotherhood on the court was irreplaceable.

Off the court was another story. Darius could be a handful, but so could I. In my eyes, he was gifted in so many different aspects. One aspect was cutting hair. Darius was a professional barber without the license and permit. He would cut his friends' hair for free, but he also worked in a barber shop at the time. One day that summer, he ran behind schedule in the shop, and our good friend Lafayette (Newt) and I were going to pick him up for basketball practice. We had practice on the Hill and we all wanted to go together on the bus. We were expecting Raj to be a little upset for arriving to practice late, but Darius was our friend, so Newt and I waited for Darius to finish work and we all caught the bus together.

By the time we arrived, Raj was more than a little upset—he was furious! He had never gone off on me like he did that day, and I was shocked. He gave us a speech about accountability. He said, "If Darius is late, why are you all late? Why not get here on time and work until Darius gets here? Darius has the job, not Newt or you. Darius is making money by working and being accountable for having a few dollars in his pocket while Newt and you watch him work and are late for practice. If Darius jumps off a bridge, are you going to jump off a bridge?" Raj was irate. He tore into us for 30 minutes, and then told us we weren't practicing. Not just that, but we couldn't touch a basketball while he was there. I couldn't believe Raj was so mad. He wouldn't even let us try and explain or make up an excuse. We couldn't get a word out. He didn't want to hear any of it. I was so hurt and upset that I had disappointed him. I felt guilty—as much as he had done for me and I couldn't even get to practice on time. His speech hit home with me that day. I was never late for another practice with Raj. Not only that, but in the future, I helped teach Future Star players about being accountable and trying to always do the right thing. Raj taught me a big lesson that day. I have to be accountable for my actions and be able to deal with the consequences. I can't put my actions off on someone else. That was an important lesson for all three of us. Raj was teaching us to be mature, accountable, and responsible young men. Lesson heard—loud and clear!

That summer on the Hill, I started going to Kenard to watch some older players play. Kenard Summer League was about a 5- to 10-minute walk from Ozanam. It was more like a semi-pro summer league. One hot evening, Darius, Newt, Gerald (another good friend of ours), and I decided to go up to Kenard to watch a few games. The night game, played at 9:00 P.M. is usually the best game of the night.

It's also usually a team from the Hill playing that game. On this particular night it was Zonk 5, a team from the Hill, against a team with Pittsburgh legend, Myron Brown, on it.

Myron Brown played at the highest level in the world—the NBA. At the time, he was playing overseas in Italy. He got a lot of love on the Hill, and mostly for being in a Gatorade commercial with Michael Jordan. Everyone loves Jordan, right? Myron had what we call, "the juice"— meaning, he wasn't from the Hill, but he got "hood love" because he was a very good player who made it big time but kept coming back to play in "the hood." People respected that and appreciated his journey to the top. On this night, I was in awe of Myron from the minute he got out of his truck. He drove up to the game and parked 30 steps from the court in a new white Tahoe truck. I was like, "Wow, this guy is rich and still coming up here to play. He is a BEAST. A brand new $60,000 truck in the hood, in the Hill district, and you're not a drug dealer." That was something to talk about and be in awe of. What's more, he got out of his truck smiling, talking to people, and just had a coolness about him that said he was going to come up here and give us a show. He would put a little work in (score some points, get a few assists, and win the game), and then go back home to the suburbs. I remember thinking, "This is going to be too easy for him. He is a pro. These are just very good college players and so-called playground legends."

As he warmed up, he just glided all over the court. He was so smooth and graceful, it seemed like the game that I loved so much and worked so hard at, came so easy for him. As expected, in the first few minutes of the game, Myron did his thing. He scored 2 or 3 buckets, made some sweet passes, and it just seemed like another easy game. Then all of a sudden, all I heard from the bleachers was "Get 'em, Byrd. He doesn't know about you, Byrd. Get 'em, Byrd. This is the Hill."

For the next 25 to 30 minutes, I watched the best display of defense that I had ever seen in my life. No, not even Michael Jordan, Michael Cooper, Bruce Bowen, or Dennis Rodman looked as good as Bobby Byrd looked playing defense against Myron that night. You have to understand, Byrd was a neighborhood baller—a "hood legend." I didn't even know that he went to Community College many years ago. All

I knew was that Byrd was a "hood hooper." What was even more amazing, Byrd was doing this in blue jean shorts. He didn't even have on basketball shorts. It didn't matter to him. No top-dollar sneakers or nice uniform, Byrd had on a pair of old-and-run-down gym shoes—AND NO ONE CARED! The only thing that everyone seemed to pay attention to was the defensive show that Bobby Byrd was putting on display.

Byrd went on to give Myron more problems than anyone had ever seen Myron have on the Hill. Byrd got in this defensive stance real low to the ground, locked into Myron's abdomen, never looked him in the eyes, and didn't let Myron shake him or get loose for another open shot for the rest of the game. I am not sure if Myron even scored another point after Byrd started guarding him. Myron tried playing it cool and laughed off Byrd's dominance but this was no laughing matter.

I was taught, either you compete and try to meet the challenge, or get off the court. I guess laughing was all Myron could do because Byrd was dominating him on this night. I was disappointed that Myron never really stepped up his level of play. I couldn't believe that smooth Myron Brown got locked down by tough-as-nails, 30-plus-year-old Bobby Byrd. This couldn't be possible, but it happened right in front of my eyes. The performance stole our hearts. My friends and I were so excited and amped up after the game, we did defensive slides from the Hill to downtown Pittsburgh. We usually caught the bus from the Hill to downtown, then home to Wilkinsburg. It's a 30- to 40-minute walk downtown from the Hill. We didn't care about that 30 minutes. Bobby Byrd made us feel alive. We temporarily lost our minds and were just truly living and enjoying the moment as teenagers. That night Byrd made me have much more respect for playing defense. He showed me that you can dominate a game on the defensive side of the ball. He imposed his will on the game and Myron. That opened my eyes to the beauty of shutting down a very good offensive player. That night Byrd made all 4 of us realize that it's not who you are, but how hard you play. Your name doesn't mean a thing when you step in between those lines (and I live by this lesson to this day). Thanks, Bobby Byrd—I appreciate the lesson. I'm just glad it was Myron (who to this day I still have the upmost respect and admiration for) and not me who got locked down that night!

The duration of my summer was spent doing one of two things: enhancing my growing passion for basketball or spending time with my first teenage girlfriend. Her name was Monique. She was a great girl and will always remain dear to my heart. She was such a sweetheart. What I really liked about her was that she was all about me. She made me feel like a special young man by displaying her feelings toward me. She had a way of making me always feel at ease and happy when I was around her. She had a great spirit and a warm, caring heart.

We would sit on my porch or sit in her house and talk for hours. She would tell me her goals of getting out of Wilkinsburg, and I would tell her my own dreams of playing Division 1 basketball. Eventually, we broke up. A lot of it was because of the distance—high school in West Virginia— but also it was my love for ball. I put ball in front of her, and at the time, we were both too young to really understand what it took to make a relationship work. I thought about her often as I got older, especially in college. I always just wondered how she was doing, and how life was treating her. I wish I would have stayed in touch with her. I am sure she would have been a great friend to me over the years. She will always remain close to my heart as a phenomenal young woman.

Coming back for my junior year at Linsly, I was a dedicated basketball player. My friend, Aarron, had decided not to return. I didn't agree with his move, but he had to do what he thought was best for him. His absence put a little more pressure on me to play football. And I was having no part in that because somewhere between my sophomore and junior years, I transitioned from a football player into a bona fide basketball player. Suddenly, I didn't want to do anything but play basketball. Linsly, the administration, and the football coach were not happy about my decision not to play football. I couldn't understand why they kept pressuring me when I didn't love it anymore. I stuck to my guns. Then, they brought up the fact that I had to play 2 sports in order to keep my scholarship. At this point, I really didn't care or even hear what they were saying. As far as I was concerned, my football career was finished. I figured I would play basketball and baseball, if they forced me to play 2 sports in order to keep my scholarship. As much as I disliked baseball, I figured I would just make the junior varsity team, or get cut.

In spite of all the back and forth conversation, after a few more meetings, and some heated disagreements, they finally decided it was OK if I didn't play baseball and football anymore. A few teachers and football coaches were not happy with the dean's decision. I was excited about the outcome—not because I got my way and the dean came to my aid, but because now I could focus all my time and energy on basketball.

I had a very solid junior year playing basketball. I earned a starting position and slowly became the best player and leader of the team. Coach Smith didn't let me run wild (by being selfish and worrying about my own stats). He kept the reigns tight on me for the most part. It was a good and bad thing. Coach Smith and I didn't see eye-to-eye on some basketball decisions, and that made for some tough times. I wanted more freedom to score and show my ability. He wanted a strictly fundamentals "Princeton-style" system that I didn't think fit my game. I wanted to play a more up-tempo style of basketball, like my summer league teams back home. In spite of this, I think we both looked in the mirror and came up with some honest answers by the end of the season.

I had no clue that this difference of opinion between us would help me in the future—enabling me to deal with coaches who may not see my game, my talent, and my ability the same way I do. I became more of a "team" guy and not a "me" guy. It let me know that winning comes first—period. Coaches coach teams to win, not individual players to score points, no matter how good that player may be. In any case, not being able to show off all my ability just kept me working hard every day. I pushed every day to be a special player. I wanted to be so good that Coach Smith didn't have a choice but to play me a lot of minutes and let me lead the team in order to win games. In the end, we had a solid season. In spite of the wins and losses, I learned a lot about myself, my teammates, and Coach Smith that season.

I finally felt that my teammates respected me. Now it was up to me to take my game and leadership skills to another level if I wanted to have a great senior season. I learned that leadership starts with actions. I don't have to say how good I am, I have to show how good I am. I shouldn't say I am working hard, they should see my hard work in practice every day.

That season, our Linsly team added a new assistant coach—Lance Bibey. He was a true blessing. Coach Bibey was a young coach who had just finished college a year or two before he came to Linsly. He could still play, so he would play with us sometimes. He had a lot of swag and confidence in his ability. He would talk a lot of junk too. He would push me to excel. He would always say, "Forget who you are playing against now, but play like you are playing against the best player in West Virginia every day." He encouraged me to follow my goals of becoming a Division 1 player. He would stay after practice and shoot for hours with me. He would come to the gym on off days to help me work on my game. He was the big brother away from home that I needed. He became my mentor. Without his help, I'm not sure I would have become the player or leader that I needed to be in my senior year at Linsly.

My junior year also had a lot in store for me as far as girls were concerned. Even though Linsly had a lot of rules, and one of them was no girls permitted in the dorms or in the rooms, I still interacted with the females at the school. Everything was just basically out in the open. What I realized very early on was that a lot of faculty and administration didn't mind students mingling and hanging out, but interracial dating was not easily accepted. I am not sure why it wasn't accepted when we (blacks) were supposed to be just like any other student, right? Wrong! I believe their true feelings were more along the lines of "We will put up with you dating the white girls, but we will not be happy about it." That made for some uncomfortable public interactions with the girls, on my part. I didn't hang out much, but when I did, I played it safe. I suppose the black athletes were there to try and dominate sports, and get a quality education. The social part of high school was supposed to be put on hold. It didn't make much sense to me, but it didn't bother me much either. I wasn't really thinking about dating girls on campus at the time. I was cool with one or two girls, but nothing serious. I was very hesitant to hang with a white girl at Linsly, at least on some dating, kissing, or affectionate-type basis. I wasn't comfortable or ready to deal with the potential problems.

Don't misunderstand me, not all faculty members were against interracial dating because some of them were very cool about it, as long as it was respectful. I know two faculty members who were always supportive of me, and always gave me good advice when it came to girls and dating on campus. Mr. Plumby and Professor Hon were very open and honest with me. They gave me a lot of good advice, and helped me understand the do's and don'ts of campus.

I struggled with some things during my time at Linsly, but that was to be expected. I was just a young boy becoming a young man, learning about myself and girls, and doing a lot of it on my own. I was away from friends and family who could have given me advice and help when it came to dating and relationships. Nevertheless, I had both good and bad times interacting with the girls at Linsly. It was definitely a learning experience. I learned a lot of positive things that I would take with me to college—simple things like good communication, honesty, getting to really know someone before getting involved, patience, school rules, priorities—things that may have been different if I were at home going to public school.

My junior year ended well. I was more comfortable and fit in better with my classmates. I had adjusted quite well to school and life in Wheeling, West Virginia (only playing one sport enabled me to go home more, and that made life in Wheeling easier to deal with). My mom picked me up from school almost every other weekend after basketball season ended. And when she didn't come, I had a few friends now at school. So, I would hang out with them and their families off campus for the weekend. However, I enjoyed going home on the weekends and relaxing with family and friends the most. It brought me closer to my family, because we really took the time to be with each other during those weekends. My sister and I would spend hours just talking and laughing together. We were always close, but I felt like our relationship was fading a little with my departure to Linsly.

I was young and felt a little alone at school. I was afraid of losing the closest person to me. I should have known my sister and I would always be close no matter the situation. Still, our time we spent together reinforced our bond and the love we had for each other. Every relationship is different and she needed to have a quality relationship with Darius in order for us to grow. By this time, Darius's relationship with my whole family had changed. He was like a son to my parents and a brother to my siblings. He always made me feel that coming home for the weekend were the best 2 days of my life. I needed that more than he knew it. He went out of his way to make me feel a part of my own family and that made our friendship and brotherhood stronger. It blew my mind sometimes, but he was beyond his years when it came to some things.

III | Focused on a Dream

GOING HOME FOR the summer was always an exciting time for me but this summer had to be different. This had to be the best summer of my life if I intended to get a Division 1 basketball scholarship. This summer would be all about ball and how I could develop into a bona fide college ballplayer. I surprised a lot of folks that summer on how hard I worked—my hunger for the game and how my game took off! I went from people saying, "Dude can shoot a little bit and he has some ability," to "that boy got game, he can flat out play!"

Playing in the semi-pro summer league, Kenard, that summer helped my progress. It is without a doubt the toughest summer league in Pittsburgh. I was only 16, but I needed to venture out and see where I stood as a ballplayer. Playing in Wheeling, West Virginia, for Linsly was a setback when it came to the game of basketball. It was a private school, and we played in a weak league with a weak schedule. We played decent teams, but nothing that would make a college recruiter say, "Wow, this kid is playing against top-notch competition." Plus, I needed reassurance that I was where I needed to be as a player to play at the next level. So, my decision to play at Kenard with some guys that I didn't have a close relationship with off the court was nothing personal against my friends. I had to test my game against the best from Pittsburgh and I had to do that any way I could. Therefore, I decided to play with a team from Wilkinsburg.

To be honest, I was surprised they even asked me to play with them. I didn't play high school ball in Pittsburgh and these were older guys who hadn't seen me really play since the 9th grade. I was unsure and curious as to why they hadn't asked any of my other friends to play with them. I didn't worry too much about that and it didn't stop me from jumping at the opportunity to play at Kenard. It was an experience that changed my life. I went to Kenard as a kid who thought he could play the game of basketball, but I left as a teenager who knew he could play the game of basketball.

It felt good gaining the love and respect game by game from the other ballplayers and fans. I was young and needed affirmation from others that I had the talent to play at a high level. Although I was playing with Wilkinsburg at Kenard, I still played with my friends and Coach Raj on the Future Stars at Ozanam. The Future Stars were like my extended family. There was no way I would ever abandon them.

One day, I had a game at Kenard with the Wilkinsburg team and a game at Ozanam with my Future Stars team. The game start times were an hour apart. So, I played the 1st half of the game at Kenard, and then ran 10 minutes up the hill to Ozanam to be on time for my Future Stars game. I had 21 points in the 1st half at the Kenard game. I was playing one of my best games at Kenard, and maybe could have scored 40 points. That didn't matter to me. I had to be on time for my family, for my boys, the Future Stars. What's more, we won the Ozanam game and that made my night a good night; a happy time. I didn't have to score 20 points with the Future Stars to feel good. It was about winning and playing basketball with my closest pals. There was just something special about playing for the Future Stars.

That summer, I also attended the famous Five Star Basketball Camp. At camp they have 2 Divisions for the high school players, an NBA Division and the NCAA Division. The NBA Division is for the best high school players at the camp. It consisted of mostly the upcoming seniors and the top juniors. I was an upcoming senior but I was placed in the NCAA Division. The Five Star counselors and staff had never seen me play before and put me in the NCAA Division. I felt slighted. I guess they figured no name, no game. I was pissed for the whole first day of camp. Then, I vowed to make Howard Garfinkle, the famous Five Star camp director, pay for his mistake. It was his camp, so it was his mistake. The only way I could make a statement was by being the best player in the

NCAA Division. Forget what others thought, I had to take advantage of being at a prestigious camp, and that was what I did.

That week I was the Most Outstanding Player in the NCAA Division. I dominated the competition. I wasn't the best player at the camp, but I deserved to be in the NBA Division. This would be the story line throughout my career. I would always be overlooked and passed over. But, I would persevere and keep pushing for a personal best. It didn't matter that I only played in the NCAA Division. I played hard and proved to myself that I could do what I set out to do, if I put my heart into it. I just hoped that I opened a few recruiters' eyes at the camp that week. Hopefully I had showed that I had the potential to be a Division 1 basketball player.

My senior year at Linsly was going to be a big year. I was not getting any letters of intent to play college basketball, but that didn't bother me much. I knew a big senior season would help me live out my dream of being a Division 1 college basketball player. From the day I gave my heart to basketball, it was all about getting a basketball scholarship. I could see nothing beyond that. My only other interest outside of ball was girls, of course. I was starting to come into my own physically. I no longer wore glasses, now I wore contacts. I thought I was too smooth. Now, I had a confidence off the court that matched my new senior year swagger on the court. I was still quiet, shy some might say, but I just was more confident about my appearance. With my confidence growing both on and off the court, my senior year was about enjoying Linsly, and earning that Division 1 basketball scholarship.

When it was time for basketball season in November, I was excited and ready to get the party started. In the first few practices, I was on my best behavior and did everything Coach Smith asked me to do. He was preaching to me that if I did what he asked, I would be a more ready and complete basketball player. I listened to him and I believed him. I took for granted that if I listened to him, he would help me get that Division 1 basketball scholarship that I yearned for.

Maybe it was miscommunication, but I feel as though he wanted one thing for the team and I wanted another for my future. So, for the first few games of the season I played a role, a smaller role, because I thought that would let Coach Smith know that I trusted him and was buying into his system. The team was doing OK, but not as good as I knew we could be doing if I did more—both offensively and defensively. In the meantime, what really hurt me was that my brother Darius was getting college letters from different schools, and I still had not seen one letter from any college. At that point, it clicked. I had to be me and do what I did best on the court—play basketball with all my heart and desire. I could not worry about what Coach Smith wanted or was doing to help me. I had to help myself. All the work I put in over the summer, all the late nights watching basketball tape on the coffee table at home, the late night dribbling sessions outside on the porch, it was time for all of that work to pay off for me!

In that first game after my new "attitude," I went for about 20 points against an average team. From there my game just took off. When we came close to my hometown to play Shady Side Academy, a private school right outside of Pittsburgh, I was hyped up to show my friends and family that I could really play the game of basketball. Plus, Shady Side had turned me down for financial aid—another reason I had ended up at Linsly. So, this game was a little personal as well.

The point guard for Shady Side Academy was Terrance Parham, the same 14-year-old phenom who went to Russia to play ball because he was so good at an early age. He was now on his way to play Division 1 football at Bucknell University, a Division 1 AA football program, in the fall. In addition to Terrance, Shady Side had a stacked team, with at least 5 potential Division 1 and 2 basketball players. They had Eugene Baker, who went on to be an NFL football player, but was first given a Division 1 scholarship to Kent State to play football. They also had Pete Sauers. Pete played for the Future Stars in the summer and would receive a scholarship to play basketball at Stanford University after he graduated from high school.

At Linsly, we had no big-time players on our team. In the end, we lost a close game in which I played my tail off and rang up 40 points. That game was a big confidence booster for me. It further reaffirmed my belief that I could do some special things on the high school level. That game I played very aggressively, with a lot of energy and sense of urgency knowing that I had to play a great game in order to have a chance to win.

Even in a losing effort, I knew there could be more on the line for me. With so many potential college players on their team, I felt like a scholarship could be on the line for me. I didn't know for sure, but I couldn't take the chance and not play well in front of college recruiters. All in all, this was one of the best high school games I had played.

I did have one letdown or bad performance that season that was very disappointing. The bad game came against a school named Bellaire. They had a player who was supposed to be all-world by the name of Scottie Coin. They hyped him up so much that I couldn't wait to bump heads with him. I didn't know how good he was, but I knew he didn't want to play me as bad as I wanted to play him. He played solidly, but nothing great. I didn't play a good game at all. I only had 8 points that night and didn't shoot the ball well. I played OK in other aspects of the game, but by my standards, I was highly disappointed in my performance. Scottie Coin was a good player, but he just didn't have "it" in my eyes. The funny thing was, many people, including my coach and college recruiters, didn't think I had "it" either. "It" to me, is the talent, the ability, and the drive to be a good player at the best level you are playing at—or being good at the highest level you've been given the opportunity to play. I didn't care what anyone else thought about me—I knew eventually I would force others to see what I already knew about myself!

As a child, when my emotions got the best of me during sports, I had my dad to keep me in check. During my senior year, there was one situation on the court where I probably could have used him. I was always an emotional player. Off the court, I am not emotional at all, but on it, I was too emotional. My dad always called me a hothead. Anyway, I was ejected from a game for arguing a bad call made against my teammate.

We were not an elite basketball team. We had soft-spoken, well-mannered players. I believed these things put us at a disadvantage. In my eyes, the referees saw us as soft, passive pushovers. And in this case, expected us to accept terrible calls made by a referee. The referee disagreed with my opinion and gave me not one but two technical fouls because of my aggressive speech and actions. Two technical fouls meant instant ejection from the current game and disqualification from the next game as well. To make matters worse, the next game was an away game in a hick town in West Virginia. I knew it would be tough not playing and having to hear unkind words said about me throughout the game. My dad knew this as well and even though I would not play in the game, he drove 4 hours to support his son. This was the type of support and love he gave me. He knew I needed him and he was there. He told me to hold my head high no matter what happened that day, and that is what I did. I kept my head held high and supported my team to the fullest. We lost the game, but the team played well.

After that game, I came back and finished the season strong. I scored, defended, and helped us win more games that year than in years past. In spite of this, I didn't get nearly the love I think I deserved in West Virginia. I wasn't selected 1st team All-State, after averaging 24 points a game! I was an honorable mention selection and that hurt. I felt slighted. I wasn't getting any respect. By the time my senior season finished, I was being recruited by 1 school—a small Division 3 school called Wheeling Jesuit in Wheeling, West Virginia. My dreams of playing Division 1 basketball were shattering right in front of me!

My mom knew my goal was to play Division 1 basketball and by now she was a little disappointed with Linsly as well. She didn't know much about recruitment, but she saw how Darius was getting letters from different schools throughout the country and her son wasn't getting any. So, she decided to take matters into her own hands. That's my mom—she would do anything in her power to make my dreams come true. She and I started a letter and videotape campaign to different Division 1 schools that I thought I could play for. We probably sent letters and tapes to 50 different schools! Some replied, but many didn't. However, one Division 1 school showed real interest in my mom's letter and the game film—Howard University's Coach Butch Beard. He was a really nice man and showed genuine interest in me as a student-athlete.

My mom wanted me to fulfill my dreams of playing Division 1 basketball but she didn't want it to happen at Howard University. She went on to explain why Howard wasn't her school of choice. We had a family member attend Howard a few years before who had been hospitalized because she drank some spiked punch unknowingly at a party. Our family member never was quite the same after the incident. Although I felt terrible for our family member and I understood why my mom felt the way she did. But I didn't care about any of that stuff, I just wanted to play Division 1 basketball.

My mom and I didn't have to discuss this situation long when Coach Beard made the decision for us—he left Howard to become the head coach of the NBA's New Jersey Nets. That left me with one school, Division 2 Mansfield. At the time, my good friend and fellow Future Star comrade Lafayette Moran was attending Mansfield. Having him there made me feel a little better about attending, and giving up my goal to play Division 1 basketball. Plus, I liked and respected their assistant coach, Adrian Townsend—AT.

AT was real cool and a very good college point guard himself. I kept trying to convince myself that as long as I didn't have to pay to go to school, I would have accomplished something. AT and the head coach at Mansfield came to my house and gave us their recruiting pitch. My mom liked AT and thought that Mansfield would be a good place for me to go to college. If not for God fulfilling my dreams of playing Division 1 basketball, I would have attended Mansfield University.

By the end of my senior year, I was so frustrated and upset with Linsly about my scholarship situation, all I wanted to do was graduate and get back to Pittsburgh. I wanted to get away and be closer to my support system back home. I had one more hurdle to jump over to get a scholarship. I had to get a good score on the SAT test. I never really performed well on standardized tests, and the SAT was no different. I didn't get above an 800 the first time I took it. A few of my teachers and administrators at Linsly thought my inability to get a better score on the SAT was nonsensical. I was a 3.5 student at Linsly. As my last days of High School were winding down, I was contacted by Bucknell University.

I had sent a tape to Penn State University, but Penn State never got back in touch with me. What I heard, and was later confirmed by Bucknell Head Coach Patrick Flannery, was that the tape was sent from Penn State to Bucknell. Penn State coaches felt that I couldn't help them but I could play at a lower level, so they sent the tape to the Bucknell coaching staff. I will never really know why PSU felt that way about my ability, but thank you Penn State!

At the time Bucknell didn't give out full basketball scholarships. That negated them from contention. I couldn't pay to go to college. Coach Flannery, the head coach at Bucknell, said not to worry about the financial stuff. He said my family financial situation would enable me to get enough financial aid and assistance—that I wouldn't pay anything to attend the school. That was, of course, if I got accepted by the university.

After graduating from Linsly, all I could think of was the possibility of getting a chance to play Division 1 basketball. That summer, it came down to two schools: Division II Mansfield and Division I Bucknell. Mansfield didn't have a chance if Bucknell gave me full financial aid. I couldn't say that to anyone, because Coach Flannery still wanted to see me play live before he made his final decision. So, early in the summer, he came to watch me play a game. He needed to see if I was worth all the aid they would give me if accepted at Bucknell. Coach was not new to city life, having grown up in Philadelphia, but my mom was a little concerned about him coming up to the Hill, on his own, to watch me play. The games are played in the projects, and my mom knew how rough it could be up there. I laugh now because Coach Flannery probably had no clue what he was getting himself into. He went to sit in the stands and was literally the only white guy anywhere near the basketball court. Everyone was staring at him when he sat down, including me. I must admit, he took it all in stride, and just sat next to mom and watched the game. When the game was over, all I remember was walking over to shake his hand—a little nervous because this was my future on the line. Did he see enough in this one game to know that I was deserving of the chance to play Division I Basketball? Would my goal be achieved or will I have to accept other options? He made me relax instantly when he cracked a smile and said, "I would love to have you play for me at Bucknell."

All we had to do now was check my future SAT scores to see if I had reached admissions standards to be accepted into school. Coach Flannery left Pittsburgh the following morning saying he would be in touch very soon and welcome to Bucknell. He was very confident that my mind was made up; he was right. I knew the second he said that he would love to have me that I would be attending Bucknell University.

IV | New Face/New Place

BEFORE I KNEW it, it was the fall of 1994 and I was about to be a freshman at Bucknell University. I felt good about my transition from high school to college. One of the reasons I felt comfortable with the transition was because I knew I would be rooming with my high-school class-mate, Jamie Youssef. Jamie and I were real cool. Rooming with someone familiar would make the adjustment to college life a little easier and more comfortable. My parents helped me move into my dorm room, and it was really nice having them there on my first day of college. When I opened the door to my future room/home, I was shocked. Jamie and I didn't just get a dorm room, we got a suite! I had no idea how we got the room, but we had the only room on the floor with its own bathroom. The room was huge. I felt like the #1 recruit when I walked in. I knew I wasn't, but I was extremely happy and grateful about our living situation!

Jamie wasn't there when I arrived. His clothes and things were there because he had been at school for a month or so for football camp. It was good he wasn't there. It gave me a chance to say goodbye to my parents in private. My dad gave me a hug and told me he loved me. My dad wasn't very emotional, but I knew he was proud of me. My mom, however, was the exact opposite. She was very emotional and outspoken. She was happy to send her son off to college, and it showed in our last few minutes together. We laughed and she shared a few mother-and-son things, like the fact that she loved me, she was happy for me, I should eat well and be good, and call her if I ever needed anything. Then she prayed over me and we said our goodbyes.

When my parents left the room, I sat on my bed just thinking about my mom. I thought about how much I loved her. She had made some tough decisions for me to get this far in life. I knew it wasn't easy for her to send her son away to attend high school at the age of 13. I knew she loved me unconditionally and only wanted the best for my future. She had 2 other biological children, and sometimes 3 or more she was concerned or worried about staying at our home. My mom had a lot on her plate and she did an amazing job with all of us. I knew she was proud to see her second-born son go off to college.

Arriving on campus a little early for orientation, I got to see the campus, learn my way around a bit, and meet other freshmen trying to adjust to life in Lewisburg, Pennsylvania. At one of the orientation meetings, I encountered only one other black face in a crowd of roughly 200 people. I am kind of shy, so I just took a seat and relaxed. I didn't mingle at all. Then, the other black face walked over and said, "Anybody sitting here? You mind if I grab that seat?"

I said, "No, you got it." His name was Gene (C. Eugene Uzoukwu). We have been life-long friends, since that very 1st encounter. As I walked around the beautiful campus during orientation, I experienced an array of emotions. I was a teenager with big dreams. I had come there to be a basketball star, but I had no idea what college life had in store for me both on and off the court. Receiving a quality education from a prestigious school like Bucknell was a given. Becoming a basketball star, however, wasn't. I knew I had my work cut out for me, but I felt like I was up for the challenge.

The first few weeks of college life were nothing special. Outside of being in Lewisburg, it felt a lot like my high-school days. Of course there were more students and more cute girls, but for the most part, it was a lot like high school. I had always been kind of a loner, so I really didn't talk to many people. I simply went to class and played basketball as much as possible. That was it.

On one day in August, I walked into the gym to play some ball during my free time, as I usually did. However, this day was different because there were enough students in the gym to play a game of 5-on-5. On most days, I went to the gym to shoot by myself. I was excited to play full

I would ask myself—was I a good mom to leave my son way up there in "no man's" land in unfamiliar surroundings in Lewisburg, Pennsylvania? The day we arrived on the Bucknell campus, I remember hearing that a young man was killed in a car accident, and that didn't help ease my fears of leaving my son in Lewisburg. Yes, I wanted my baby boy in college, a good college, but at what cost for the family? I knew we really couldn't afford this college, and as a family, we still had financial responsibilities to our son at school (his books).

His siblings missed him during the years he was away at high school. I worried about Booper and if he would be okay; ALONE and in a mostly white environment (again). Going to college was something I never had a chance to do, but always wanted to do. However, it was in my heart for all my children (and any children living with me) to attend college. My feelings once we got to the campus were good. The people were friendly, but again, not too many African-Americans. In fact, I don't remember seeing ANY. So I kept trying to convince myself that this was a GREAT opportunity for MY SON! His dad and I had talked about Bucknell, a university which neither one of us had ever heard of before. Robert researched the college history, and it was far greater than we felt worthy of. He reminded me that Booper didn't get offers from the colleges he wanted, so we should do the best we could with the offers he had.

Well, I decided that this would do, but if Booper was unhappy we would simply CHANGE SCHOOLS immediately. If at any time our son came home and didn't want to return to Bucknell, it would be okay with us. Coach Terry Conrad reassured me that he would look out for Booper. Head Coach Patrick Flannery was thrilled about having him as a player, and excited about the opportunities he would have both on and off the court. He explained to me that after graduating from Bucknell, Booper would have many career options and a very good salary. I believed that my son would be able to live a life that I only could dream of. Leaving my son at Bucknell that afternoon was not easy. Once I left all I could do was pray and put it in God's hands. I remember promising God that if He protected my son that I would give my life totally to HIM. I would do and go wherever HE wanted me too. I trusted God with my son's life.

court against some competition. Because there weren't any players from the basketball team in the gym, I figured I would dominate these pick-up games. One of the students in the gym was my buddy from orientation, Gene. He told me he used to play ball. He said he had quit his senior year in high school. He was at Bucknell on an academic scholarship. So, I just assumed he was OK, but nothing special. Boy, was I in for a surprise! Gene wasn't just average, he was really, really good. He was giving me fits. I couldn't stop him from doing the things he wanted to do on the court. Gene was small, quick, had all types of moves, could shoot the ball really well, and was left-handed. My thoughts of dominating when we first started were quickly diminished by this guy standing at about 5' 9". I could score on him, but not easily. On the other hand, I could not stop him. He hit me with move after move, basket after basket. I couldn't believe he was better than I was and HE DIDN'T EVEN PLAY BALL for Bucknell! What would a college junior who played basketball do to me?

That was my wake-up call—an immediate indication of how hard I would have to work to become a better player. That pasting kept me in the gym religiously. In addition to my normal workout routine, I would talk to Gene about his moves and ask him for advice. He openly taught me different moves and how to do them on the court. Then, I would go to the gym and just work, work, and work some more. I was determined to get better.

About a week or so before official practice started, everyone was in the gym playing a pick-up game. All the upperclassmen from the team were there, a few Bucknell students who could play a little bit, and then Gene and me. The upperclassmen were trying their best to control the court and assert themselves and show their seniority over the rest of us. They weren't trying to pick freshmen or regular students to be on their teams. The way it worked was that if you lost, you had to wait to play again. Usually you had to sit out for 2 or possibly 3 games, depending on how good you were or how good people thought you were.

Gene was confident in his game and quite outspoken. He was like, "Hey, we got next game. We sat watching 2 games and it's our game next." The upperclassman kind of snickered like, "OK, y'all got next game. We will beat these young chumps and keep dominating the court." Gene had something else in mind. We had no big guys and no upperclassmen on our team—just 5 freshmen! As soon as the game started, Gene looked at me and he said, "Let's go, it's your time to show them what you can do." Remember, I had been working on my game for the past month or so. I was ready. We went down 2 points early in a game to 9. Before you knew it, I hit a jump shot, a lay-up. Gene hit a few shots and then the game winner. Game over, who's next? The upperclassmen were surprised and pissed. They were like, "Who are these kids, thinking they can come in here and win?" Gene was enjoying every minute of beating them. As we won game after game, Gene started yelling out, "Young Guns." Now, the gym was quiet except for Gene yelling, "Game, young guns baby." We didn't lose a game that day. We left the court undefeated and with the respect of the upperclassmen. Gene had set the tone that day for the rest of our 4 years at Bucknell.

First, no one would be disrespected if they wanted to play ball in the gym. Your skills and your talent would either get you more opportunities to play or to not play at all. Second, Bucknell was my team for the taking if I had the heart and desire to take it—maybe not as a freshman—but soon. I had the ability to achieve my goals at Bucknell if I had the desire and work ethic to accomplish them.

When practice officially started in my freshman year, I was ready to compete and earn minutes on the floor. Head Coach Patrick Flannery recruited me because he knew that I had the talent to play at this level, and I was there to prove that every day at practice. I wanted to show the upperclassmen that I belonged. I didn't have a clue what to expect from Coach Flan or the team because this was Coach's first year as a head coach at his alma mater. Most of the players on the team were used to the old regime and assumed that all freshmen would play their freshman year on the freshman team. I didn't know anything about that and never intended to do anything but play basketball for a Division 1 program.

I worked my tail off at every practice and I earned my spot on the team as the back-up combo (both point guard and shooting guard) guard. There were two guys in front of me: Sekou Hamer from the Bronx, New York, was the starting point guard, and Kevin Wenk from Vienna, Virginia, was the starting shooting guard. Sekou was better than me—no doubt about that. Kevin wasn't the most talented player, but he was a hard-nosed, hard-working ballplayer who played his tail off every minute he was on the floor. Kevin was the leader of the team. He was the steady, heady player that the team needed in the starting lineup to help us play more together—like a unit.

One of my first college games was against the Maryland Terrapins in College Park, Maryland, at Cole Field House. They had a phenomenal freshmen in Joe Smith (a future #1 pick in the NBA draft), Johnny Rhodes, Duane Simpkins (a highly recruited phenomenal point guard out of DC), Exree Hipp, Mario Lucas, and another freshman who would end up having a great professional career, Lithuanian Sarunas Jasikevicius. I remember that game because when we ran out, I couldn't believe that 15,000 people came to see a basketball game whose outcome was known before the game was even played—Maryland would win. I knew I wasn't going to play that much, but I was extremely nervous!

During the lay-up line, I kept looking at all those fans and students like, "Wow, this is big-time basketball!" That game taught me something about myself. After a blowout loss where I got to play some minutes when the game actually still mattered in the 1st half, I realized I could play college basketball.

I stood toe-to-toe with Duane Simpkins, and I had no fear. He picked me up full court, and I had no trouble getting the team into our offensive sets. There was no doubt that he was better than I was, but he didn't expose me or make me look like I didn't belong out there on the same court. That realization kept me working every day in practice to become a better player. I kept on believing that one day I would be part of a big game against a big team, with Bucknell being on the winning end. I wanted to be a part of something special at Bucknell, but I knew that first I had to be special.

That freshman year was a blur on the court. We had a phenomenal regular season. We won the Patriot League regular season in Coach Flannery's first year. We got better as the year progressed. I only played about 10 to 15 minutes a game, but I felt good about myself because I was the only freshman who played a quality amount of minutes when the game still mattered. That was a feat in itself, especially as I wasn't even the #1 freshman recruit. In spite of the positives, the season ended on a sour note. We were the #1 seed in the Patriot League tournament and felt we had a good chance to make the NCAA tournament. In the first game, we would face the host team—the last-place team in the conference, Army. To our surprise, they played a great game, defeating us handily, ending our season. It happened so quickly that I don't believe anyone realized our season was really over until we arrived back on campus. It was a bittersweet ending. However, I was looking forward to next year. I knew that next year, expectations would be even higher for us. We had a few seniors, but they didn't play very much. All 5 starters were juniors, so we would have the same team back next year. This meant more success and more pressure next season to perform at an even higher level. What's more, I knew I had to get better if I intended on being a starter next year—and I expected to be a starter!

I met good people during my first year at Bucknell and established a few good relationships. At college, I had to get used to balancing my course work with my social life. I had 100 percent freedom. I could do whatever I wanted, whenever I wanted to do it. That was cool, but at times I would procrastinate, thinking I had time to do my school work later. It didn't happen often but it did happen. Boarding school taught me discipline and I learned to do the right things, the right way.

I did get out and have fun in my freshman year. I attended a few house parties that the multicultural students would throw at the 7th Street House. I even dated a senior for a few months. She was a mature, genuine, supportive, sincere sweetheart. She taught me how to be in a healthy, fun relationship that didn't involve sex. We never crossed that line. But, I was a young, naïve, immature, horny, teenager who didn't know how to be in that type of a relationship with a good woman. I pushed her away and did something stupid. I don't even remember what I did to disappoint her. We never recovered from my mishap. I regret mishandling that situation as a young buck. She was a good woman, and I wasn't as happy chasing other women as I was spending quality time with her. You live and learn, and I guess I learned that lesson the hard way.

As school ended, it was time to get ready for the summer. That meant basketball, basketball, and more basketball. I met with Coach Flannery before I left for the summer and he gave me a few pointers that I needed to work on. He also told me that I could do some great things at Bucknell, but it would take a lot of hard work. I vividly remember him saying, "You will be as good as you want to be here. I decide who plays, but you can show me who deserves to play." That was all I needed to push myself to extreme measures that summer. I knew I would work harder than any other player. That would start with hours of playing ball any and everywhere I could possibly get to.

After a productive summer, I was excited to get back to school and show off all the skills I had worked on. I wanted to show the coaching staff that I was ready to be a starter. As the preseason began in my sophomore year, I was confident—a little cocky—and ready to show and prove to everyone that this was my year to step up. It was evident early that I was not backing down from anyone. In a preseason pick-up game, I got into an altercation with Brian, our starting center and All-Patriot League performer. He called a foul on me that I knew was a soft call. I thought he was very talented offensively, but a bit of a cry baby. So I refused to give him the foul that he had just called on me.

He said, "Check ball, our ball."

I had the ball in my hands and I said, "No, you can't get that."

He said, "Who are you? You're a nobody around here. Our ball, underclassman."

I said, "Who am I? Who am I? I am better than you, and one of the best players on this court. Underclassman! What's sad is an upperclassman being a soft hooper." He was pissed, but I didn't back down. Brian was about 6' 9", so he tried to just stand over me. I just laughed and stood there like, "What are you going to do?" The team kind of jumped in and made sure nothing happened. Yes, they got the ball and I was OK with that, but my point was proven. Now Brian and everyone else knew I was about business, and I wasn't accepting the same passive role I played last year. I was going to be a major part of this team whether they liked it or not.

School went very smoothly my second year at Bucknell. I had adjusted to the rigors of school work and started to fit in socially. Gene, Willie Hill (who played football), and I were getting closer as friends.

I hung out with them the majority of the time. Outside of that, not much changed for me. I went to class, partied very little, and hung out with a few female friends from time to time. I did start developing a good friendship with a young woman back home named Toya. We had known each other for a few summers at this point. I mostly saw her at the hoop courts I played at during the summers, but we had recently started talking regularly on the phone. It was only friendly banter. She was on her way to college the following year, and she wanted to talk and bounce ideas off of me. I secretly had a crush on her, but I didn't say anything. Being a good friend to her was enough for me because I knew that was what she needed and all she could offer me at the time. The more we communicated, the more diverse our conversations became. We talked about what she wanted to study in college, her love life, and what she wanted from a current boyfriend. I enjoyed our friendship and she gave me a piece of home while I was away at school.

Sophomore year was good off the court, but even better on it. Early in the season, we headed to a tournament in Wichita to face a ranked Alabama team. They had players on their team that I'd watched on television the season before, and even looked up to. I was a fan of Marvin Orange, the Crimson Tide point guard. He was a smooth, nice-shooting combo guard. They also had Roy Rogers and Eric Washington, both of whom would go on to play for a few years in the NBA. Two days before the trip, our starting point guard Sekou Hamer went down with a sprained ankle. The look on the seniors' faces when Sekou got hurt was priceless. It was as if they thought we would lose every game until he came back. I never liked to see a teammate get hurt, but when Sekou went down, I knew it was my chance to show I could lead our team. I was very confident in my abilities. I didn't know if we could beat Alabama, but I knew that game could change everyone's opinion of my ability and potential to lead.

On the plane ride to the tournament, Coach Flannery had a talk with me. He told me to be patient, not to force things, not to get down on myself, and last but not least, "Go get 'em buddy." That conversation relaxed my nerves, and the following night I proved that I could play, compete, and defeat some of the best players in the country. We went toe-to-toe with Alabama. I had a great game with 16 points, and we defeated the Crimson Tide 72–64. It was the biggest win in Coach Flannery's tenure to that point, and the biggest win in Bucknell history. Bucknell went on to win bigger games and beat bigger and better teams, but at that time, we had accomplished something never done before.

I tried to play it cool right after the game around the team, but I was the happiest man on the planet. I felt like I had proven my point. I was not a talker, but a doer. All the hard work I had put in over the summer paid off. All the times I'd dreamt about playing big in a big game—I'd done it! I didn't know what the future held for me, but I knew I had played a hell of a game at the right time. I must say, not much changed after the big win, as far as my role on the team. I went back to coming off the bench. In the end, we didn't live up to our expectations that season. We definitely underachieved as a team. This was an average season, and I didn't come to Bucknell to play on an average team. I knew next season it would be my team and my time to shine.

An incident happened during my second year at Bucknell that could have forever changed my life. Coach Flannery called my room saying he wanted to talk to me immediately. He had never called my room before, so I thought I was in some type of trouble. I didn't know what I had done, but I was nervous, thinking that it must be bad if Coach was coming to my room to talk. When he walked into my room he got straight to it.

Coach told me that my cousin Nelco had been killed a few hours ago. I looked at him speechless for a few minutes and then started crying. Coach gave me a hug and consoled me for more than an hour. I sat there crying, just thinking about what I should do. I had just talked to my cousin a week ago. We talked about him coming up to Bucknell to get away from the streets. We laughed and joked about the girls he would be talking to when he got here. Now he was gone from this earth and I couldn't believe it.

Nelco was a cousin that trouble always seemed to find. In spite of this, he had an untainted and pure love for my family—indescribable. I had so much admiration and respect for how he had persevered through a rough upbringing. All he knew was the streets, and the streets ended up killing him. He was shot on New Year's Day. After hearing about his death, I wanted to go home. I couldn't imagine not being home, surrounded by family. However, my mom had talked to Coach; she didn't want me to come home. She felt it was best that I stay at school. I didn't agree with her decision, and for about 3 or 4 days, all I could think about was transferring. Coach Flannery and I went back and forth on the matter for hours—even days. He never wavered in saying that Bucknell was the place for me, and that if I left school, I would never be the man or player that I could become.

In his office one afternoon Coach said, "J.R., leaving will be the biggest mistake of your life. Why hurt your family more by going home?" I sat in silence for a few minutes, and when I got up to leave his office Coach Flan said, "I love you kiddo." I turned and walked out, knowing that Bucknell and playing for Coach Flannery was where I was supposed to be. In the end, I never transferred to Duquesne University. I didn't even go home for the funeral. It would have been too much for me to handle at the time. Coach Flannery saved my life by caring about me as a man. He didn't put my athletic ability first. He wasn't thinking about himself or the team but he put my family and me first. That meant a lot to me and from then on I never wanted to let him down or disappoint him.

Knowing that I only had 2 years left in college, that summer I put immense pressure on myself to get better as a basketball player. I didn't want to be good; I wanted to be *really* good. I wanted Bucknell to be MY team next year, and I knew in order for that to happen, I had to work even harder than I did the summer before.

Coach Flannery set up a trip for our team to travel overseas and play a few games. I didn't know what to expect as far as the games were concerned but that wasn't my first priority. My primary focus for the trip was to play well and become more of a team leader. That trip was important to me, and although some of the players were excited at the chance to tour Europe and enjoy the sites, I was there strictly to play the game I loved. I don't even remember all the places we visited, but I do recall playing in both Sweden and Finland. We won most of the games. The competition wasn't very challenging. What I didn't know was that we weren't playing the best players or the best European teams. Nevertheless, the trip was a success and it was nice to be able to play ball competitively and see another part of the world.

After returning home from Europe, I spent the rest of the summer playing basketball. I participated in 3 summer leagues in Pittsburgh, and spent a lot of time working on my game with Darius. One hot summer day, Darius, a few of our friends who played college ball, and I went to play basketball at the park. We ended up playing all day. Samba Johnson, a fiery point guard who'd just graduated from Chaminade University in Hawaii was there. He was a player that Darius and I looked up to.

On this particular day, it was evident that I was coming into my own, and I was the best player on the court. My team had been winning all day before we decided that we would play one last game. We were all a little exhausted going into the final game. I was playing the last game a little lackadaisical and my team began to lose for the first time that day. Out of nowhere, Samba started barking at me. He was talking trash and said, "You are about to lose, you only have 1 point, 1 rebound, and 1 assist. Your team ain't winning this game, you ain't sh★★ Boop!" That caught me off guard. He was telling the truth, but he knew I was going through the motions. I had been destroying him on both ends of the court all day long. Now, during the last game he started talking because he was going to get 1 win out of 10 or more games. It ticked me off, but what could I say? He was right. Every time I step on the court, I have to play with heart, desire, and a sense of something to prove. Many times fatigue causes you to relax, take a break and succumb to being tired. Samba's outburst made me realize that others are always working to beat me. You're only as good as your last game, so play every game like it's your last.

I laughed it off that day, and told him, "About time you got a win, Samb." However, he taught me a valuable lesson—never step on the court unless you are going to try and play your best and win—period!

I knew going into my junior season there would be a lot of pressure on me—pressure that I wanted—pressure that I put on myself. My first goal was to play during March Madness in the NCAA tournament. I knew I only had 2 years left to fulfill that goal. Time was ticking. The other goal was the NBA. That was not truly a goal of mine—sort of pushed on me by others. I just wanted to be a good college player and an elite Patriot League performer. Others were talking that NBA babble.

All I wanted to do was play well individually and try and take Bucknell's basketball program to new heights.

As for college life, I started doing things a typical 20-year-old college athlete wanting to enjoy the "glory years of college" would do. I became more socially active and started traveling off campus to enjoy other colleges and universities as well. I didn't have a car or a driver's license at the time but that didn't deter me or disrupt my fun. A good friend named Carrie used to let Gene and I borrow her car to travel to Bloomsburg, Penn State, and even Howard in DC from time to time. Gene had a driver's license so we were good to roll in Carrie's car—legally. Carrie was my girl. Not my girl as in my girlfriend, but my girl as in a true friend—more like a sister. She had a kind heart and I will always have love for CJ (that's what I called her).

That year I also had my first-ever experience partying at a white fraternity. I had no idea what carefree, unadulterated fun was, until then. I was totally surprised by what I saw. There were nothing but kegs of beer, dirty floors, and college kids getting drunk and acting crazily (good crazy)—listening to hard rock, heavy metal, and Top 40. I had no idea it was like that! I mean, no one was dressed up or trying to look stylish like at other parties—like the black parties I had attended. They just jumped around, danced with no rhythm, spilled beer on each other, screamed and yelled—just truly having fun in their eyes. Surprisingly, I enjoyed it! It showed me that it wasn't always about looking dapper or trying to impress others when it came to having fun. Don't misunderstand me, I loved the black parties and get-togethers at Bucknell as well. I went to them far more often than I did the white frat parties. I just felt more comfortable in an element that I was familiar with. Also, I took pleasure in and benefited from the parties I attended at other schools. I enjoyed meeting new people and seeing new faces—OK, I really just enjoyed seeing beautiful women! There was nothing like an attractive woman dressed up, smelling good, and just doing her thing. Now I wasn't a guy that was smooth with the women by any stretch of the imagination. I didn't have what my friends would call "game." I was happy with a good conversation and quality company. I simply enjoyed the presence of an attractive woman.

Getting a degree from Bucknell was no easy task, and even though I was enjoying the college social life, I wasn't willing to compromise getting a sound education. I continued to focus on my academics first and basketball second. I had decided the previous year that business management would be my major. I enjoyed the business classes I had taken previously and wanted to pursue that degree. Consequently, I really buckled down in the first semester of my junior year and embraced learning. The opportunity to learn from experts (professors) in their fields would not last forever, and I wanted to take full advantage of that. A degree in 4 years was my goal and I was determined to accomplish this feat.

On the basketball floor, I had an exhilarating year. It didn't end with a trip to the NCAA tournament, but we came very close. Before the start of the season, Coach Flannery, in the Bucknell media guide, said these things about me, "*J.R. is a bundle of energy. He's very unselfish, very vocal, and very smart, and those are the things you look for in a point guard. I'm excited about working with J.R. as with any point guard I've had. He's worked extremely hard in the offseason and ready to assume the role of running this ballclub. He sets the table for us.*" We had a tough schedule ahead of us that season. We lived up to our own expectations with some big wins; conversely, we played below our standards a few times that season with some disappointing losses. It was a roller coaster regular season but we grew immensely as a team.

By the time the Patriot League tournament rolled around, we felt that we were the best team in the league, despite the doubters and critics saying that we would go no further than the second round. We would soon face Colgate and their future first-round NBA draft pick, Adonal Foyle. I loved being the underdog and this gave me added motivation to shock everyone and defeat Colgate. Our mentality going into the tournament was why not us, why not now? We rolled in Game 1 with an easy win and then stunned everyone by defeating Colgate in Game 2. That Colgate game was a special victory and moment for my dad and me. I had a very good game and as I walked off the court I looked up at my dad smiling, he screamed, "That's right son, way to spoil the party. We're not supposed to be here."

I couldn't hold my excitement, I was pointing at my dad bobbing my head, bouncing around smiling, thinking to myself, "This is our year!"

Right before I ran to the locker room I saw my dad pointing at me proudly with a big grin on his face. It felt good knowing that I had done something special and that he was there to experience it. We had one more win to get before reaching my ultimate goal—playing in the NCAA tournament. Before that step, we had to travel to Annapolis, Maryland, to face the home team, Navy, in the Patriot League championship game.

The week of the game I dreamt about me smiling with my hands up in the air swaying from side-to-side like Jalen Rose did at Michigan, when his team won an NCAA tournament game a few years ago that they weren't expected to win. I also talked to my friends back home that week, and they couldn't wait to watch the game on ESPN. My mom was throwing a get-together at the house to have my friends and family over to watch the game. I was excited that everyone back home would be watching the game on TV.

The night before the game I could barely sleep. I couldn't believe what I was about to accomplish. I had dreamed about this moment as a child. Running onto the court the night of the game, I knew it was my time. I had waited long enough to lead this team at Bucknell, and now it was my time to get us to the promised land. It was a tough, hard-fought game. Both teams played with heart and desire, but one team had to lose. That night, it was Bucknell. I was heartbroken. I had failed. I didn't accomplish my goal. I didn't push my team over the hump. I asked for the responsibility to make this a championship season and didn't achieve success when it mattered most. I had let my team, my family, my friends, and myself down. I played a solid game but not the extraordinary game that I needed to play for us to win. As I sat in my locker after the game, my eyes were full of tears. It was as if a weight had been dropped on my chest and I couldn't breathe. My life pertaining to basketball felt like it was flashing in front of me. I didn't think I would ever get over the pain I felt at that moment.

Losing an important game is tough, but how you bounce back is what shows your true character. Well, let me tell you, I was in the dumps for more than 3 weeks. I was depressed. I missed classes. I didn't eat much. I am a sore loser and, at that moment, I was sick. I was sick about losing and I didn't have the energy or strength to fight back. My dreams had been shattered.

I didn't know how to deal with such a disappointing basketball experience. It took a childhood friend to help me get over this tough time.

Darius called me and left this message on my answering machine, *"Go to that place where everything makes sense. Don't sit in your room, but get out and smell the fresh air. Man, I can only dream of making it to where you're at. It's going to be alright. This is a test. A test to see if you have what it takes to persevere."* The next day I woke up and took his advice. I went to that place of refuge, my sanctuary, the basketball court! I dribbled the ball and shot jump shots with tears in my eyes for more than 2 hours. It was the cleansing I needed. I had put so much pressure on myself to succeed. I learned a lot about myself during this time, and failure like this is one reason I love the game so much.

After a good year in the classroom, it was time for the summer break—always critical to my development as a player. This summer would be different, and I knew it. It could be the last time I would call myself an athlete. I had one more year to prove to the world that I could compete with the best players at any school in the country. I was so close last season to doing something extraordinary. I couldn't stop or give up now. I had to work harder and smarter; that started the first day of summer. I expected a lot of myself, and I was taking my upcoming season very seriously. Nothing was a joke when it came to ball. My buddies on the Future Stars thought I was so serious and crazy when it came to the game that they started calling me HC (for Head Case).

What pushed me even harder that summer was Dick Vitale having said my name wrong on national television, during our PL championship game last season. Dick Vitale, the famous NCAA commentator and "the man" when it came to college basketball, called me RJ instead of J.R. at halftime of the Patriot League championship game. He was giving me love, but he didn't even know my name—for real! I took that personally, and I worked all summer saying to myself, Dickie V. will know my name next year! There will be no mistaking who I am or how good I am. I will be good enough that he will know my name AND say it correctly next time—something that pushed me and drove me even harder throughout the summer.

I worked myself to exhaustion on more than one occasion. I was obsessed with putting in the work required to play better on the big stage.

I had played well many times against bigger schools, but I failed when it mattered the most—at last season's Patriot League Finals. Many of my close friends and associates started talking about my making it to the pro level. I didn't care about being a professional basketball player, I wanted to get to the NCAA tournament. Furthermore, all their talk and uncertainty of my future concerning basketball caused me to close myself off from my friends. All this pressure from the outside world caused my emotions to run wild all summer long when it came to the game of basketball.

I didn't have much of a social life that summer. I was either playing ball or watching it. One evening, while at a Kenard game, sitting in the bleachers getting ready to play next, I saw a friend of mine. Mike was his name. He was sitting in front of me with his friend. He introduced me to her.

She said, "Hi."

I said, "What's up?" She was sexy and had this look about her that I can't even describe. It's hard to explain, but I knew she wasn't from Pittsburgh. She was 5' 10"(which I didn't know until she stood up), light skin, cute face, and had this skirt on with those long legs that had me, like "Wow!" Her accent and inviting smile had me staring at her. She had me in a daze. Anyway, she asked me who I played for and when was I playing. I told her I played for the Future Stars and that I was playing next against D. Wade's team. D. Wade is a legend in Pittsburgh, so she knew exactly who I was playing against. She chuckled and said, "Oh, OK. You got your hands full next. Don't get hurt out there."

I just smiled and responded, "I hear you."

A few days later, while downtown, I bumped into her again. As we crossed paths, she said, "Hey cutie, good game the other day, when do you play again?" She caught me off guard. I didn't think she stayed for the game and did she just say "cutie"? She had so much flavor that I had to gain my composure before opening my mouth. I said a few words and then kept it moving because she seemed to be in a hurry. As she walked away, I thought, "Man, I blew it. Why didn't I ask her for her telephone number? Why did I freeze up like a sucker?"

Walking away I thought to myself, "Oh well, it's over now." That weekend while at a 21-and-over club (I was not quite 21), who did I see walking in the club?—none other than my mystery woman. She walked in.

No, she floated in! It looked like she was in a scene from a Spike Lee Joint where people are supposed to be walking but they are gliding effortlessly on the set—that was her that night! She seemed to be on a different level from every other woman in the club. I played it cool and stood near the bar. I was sure she would come get a drink. Five minutes later she was there. She said, "Hey," and from there we shared a few drinks and conversed until the lights came on signaling closing time.

Her name was Nicole. She was from Delaware but spent most of her time in Philadelphia. She now lived in Pittsburgh, had a daughter, and didn't have time for the BS. We spent the whole night vibing with each other, but I can't lie, she was intimidating. She could sense I was shy and probably wouldn't ask her for her telephone number. Before she caught up with her friends, she gave me her number and said to call her. I wasted no time; I called her the next day. She was everything I thought she would be and more. She became my friend, my confidante, my woman, and many more things over the next 5-plus years that we spent together.

My senior year of college had finally arrived. What would be the outcome of my collegiate basketball career? Would I have a good season? Would I lead Bucknell to the NCAA tournament? Would I get a shot at playing in the NBA? I had so many questions at the time but no answers. It was time to find out what I was made of.

The basketball season started with a trip back home to play two schools: Robert Morris College and the University of Pittsburgh (Pitt). Robert Morris wasn't a big deal, but playing at Pitt, in the Fieldhouse— Wow! That was huge for a kid who grew up idolizing Pitt players. I knew of a few hometown kids who came back home to play against Pitt. None of them played well. In spite of this, I planned on having a great game for my homecoming. What did make me nervous was knowing that I would have all my family and friends attending the game. In addition, all of the hood, the Hill district, and my haters would be there to see if I was as good as I thought I was. A few days before the game, my close friends would call me throughout the day to say things like, "What's up, Boop? It's on, baby! You coming back home! You gotta come back and destroy these boys."

Trying to play down my excitement I would reply, "Yep, we are going to go in there and try to get a win, man."

In their excitement for me they would be like, "Naw, Boop, you better do your thing."

Again, I would say, "I am, man. It's going to be fun." I was a little nervous, but I would never let on what I was feeling. Honestly, I just didn't want to come home and get blown out. I wanted to come back home with a bang and represent my family, friends, loved ones, and supporters to the fullest.

It seemed like it didn't take long at all for game day to arrive. Before I knew it, it was showtime! I was running out onto the Pitt Fieldhouse floor, with the lights beaming down on the court, getting ready to face one of my toughest challenges of my senior year. This was it! The pressure was on from the moment I ran onto the court. I remember hitting the floor and seeing my mom in the front row. She loves me to pieces. She was proud of her son but, boy, was she making it hard for me to be that low-key assassin. I love her to death, so it was all good. Needless to say, I would feel like crap if I came home and played terribly—with my mom in the front row making a big scene. She was holding up signs, screaming my name, wearing my jersey number and had everyone in my family wearing T-shirts with my number on them. As soon as the ball went up for the opening tap, the nervousness was gone and I didn't care who was in the gym watching—it was time to get down with the big boys.

Although we didn't pull off the upset, we battled hard and lost a close game 74–67. Unlike the others, I came home and represented well. I did a little bit of everything in this game. I hit a half-court shot before the half-time buzzer. I hit a few tough shots throughout the game. I even got a dunk (my first collegiate dunk in a game). I finished with 27 points and a few assists and rebounds. I left the court emotionally drained but proud—pleased to have represented my family and Bucknell University well.

When I walked out of the locker room after the game and saw my then girlfriend, Nicole, smiling and my family just so happy and proud, it warmed my heart. I hugged my mom, sister, and the rest of my family before I had to catch up with my team. Seeing my family together like that, just happy to have seen me play a game, was a true blessing. Their support and love was all I needed to succeed. I knew that God had His hands on my performance that night.

I can't say there was a lot to do in Pittsburgh in the summer but because I love basketball, I couldn't pass up the opportunity to check out the summer league games. My boy, Mike James, was playing for Duquesne and told me to check out the events at Kenard. He made a point of letting me know that it wasn't Sonny Hill (the summer league games in Philly), but that I would enjoy it for sure.

Mike and I were chilling in the bleachers and he introduced me to a few of the guys sitting around. The one guy was a little cutie—they called him Boop. Some even said Booper. Now that was interesting in itself, but what was more interesting was that Mike told me he went to Bucknell. So in my mind, "I'm like, oh, he got a little hoop game AND he has a brain—now that could be dangerous (in a good way)."

We sat and chatted with the crew because Boop's team was playing next. I talked a little trash to him because he was playing D. Wade's squad next. D. Wade was straight hood and had mad handle. I teased Boop a little bit to let him know that I didn't think he could handle D. Wade. He had this little smirk that said, "Yeah whatever!" I stayed around and checked the game out—and I had to admit that Boop had some game. Now I thought his pat was a little high and hard, but it worked for him. He was definitely fast and could throw off some assists with ease. I got a chuckle out of watching his team hit D. Wade's up for a win.

A few days later my girlfriend Michelle and I were walking down 5th Avenue at lunch-time and I saw Boop walking up with one of his friends. I smiled at him and asked him when he was play-ing up at Kenard again. He gave me a puzzled look, but then replied that he was playing the next day. I went to Donzi's on Sunday night—that was the local hot spot in Pittsburgh at the time. I saw Boop standing right by the door. He gave me the once-over and I did the same. He had the preppy college boy look that I loved, so I stopped to converse with him. I knew he was young, but he carried

(Continued on page 248)

We started the season a miserable 1–4. However, we would regroup and by the end of the season, we had developed into a pretty solid team. On Senior Night, the last home game of the season for a senior, the university and my team made sure it would be a special night. Earlier that week, all I could think about was the feelings of my then-girlfriend, Nicole. My mom wasn't a big fan of Nicole early in our relationship. However, I knew that Nicole was a good woman.

Not inviting Nicole to Senior Night would hurt her feelings, and I felt terrible all week thinking about it. But Senior Night was about my parents. It was their time to bask in the glory of the bright lights for all they had done to raise me. Anyway, I was the lone senior and the fans, students, and alumni showered my family and me with so much love they almost brought me to tears. My mom enjoyed every minute of it. She walked out to mid-court with her son, waving her arms as if she were the Queen of England. She was waving to the crowd as if they were her successors. I could only smile and chuckle. She deserved every minute of the praise and adulation of the crowd and I was happy she was eating it up.

She had made all the key decisions to get me to Bucknell. She didn't always do what others thought was best, but she did what she knew was best for her son. And in the end, it all paid off. I was happy that she got a chance to enjoy such a moment. Matter of fact, we enjoyed it together. That made it all the more special. My dad, on the other hand, was his usual cool, laid-back self. He just had his arm around my shoulders and told me a few times how proud he was of me. The icing on the cake was we won the game. It felt good to finish my career at home the way I did—with a win.

Before I knew it, it was tournament time and my last opportunity to reach the NCAA tournament. This was no time to be cool or worry about anything but playing ball—to the best of my ability. My intensity and my passion were on display from the very beginning of the Patriot League Tournament. My only thought was that this could be the last time I play organized basketball. I had to give everything I had on the court. Game 1 of the tournament was a tough game that we won 60–56. A win is a win and we were moving on to the semi-finals against the home team, Navy—the same team that had beaten us last year in the finals. I came out that game with the mindset that losing was not an option. No one was going to stop me from fulfilling my dreams of making it to "March Madness." Then in an instant my college basketball career was over. Was this really happening? Was this really how my career was going to end?

A Navy player and I got tangled up, and he went a little overboard by getting in my face. He pushed my shoulder and then pointed his finger at me. I didn't back down. I gave him a serious look, but I didn't touch him. I told him, "It's a motherf★★★in' war out here today baby and we ain't going nowhere. We're here to play today." I thought this was harmless, just 2 guys battling and trying to get their teams over the hump. Plus, I didn't touch him. I just pointed back at him and let him know this game was serious and that this wasn't last year. This happened with about 15 minutes left in the game and we were ahead by 2 or 3 points. I already had 20 points and felt like I was on my way to 40. I was unstoppable. In any case, the referee jumped in and gave us both a technical foul. OK cool, no big deal, right? I was at half court talking with my team, then, out of nowhere the referee said that I had to leave the court. He was kicking me out of the game. What??? What was he talking about? I didn't do anything. This couldn't be happening. Was he serious? This was not happening.

The referee touched me and told me I had to leave the court. I was in complete shock. I walked off in disbelief. My legs started to shake and tears were forming in my eyes. Before I left the court I took off my jersey and threw it into the crowd. I was hurt and disgusted. I knew my team couldn't play without me for 15 minutes against this Navy team and win. I was so disgruntled when I walked into the locker room that I went berserk. I started throwing things and screaming at the top of my lungs. I was in such a rage! I just couldn't believe what had happened. Why was this happening to me? What did I do to deserve this? I had done nothing wrong. I didn't touch the other guy. All I did was stand my ground in retaliation. Why didn't he get kicked out? Why did the referee do this to me? Did he know I was a senior? Did he kick me out because I was black and the other player was white? All these thoughts ran through my mind.

In the middle of my rage, my father walked in. He could see the hurt, pain, and the distraught look in my eyes. He walked over to console me, and I collapsed in his arms. I cried uncontrollably. He just held me and told me how proud he was of me and that he loved me. At that moment, I didn't know what to think about the hand I had been dealt concerning basketball, but I did know that my dad would always be right by my side no matter what. He had attended almost every game in my junior and senior years—both the home and away games. He was committed to his son and what more could a young man ask for? I would look up in the stands before every game to seek him out. He would usually be in the corner with a hat on. He would point at me and say, "It's time." It always made me feel good knowing he was there.

Sitting in that locker room at Navy, I had reached a new all-time low. I thought I couldn't feel any worse than I did last year. I felt like life was truly unfair. What was God telling me? I knew God had a plan for me, but I didn't see it. In spite of what I was dealing with in the locker room, my team fought hard without me, but lost the game handily, 80–61. My college career was over and for the second time, I didn't do enough for my team to get to the NCAA tournament—something I watched on TV as a kid for years and dreamed about had been snatched right out of my hands.

I went back to Bucknell and disappeared. There was no answering the phone, there was no consoling me—my career at Bucknell was over—and I had probably played my last official game as a basketball player. As a consolation prize, a few months after the Patriot League Tournament, they suspended the referee who kicked me out of the game from doing Patriot League games for 3 years or something like that. I couldn't care less about that or the referee. I was hurt, and that pain stayed with me for months, even years after I graduated from college.

During the last few months of school, I hoped and prayed that a possible basketball opportunity would present itself, or an agent would call and tell me I was the best player he had seen come out of Bucknell—but neither happened. Although I did purchase a reasonably priced blue suit from Burlington Coat Factory for a few job interviews, I did not get any job offers. I didn't want to work in corporate America after I graduated; I wanted to play pro basketball. Coach Flannery had made a few calls on my behalf, but nothing came of them. I am not sure why, maybe it was the upcoming NBA lockout, or just that no one thought I had the talent or ability to play at the next level. Either way, it was starting to look like my career playing basketball was over; I wouldn't play beyond college.

I didn't know much about playing ball overseas, so I continued to focus on getting an invitation to an NBA Summer League, an NBA camp, or even an invitation to hoop in some NBA invitationals such as Portsmouth. I had talked to a few agents, but none of them were really interested in representing me. It seemed as if they were conversing with me as a favor to someone else. I had not quite given up on my hoop dreams yet, so when I went home, I would work out at Duquesne University to stay in shape. I figured that I had better be ready if an opportunity ever presented itself.

One afternoon while sitting in Darrell Porter's office (he was the head coach at Duquesne University and a role model to me for many years) talking about ball and life after ball, he had to leave to attend to something urgently. He told me to come back tomorrow to talk, but I could chill in his office if I wanted to. He told me to make myself comfortable. So, I grabbed some reading material off his desk and was reading different things when I came across something about playing ball in Europe. I grabbed it and put it in my pocket. Later that evening, I filled out the application form and put it in the mail the following day.

Off the court, my senior year was pleasurable. I did more in my senior year than I had in all 3 previous years combined. I took advantage of being the "big man" on campus. Also, I laughed more and I enjoyed the little things more than I had before. It was as if I finally realized how special life was at Bucknell. I sensed that the people I met and spent time with would probably be life-long friends. I took pictures around campus with friends, wrestled with the fellas in the hallway of the dorm, sat outside, and joked around with people. I totally embraced being a senior at Bucknell.

I knew that my college days were coming to an end. I wanted to take it all in. I also did things that I shouldn't have done—like driving in a snow storm. One night, during the winter break, my teammates and I were bored and tried to go out and have a good time. The weather was awful, but we were thirsty for some fun! I had a white, paint-chipped, could-drive-for-a-month-on-a-full-tank-of-gas, 1985

Chevy Celebrity. My grandma owned the car before me. I was thankful for it. It was one of the cheapest cars on campus, but that didn't bother me in the least. We called the car "the Ubie" and I loved it.

One night as we drove slowly to Penn State, about 45 minutes from Bucknell, the Ubie slid off the road. The car had bald tires and I knew that I shouldn't have been driving in such bad weather. We got out, pushed the Ubie back on the highway, and kept driving. The car suffered a little dent on the side from sliding into a ditch. I wasn't happy about it but it didn't bother me much either. I just wanted to get to Penn State to have some fun.

Two hours later, when we finally made it up to Penn State, we had a blast. We drove back early the next morning, laughing, joking, and having a good ole' time, not even thinking that what we just had done was stupid and dangerous. The weather was bad, the tires were bald, the car slid off the road, and someone could have been seriously hurt. It definitely paid off having a mom and family always praying over me. We should have been smarter, especially me being the leader and the oldest. But, we were all living in the moment. I won't forget that ride, sitting in the car laughing with my teammates about life. I saw another side of them that night. They had dreams and hopes about basketball and things outside of school—the same way I did. It was a great learning experience for me, including the dangerous car ride.

On one of the last days at Bucknell, Gene and I were in the gym by ourselves shooting ball and talking. By now, I was better than Gene at hoops, and he was no longer that freshman who crushed me. I was now the senior crushing him.

Gene said, "What's up, let's play 1-on-1." He wanted to play one last game for old time's sake.

I laughed—like "OK." I figured that I would dominate the game pretty easily. As the game went back and forth, and Gene made every shot, I shot mostly jumpers because I felt I was the better player. He smiled and hit jumper after jumper, matching me point for point. He got excited because he thought he could win. By then, the game had tied, and the next person who scored would win the game. Gene had the ball, so victory could have been his. I was playing defense for real now. I'm talking defense like it was the NBA Finals. I couldn't let Gene defeat me. I knew if he won he would rub it in my face and never let it go. I had to stop him! With the ball in his hands and the game on the line, he took a step back after we checked the ball. Now he was about 3 steps behind the college 3-point line—he made his move—pump fake, jab step, pump fake, jab step, cross over hard dribble between the legs, in and out—step back—and launched a three-pointer. As the ball was in the air, I turned to get the rebound and Gene said, "That's good." The ball seemed to be in the air for 30 seconds. I thought "Hell no, I can't let Gene beat me. I will never hear the end of this." The ball went in—and out—and Gene was crushed. He knew he couldn't stop me from game point. I was not going to shoot a jumper to win the game. I was going to drive to the basket and Gene knew it. So he basically quit and just lay on the court screaming and laughing. He kept saying, "You were scared as hell." He was smiling and laughing, but for that split moment, he thought that he had knocked me off my pedestal. We laugh about that game to this day. He says if he had beaten me, I wouldn't be the person or player I am today. I just laugh. Maybe he's right, maybe not. But, we will never know. More important, we don't have to know because I won.

I am amazed at some of the great memories I have of Bucknell University. Bucknell was good to me. I made life-long friends and met a lot of phenomenal people. I wouldn't change a thing about my experience there, especially Gene missing that shot.

I graduated from Bucknell on a beautiful sunny day in May of 1998. It was a wonderful occasion. It was a time to say goodbye to college life and hello to the real world. Many of my classmates were ready to leave but were afraid of what lay ahead. The last few weeks of school were a blur. One minute I was talking to professors about jobs and new endeavors, and the next I was partying like I would never party again—college was coming to an end. It was a wonderful time. I was ready to move on to the next phase of my life. So on that beautiful day in May, surrounded by loved ones, I left Bucknell with memories of time spent learning, growing, and maturing into an educated young black man. That afternoon, I said goodbye to Bucknell and hello to my new life—an unknown.

75

Three years had passed since our first official 1-on-1 game! When Jon and I first met on the court, we played 2-on-2 and we were on opposite teams. That day was a workout for him. We would have a series of 1-on-1, 33s, and 5-on-5 match-ups that would follow. I was victorious in all of our match-ups. As we progressed, the games got tougher.

By sophomore year, we were pretty much even. Our games were no longer a walk in the park for me. Our match-ups became a sort of a spectacle, and he was making a name for himself in the Patriot League. Besides Adonale Foyle, J.R. Holden was a household name! By junior year, he began winning all of our match-ups—1-on-1s, 5-on-5s, 33s, etc. All these match-ups were still very competitive, but he had the edge. The training, discipline, strength, and game experience to win had begun to take over.

In the remaining days of our senior year, I would peep at him on the court and say to myself, "I still got this cat FOR REAL— I don't care how many games he's played, sprints he's done, or weights he's lifted, I got him, if for no other reason, because I'm just that nice." As we moved around in the gym, looks were shot back and forth—the confidence, the ego, the pride, the ability, the respect, the admiration, the competitive spirit—the teacher— the student—the student-soon-to-be-teacher—and with that, we went from shooting around to "CHECK BALL—GAME 12 STRAIGHT UP"! This game was epic because no one knew our history and our friendship better than we did. No one knew how to get under J.R.'s skin better than I! You would have thought this game was on ESPN. Funny thing though, the gym was empty— just us 2. Finally, the game wound down, the score was tied, 11 apiece and I HAD THE ROCK! I think he was pretty nervous.

Unsure of what the next move or shot could hold, he boned up pretty tight. In my amusement, I sought to rub it in by saying, "You know what this means if I hit this last bucket right? YOU

(Continued on page 249)

V | A Leap of Faith

A MONTH OR SO after graduation, while sitting at home unsure of what I was going to do next, I got 2 offers to play ball. That should be a great thing, right? Wrong. I did not accept either offer. One agent, Michael Garner, got me a deal for $1,200 a month to play ball in Hungary. I said, "No way, that money isn't worth it. I have a Bucknell degree." Then I got a call from another agent, Harold Woolfolke, around the same time offering me a deal in Holland, or somewhere like that for $1,500 a month. Again, I said, "No way. No need to go that far away from home for that little money." I mean no disrespect to the offers or the teams trying to provide me with an opportunity to play professional ball, but I thought I could get a 9 to 5 job right here in the United States for more money.

Consequently, I didn't sign with either agent. I don't believe they were pressed to have me as a client. I wanted someone who really wanted me. I wanted an agent who believed in me and thought I could excel at the professional level. I didn't want to be an afterthought. I have always been an afterthought as a basketball player.

A week before my 22nd birthday, my mom came to me and said it was time to start looking for a real job. Plain and simple, she said that it was time to be a man. She was right, and I decided that chasing this basketball dream was for the birds. I would start looking for a job the day after my birthday. To my surprise, the day I started looking for a job, I got a call from a man named Petri, from Sweden. He said that if I had a passport, then he had a basketball offer for me. I told him I had

a passport. He said that he had looked up my career on-line after reading some information about me. I said, "Well, I'm glad you looked me
up," and asked him where I was going to play. He said that it was only
a try-out, but I would have to leave the next day if I wanted to do it.
I told him that was no problem. He said they would pay me $400 for
the try-out week. Then, if they liked me, I would sign a contract worth
$30,000. I thought to myself, "Hell yes, better than a real job." Before
hanging up the phone, he said he would call me in a few hours with
the details about the flight. I jumped off the phone and ran upstairs to
my room to start packing. I didn't have any suitcases so I grabbed my
trunk from college. I figured this would only last for 1 week anyway—
taking my trunk would be fine. Plus, I didn't have the money to go buy
suitcases.

I didn't even know where the hell I was going or if this basketball
offer was real. After that quick reality check, I decided to wait until he
called me back before I started to pack in earnest. I called my then girlfriend, Nicole, and told her about the phone call I had just received.
She was excited and started preparing me for the next time Petri called.
She gave me a list of questions to ask, a fax number he could send any
information to, and a list of other things that she had on her mind. I then
told my mom, sister, and Darius about Petri. They were happy, but they
were fearful and unsure of what was going on. I didn't blame them for
how they felt; I really didn't know what was going on either. But, true
to his word, Petri called me back an hour or so later with the details of
the offer.

Petri said that I would be going to Riga, Latvia, to try out for one
of the top teams in Latvia. He told me to pack for a few months, just in
case I made the team. I wouldn't be able to come home until November
or December if I made the team. I was happy, shocked, and fearful all at
once, listening to him on the phone. I was in such a daze that I forgot
to ask him the questions that Nicole had suggested. I just said yes and
OK to everything and got off the phone. Quite stunned, I sat on my bed
in my room for about half an hour before I started packing. I had been
to Europe before to play ball, but this was different. This was my life,
my future—a job was on the line this time. I had no idea where Latvia

was located, or what I needed to survive there. It didn't matter anyway because I could only pack the belongings that I had. This was about surviving; I just needed enough stuff to survive. I just kept saying over and over in my head, "This is it. This is my chance to make it out of Pittsburgh. I don't know where I am going or what I am doing, but I am getting out of here and this is my starting line."

As I got on the plane for Riga, I was the most nervous I had ever been. *Riga is the capital of Latvia, situated on the Baltic Sea coast, on the mouth of the river Daugava. It's the largest city in the Baltic States.* I had traveled before, but not for a job—not to become a professional basketball player. As I walked onto the plane with jitters, I realized that I had 12 to 15 hours to think about this journey. I reached my seat in the back of the plane and discovered that I was the only black person on the flight. Right away it hit me—I was doing this alone. Part of me wanted to run—I couldn't do it. I heard the flight attendant say that the door would close in a moment and reality set in; this journey has begun!

Unable to sleep and cramped in coach class, the 12-hour flight felt like 3 days of cross-county driving in a pinto. I'm not the tallest guy in the world—6' 0"—but coach class and flying that far killed my knees. By the time the plane landed, I was exhausted. All I wanted to do was sleep. Unaware of my surroundings, I was on edge. I hoped everything would be OK. After grabbing my trunk from baggage claim, I felt alarmed. I thought, "What if no one was there to pick me up?" I had $150 in cash, 1 Discover credit card that I could put $500 on, and that was it. I guess at the very least I could get on the next flight back home if worst came to worst. I started to relax a bit as I walked and heard a voice say, "Jon-Robert." I looked back, and he smiled as he said my name again. He said my name with a bit of an accent—not too strong, but strong enough. I thought to myself, "Who is he and does he work for the team?" He shook my hand and introduced himself as Edger Sneps. He was a smooth-looking dude, real friendly and hospitable. As we walked to his car I felt like I was in a time machine. Everything looked so old and out of date. We got into a mid-sized vehicle that didn't look too shabby compared with the other foreign, old, dirty-looking cars in the airport parking lot. As he drove me to the gym we had a light-hearted conversation. I looked out of the window and thought, "Where the hell am I? And what have I gotten myself into?"

You could really tell Riga was not an affluent city. Most of the buildings looked old and run down. It didn't look like the other European cities I had visited with my college teammates 2 years ago. This made me even more uncomfortable. When we arrived at the gym, I felt a weight off my shoulders. My heart rate slowed and I cracked a smile to myself, "Yes, basketball—the place where I am most sure of myself and what I can do." A gym for a basketball player is like a safe haven. It's the one place that no matter where you are in the world, it can make you feel at home.

I introduced myself to everyone. My first thought was, "OK, no other blacks on the team." As I met my teammates, I met another American. That put me at ease a bit. He seemed pretty cool but you never know; I would have to wait and see. Sneps then tapped me on the shoulder and said he would take me to my apartment, but first, I should meet the coach.

Coach Valdis Valters was in the gym with his youngest son, Kristaps Valters, when I walked in. His son, hard at practice, looked like he could really play. He was about 16 years old. I introduced myself to both Coach and his son. Coach Valters and I exchanged small talk for a bit (the flight, my health, etc.). He didn't speak English very well so Sneps translated all of our 3-minute conversation. Coach suggested that I get some rest and that he would see what I could do later that evening. Anxious, nervous, and ready to show him what I could do, I said, "OK, tonight." I left the gym excited, anxious, and looking forward to that evening practice. This was no longer just a game; my livelihood was on the line.

When Sneps pulled up to my apartment building, I was shocked. From the outside, the place looked run down. Four shabby buildings stood side by side. One building was torn apart—clothes were hanging on the line outside—it was just a dirty looking place. We walked inside and then I was officially scared! I hadn't seen one black person since I had landed in Latvia, and the people inside the building were staring at me like I was an alien. The elevator smelled of pee and felt as if it was going to stop working at any second.

When I got to my apartment it had 3 different locks on 2 doors. With all these locks and thick doors, no one could break into this place, but on the flip side, it would take me forever to get out of here if I had to leave in a hurry! As we walked in, I realized the place wasn't half bad. The hardwood floors were nice, and the kitchen was OK—small, but not bad at all. As I checked the place out, I noticed clothes, magazines, and things already in the apartment. I thought to myself, "Hmm, weird." I did not realize that the other American and I would be living together.

I didn't have much time to sit and enjoy my new place because it was soon time for evening practice. Do I have the ability to be a pro basketball player? Can I play ball in Latvia? Will I make this team or will I be cut after 4 days? These were some of the questions racing through my mind as I got dressed for my first professional practice try-out. I was nervous, but in my gut I knew I was ready to perform. As I warmed up, I sized up my competition. As the warm-up came to an end, I said one thing to myself—"Don't think, just play."

Most of practice consisted of nothing but 1-on-1 drills. We played 1-on-1 and if you scored, you kept the ball and the next guy in line played you 1-on-1. On my turn, I went to work. I tried to beat everyone. And indeed, I showcased all my skills. I showed off my crossover, my jump shot, and my ability to get to the basket. Every time I did something impressive, I would look over to the coach to make sure he was watching. I laugh now because, of course, he was watching; I was on a 1-week try-out!

I performed well that day, and in my heart I thought they would keep me, but you never know, it was just one day. So, I just kept my mouth shut, played hard in practice every day and went about my business. The hardest thing to deal with that week had nothing to do with basketball. It was the language barrier. I couldn't communicate with Coach Valters to see how he felt about my game and my chances of making the team. So that whole week I was on pins and needles not knowing if what I was doing was enough. I needed this job—AND I GOT IT!

After 3 days in Latvia, I ended up signing my first overseas professional basketball contract. I was the happiest man in the world that day! You couldn't tell me anything. I would be getting $3,000 a month in cash. I thought I was the man! But with all the excitement of being the man, I was taught a valuable lesson about playing ball overseas—get any money promised to you up front! I was told that I would receive the try-out money whether I made the team or not. I never received that $400. Nevertheless, I had a contract in my hand worth $30,000, and a valuable lesson in my heart, so I was happy.

My American teammate turned out to be Dan Kreft, a 7-footer from Northwestern University. The thing I remember most about meeting Dan was that he wore a pouch. A pouch back in 1998 was like a purse for a man! A man's purse is hip now (although I have some close friends and relatives who may disagree), but not many brothers wore them in 1998. Anyway, Dan was a good guy, just a little different. He was very business-like off the court. He always talked about a business he was going to get started while he played ball overseas. He was very intelligent and deeply religious. The spiritual part of him was what I really needed, and it rubbed off on me. He encouraged me to read the Bible every day. For the first and only time in my life, I read the Bible from front to back. He was a true blessing and I will forever be grateful for his encouragement.

Dan, however, didn't share my passion for basketball. To him, ball was just a means to an end. He could make some money and get his business started. Ball wasn't all or nothing to Dan. He didn't have the fire or drive that I think you need to be a professional in Europe. Nevertheless, he was my teammate—an intelligent young man from whom I learned a lot in our short time together.

After only 2 weeks of practice and a couple of exhibition games, I received a shocker. The coach and management had decided to cut Dan Kreft. I couldn't believe it! Dan had told me that he couldn't be cut and that his contract was guaranteed. I learned my second lesson right then—no overseas contract is guaranteed! If a team wants you, then you stay; if they don't, they send you home and that's it. Dan was very dis-appointed that he had been cut and I felt for him. I was going to miss him—and his laptop computer. E-mail and letters were the only way I could stay in touch with my friends and family back home. I didn't make or have enough money to call home often, so Dan's laptop was my connection to America. Now that was gone I didn't know how I would survive. I knew tough times were ahead. In spite of my own selfish needs, seeing Dan leave the apartment with all his bags and his head down, hurt my heart. He had really expected to be there the whole season and now it was over in a flash. Once he waved goodbye, that was the last I saw of him. I'm sure that whatever he chose to pursue after ball, he would have been successful at it.

In an exhibition game against a team from Estonia, I met a great guy from Detroit named Larry Daniels. After we played against each other, he took me out to eat and we went for a walk afterward. During this walk he educated me about a few things he had experienced playing ball in Europe. He told me to save my money, to play hard every game (exhibition games included), and not to let my family and friends take advantage of my kindness. He said, "Just because you play ball doesn't make you rich." And clearly, I wasn't close to being rich. I took the things he said to heart. I was grateful he took the time to talk with me. He was my first mentor—the first African-American whom I had met overseas; he instantly became a friend.

I had no idea how many leagues, cups, and so on, they had in Europe. So when I got to Latvia, I didn't know who we would play, or if I would see any place outside of Latvia. However, I was very fortunate that the team I was on played 2 to 3 games a week—a Latvian game, one in European competition, and another in the NEBL (North European Basketball League). The European Competition meant that we got to travel every other week to play against some of the top teams in other countries. There are a few European Cup competitions, and I was in one of the lower ones at the time called the Korac Cup. Also, it was the inaugural season for the NEBL. This league was started by the former NBA star, Sarunas Marciulionis. The NEBL gave me another opportunity to travel to other European countries to play ball—an opportunity of a lifetime.

The first game in the Korac Cup was a phenomenal experience. We played in Poland and I had no idea who was on the other team. It wasn't as if the coach gave us a scouting report. So, I had no idea what a treat I was in store for. As I ran out to warm up with the team before the game I turned to see none other than LaBradford Smith running out for the Polish team. Yes, the University of Louisville LaBradford. He also played in the NBA with the Washington Wizards (at that time, the Washington Bullets). I was mesmerized. I thought to myself, "Wow, I looked up to this dude. I watched him on TV at home in the States. I remember he could jump out of the gym. Could I compete with him? He was probably the man on his team. I was not the man on mine, at least not yet. This is just my first year overseas."

After my brief moment in the daze, it was time to play ball. Once that ball went up, I was there to show and prove. After the first 5 minutes, I realized, no matter where you are, no matter who you are, basketball is basketball. My team won and I played really well. After that, I felt like I could play against anyone. I was young and ambitious. I wanted everyone to respect my game. I went all out that night knowing that I had something to prove. There is nothing like being the underdog. I was then, and I still play like I am, now.

I have to admit, the first few months in Latvia were tough on me. It was all new and I was very cautious. I didn't have any friends, and I never left my apartment to do anything but play ball and eat. I thought I would have a little more of a life than this. It was simply practice, games, trips to games, and back to practice. That was it!

The team gave me a car to drive but it was a stick shift, and I couldn't drive a stick. So the car mostly sat! And if I wanted to go somewhere to have fun, outside of basketball, I would have to catch a taxi. I was scared to travel in a country whose language I did not speak. I was afraid the taxi driver would try and kidnap me or try and harm me in some way. I felt more comfortable being in the hood as a child among gunfire! And as if that wasn't bad enough, I was also told not to buy red meat or certain other products from the grocery store close to my apartment. Sneps said I would probably get sick if I ate these things. So what did I do? I ate McDonald's almost every day. Can you imagine trying to be a healthy, strong, and productive professional athlete and eating nothing but fast food? Or going into a McDonald's and no one speaking English?—pointing to the food you want and hope they get it right. I couldn't make any special request like no pickles or no onions—they were having none of that! It was crazy but I got used to it. Sneps also told me not to drink the water from the faucet in the apartment. He said it ran dirty sometimes and was very unhealthy. So, I bought bottled water all year—small things that we take for granted living in the States. I had to adjust to living in Latvia. Most of my check was spent at Mickey D's and on bottled water. But again, I adjusted and constantly reminded myself that I was making a living doing what I love—playing basketball.

I found out early on in the season that it wasn't just the water in Latvia that was primitive. At an away game in some small nowhere town in Latvia I found out just how primal some people in Latvia were. The gym was really small, like a middle-school gymnasium in the States. In spite of this, it was packed—like a cage. It was evident that I was the only black man in the gym—maybe in the entire city for all I know. Anyway, in the lay-up line, all I kept hearing was, "Hey nigger, hey nigger." I tried to ignore it and play it cool, but the gym was small so everyone heard it. My teammates also tried to ignore it. By the middle of the first quarter, it was just one or two guys yelling those words repeatedly. That didn't matter much because the gym was so small it sounded like every fan in the gym was saying it. By the start of the 3rd quarter, my teammates started to feel bad for me. Throughout the rest of the game, they would put their arms around me and encourage me to keep playing a good game. I played a good game, but I felt like crap when the game ended. I wanted to spit in those guys' faces; I wanted to fight them and everyone near them who smiled and laughed at me. I felt disrespected. I had done nothing but listen to racial epithets for 40 minutes. It was a long, rough ride home for me after that game.

I started wondering if every away game was going to be like this. Was it worth it? Did everyone in Latvia just see me as a nigger? Did they know my history or the history of that word? Did they know that those words coming from a white face hurts? I had many thoughts and ill feelings about the whole situation. An obstacle that could have hindered my progress as a man and a basketball player was conquered by God and love. With the help of my family and loved ones, I overcame that setback. They helped me see that blacks have been through so much all over the world for hundreds of years. My incident was minor. Even with my mental frustration I knew I could endure this, persevere, and come out on top. I just had to keep God first and continue to focus on my goals and aspirations. After a few weeks, that game became a distant memory. I had bigger fish to fry—not just one battle to fight—but a war to win.

My next American teammate in Latvia was from the DC area. His name was Jermall Morgan. He was the total opposite of Dan Kreft. Jermall had more street sense and more of what I'd encountered while growing up playing ball in Pittsburgh. He didn't play games as far as the business side of things were concerned. He made sure he got his money on time and was all over management to make sure they did whatever they said they were going to do for him. When Jermall joined the team, my social life picked up as well.

Jermall didn't hesitate to smile and say hi to a woman staring at him. I wasn't like that, but his approach helped me to meet a few Latvian women. They would see me, the little guy, and be like, "Awe, he is so little and cute." I laugh about that; they only said that about me because he was 6' 7" tall! Very few of these women spoke English, and the ones who did were usually younger, aged about 18 to 22.

I was only 22, so as long as they were at least 19, I was cool with hanging out. I can honestly say I started feeling more comfortable in Latvia when Jermall was there. The women's company made the time go faster. The most I would do was meet a woman at the mall, at McDonald's, or she would come over to my place to watch TV. Television consisted of two English-speaking channels—CNN and MTV-Europe. I had no choice but to keep up on world events that season. Jermall and I had some good times together. He was a blast to be around and fun to play ball with. Unfortunately, he had only signed a two-and-a-half-month contract. So, it was bye-bye to another American, and I was back on my own again.

My first Christmas as a professional athlete will always hold special memories. I would be spending the Christmas holidays in Dubai, United Arab Emirates, playing in a tournament. I was not excited about being there for Christmas, but once I got there, I saw that it would be a worthwhile trip.

There were some good teams in the tournament and if I played well I could possibly impress the coaches from the other teams. And with that came the possibility of securing future employment elsewhere, next season. I also realized that I didn't need to look too far into the future and forget the task at hand; I needed to play well and simply enjoy the trip. And fortunately for me, I thoroughly did both. I had the privilege of spending a few days with former NBA veterans Tyus Edny and Anthony Bowie. And with these two men, I experienced what it was like to hang out with individuals who were successful ballplayers overseas.

I knew a little more about Tyus's career than Anthony's. I was aware that Tyus had won an NCAA championship at UCLA, had a great rookie year in the NBA with the Sacramento Kings, and was a heck of a point guard. I looked up to him as a player and wanted to learn as much from him as I could. Because we had similar personalities and I was young, he took me under his wing instantly. I asked him a lot of questions about life and ball and he answered me openly and honestly. I truly appreciated that because he definitely could have brushed me off. Anthony, I called him AB, was a true blessing. He was a happy-go-lucky guy. Always smiling, he was the life of the party. He gravitated to me and he became an advisor of mine after our first conversation. He called me "young fella."

"Young fella, let's go eat," "Young fella, going golfing—you coming?" "Young fella, quit acting like this is championship week and have a drink with me at the bar." I would just smile, go along with whatever was happening and soak it all in. I was like a little kid with AB and Tyus.

One night while at the bar in our hotel having a drink, AB and Tyus initiated me into life as a "young fella" and gave me an experience I wouldn't soon forget. After about an hour of talking, laughing, and drinking, two nice-looking women walked in. They walked to the bar, ordered drinks, and started chatting with each other.

I looked at them like "Yo—AB, I might have to go holla at one of them."

AB started to laugh at me and said, "Sit back young fella and let the vet handle this."

I started to laugh and continued talking with Tyus. After about 15 minutes, AB nodded to Tyus and 2 minutes later Tyus said, "Let's roll young fella." Not knowing what was going on, I left with him and we headed to his room. Ten minutes later, there was a knock on the door. Tyus got up and walked out of the room. I sat on the couch like where the hell is he going? The tall, cute brunette from downstairs walked in.

Now I was nervous and skeptical about what *was* going on. I was a 22-year-old man who knew nothing about "the game" (and I'm not talking basketball here). I had never been in a situation like this before. I was naïve and inexperienced. She could read me like a book and broke the ice by saying in perfect English, "Let's have a drink." So, we had a drink from the mini-bar; I became more at ease, and the rest is history.

The next morning I walked in to breakfast and saw AB and Tyus falling over in laughter at the table.

As soon as I sat down AB asked, "How did you like your Christmas present young fella?" and Tyus started to chuckle.

Tyus said, "I hope you enjoyed it because you only get one." I was quiet, now embarrassed, and honestly didn't know what to say or do. They both sensed my uneasiness and just broke out laughing again. All I could do at this point was laugh with them. Uncomfortable but appreciative of the gift, I thanked the guys—and on went our time together. To finish off an amazing trip, I was the MVP of the tournament. We lost a close game in the finals to Zalgaris—a team from Lithuania that AB and Tyus played for.

I went into this Christmas tournament with very little excitement about being there, but by this time, I did not want the trip to end. The few days I spent with AB in Dubai were enlightening and uplifting. I watched and listened to everything he did and said. But it was one thing that he asked of me that I took to heart. He said to me, "You take care of and look out for the next young fella, the same way I am looking out for you. It's only right, you never forget that." And just so you know AB—I always try and take care of the next "young fella"!

Over the years, after our first encounter, I followed Tyus's career overseas to see how well he was doing, and he didn't disappoint me in the least. He was definitely a great player and a winner. He had some great years playing in Europe. To me, that first Christmas as a professional athlete was one for the ages. I had met 2 great guys who took the time to educate me, include me, and explain to me that playing ball overseas is an opportunity that many players would kill for. Thank you so much gents!

By the end of the season, our team had 2 more foreigners come and go—a guy from the Virgin Islands named Vincent Knowles, and an

American named Alex Sturms. By the end of the season, I was the only foreigner to survive the entire season. I realized then how cutthroat playing ball overseas was. I thought to myself, "My goodness, if you don't play well or you don't fit in, you go back home quickly!" We ended up winning the Latvian championship that year. We beat Ventspils in a best-of-5 series, 3 to 1. It was a good series, but we were the better team. I played well that series, and I enjoyed every minute of victory after it was over.

A few hours after the game, while celebrating with the team at a local bar, Coach Valters asked me to come back for another season. I was happy with the season's outcome and the way I had played. I also enjoyed playing with the guys, but I really didn't think I could handle another season in Latvia. When I thought about having no real American TV, running in the woods in the winter to stay in shape, not being able to drive, eating McDonald's almost all year, not having the money to stay in contact with my family and friends on a regular basis, practicing and playing in cold gyms all winter, and not having a consistent U.S. teammate to play with (most teams had 2 Americans), I told Coach Valters that I would have to think about it. He told me they could pay me $40,000 next year. He said if I played one more year under his coaching, I would have good offers to play on bigger teams. I had heard that before—"sacrifice now and I will take care of you later"—same theory my high school coach had—only this time, I wasn't really feeling it or buying it! I smiled though, and said I would think about it.

In parting, I told Coach Valters that I would see him soon and thanked him again for everything that season. I knew in my heart that I probably wouldn't continue playing ball if I had to come back to Latvia. I had met some great people and truly enjoyed the experience, but being there for 10 months was difficult. There were times when I cried in my room alone—times when I thought I would break because I felt so restricted and confined. It was nice to just have the option to do something—to go out, to go bowling, to shoot pool—just something that resembled a normal life. But in my first overseas experience as a professional, I had none of those options. I also missed seeing people like me—black people. I missed speaking English, I missed my family, I missed home, and I didn't think it would be in my best interest mentally or emotionally to stay in Latvia for another season—but, I would think about it.

My first professional basketball season was over and I was heading home to spend some quality time reconnecting with the people I loved. It was during that summer of 1999 that I got a call from an agent in Finland named Rauno offering me a job in Belgium. He said the team was a good team, but they were rebuilding and didn't want to spend a lot of money this year. The only catch was that they wanted me to report to training camp on July 10. That was a month before most American players usually reported to training camp in Europe. Rauno said the contract was for $55,000 for the season. As soon as 55K came out of his mouth, it was a done deal. I was going to Belgium.

It didn't matter that I had to be there in July. I would have left right then and there! I had just returned home not long before I got the call, but I didn't have much money left from Latvia. I had purchased a Jeep Cherokee that summer, and my money was running low. That didn't really bother me much because it was the first time I had my own money. I was finally able to go places, eat out, and enjoy things I really never had the means to do. I took full advantage of being home in Pittsburgh that few weeks in the summer. Before I knew it, it was time to go back to work. Playing for $55,000 in Belgium was better than going back to Latvia for $40,000. Playing in Belgium for $40,000 would have been better than going back to Latvia. I knew nothing about Belgium or the team, Oostende, but I was hungry for more professional ball.

Let's just say I was a lot more relaxed when I arrived in Belgium for my second season overseas. When I got off the plane, everything seemed different and a lot more modern than Latvia. I was different. I actually had suitcases now because I had made money last year. I'd come a long way from that scared kid with a few dollars and a trunk! I was calmer and more sure of myself. I was becoming a man.

As I claimed my suitcases, I saw an older gentleman from the team I suppose, holding a sign with my name on it. The sign made me feel like a superstar. There was no one calling my name like in Latvia. I had come to appreciate a small gesture like a man holding a sign with my name on it when I arrived in a foreign country. As I walked to the car, I noticed the city was clean and the people smiled at me as if I belonged. I felt right at home the minute I walked out of the airport. As I rode to my apartment, those feelings intensified. I was extremely happy to be in Belgium. I was living and playing in a small city near the ocean called Oostende. Could things get any better?

A day or two after I arrived in Belgium, the team manager took me to a car lot to give me a team vehicle. When he pulled out a Peugeot, all I could do was laugh. It was a really nice car but you had to see it. It was blue with big orange basketballs all over it—with the team name on the side. I stood there for a moment staring at the car like, "Wow!" I was a moving billboard. There would be no being inconspicuous while driving this car. To make matters worse—the car was a stick shift. I told the team manager that I could not drive stick. He smiled at me and said, "You'll learn and you'll learn right now."

My teammate, Ralph Biggs, who was with us laughed at me—he could drive stick. Biggs, a good teammate, taught me the basics and said, "Let's just ride around the parking lot for a little bit." I picked up the essentials quickly but I was not ready or prepared to drive home in traffic. After roughly 15 minutes of practice they both said, "That's it, let's go." I was stunned but I didn't have a choice, so I took to the streets driving behind Biggs. As soon as we hit the streets, I had problems. People were honking their horns and staring as they drove by. I kept stalling. Shifting gears was difficult. To this day, I don't know how I made it back to my apartment. One thing I will say though, Biggs didn't know me very well, but he patiently kept pulling to the side of the road and waiting for me every time I stalled. I was both thankful and appreciative of his concern. He was down for me and that enabled me to be down for him from the very beginning.

Getting to Belgium so early in July meant that the season would last forever. Once I met Ralph Biggs, Coach Lucien, and the rest of the team, I knew everything would be good here. The team I was playing for—Oostende—had a history of being a very good team. They had won a few championships in Belgium but the year before I arrived, management had spent a lot of money for quality players who didn't meet their expectations. Actually, they had a terrible season. Thus, the GM decided to clean house and start afresh. He picked a new coach who picked new players, and the GM was happy to be spending a lot less money. As a result, expectations weren't very high for the team that season. I didn't care about the financial stuff or the expectations of management. I came to Belgium for no other reason than to play well and to win a championship.

Our team was made up of unknown "marginal" players who would, hopefully, not disgrace the Oostende tradition. We all knew that we weren't considered the cream of the crop. However, that brought us together as a squad to compete, fight hard, and win or lose—play together as a team. We were young and could relate to each other. Then again, this didn't mean that things didn't get testy and intense between us at times.

My basketball background gave me a sense of pride and the attitude to never back down on the basketball court. We had a guard named Dimitri Lauwers who tried his best to compete with me and out-duel me every day in practice. Dimitri was a tough-nosed player with a lot of heart. He was a big fan of the NBA, and he would try an emulate players who played at that level. Dimitri wanted to be a starter on the team. So, in some practices, I think he went above and beyond just playing hard. He wanted to prove that he could be a starter.

On most days I would just let him be, I understood he was probably frustrated. But, one day in practice early in the season, he went beyond two professionals competing for a starting position. It started with me making a few shots in a row. I was young, exuberant, a little cocky and passionate about the game. If I made a few shots in a row, I wouldn't say much but you could tell from my body language what I was feeling. And that day, my body language told him, YOU CAN'T COMPETE WITH ME!!! NOT TODAY, NOT TOMORROW—NOT EVER! I'm not sure that he read it that way, but I was definitely trying to say that. I could sense his frustration because he started fouling me. One foul, 2 fouls, 3 fouls—it was starting to be deliberate. At this point, I didn't see him as my teammate anymore. I felt as though he was trying to hurt me. In straight attack mode, I wanted to destroy his hopes and aspirations of ever being a starter as a professional basketball player. I wanted him to know that he was not on my level. And to my surprise, he didn't quit.

He kept competing with me. Irritated and aggravated by the end of practice, he started venting to our teammates in Flemish and Dutch. I didn't know what he was saying so I just smiled at him. Then he said a few words in English as if he wanted to fight. It didn't even make me flinch; I knew he was upset. He was just running his mouth. Then, he crossed the line by getting in my face. At that point, I had to protect myself and let him know, we could fight—that would not be a problem. I didn't budge from where I was standing. A few players came and stood between us. Nothing happened but it was a pivotal day for me. I had never been in an altercation with a teammate overseas. It was small but this was important. I took his competition with me personally. It pushed me to work harder and to never take anything for granted—not even being the American player who was supposed to be the starter. Dimitri helped make me that much more hungry to become a better player. Where I played, you either ate (took what's yours), or sat back and went hungry. In the end, I'd like to believe that we challenged each other to be the best players we could be at a game we were both passionate about.

Within months of being in Belgium, I had an experience that changed my life. It taught me to live life to the fullest, and that professional basketball was not personal but about business. At this time, I was still pretty much a virgin to driving a stick shift. Most times I just followed the cars in front of me. I couldn't focus on too many things at once because my driving wasn't very good.

I had to cross a set of trolley tracks to go from my apartment to the gym for practice. I had never seen the trolley-crossing awareness signs before that day. At any rate, as I followed the cars in front of me, I didn't notice what was happening. When the cars sped up in front of me, I did the same, not realizing they were speeding up so they didn't have to wait for the trolley to pass. As I sang along to the music blaring on my CD player, I never heard the trolley honking its horn or beeping. I was half way across the tracks when I saw it.

I just closed my eyes and slammed my foot on the gas pedal as hard as I could. It was too late! This was not a movie. There was no director yelling, "Cut"—no second takes—this was my life! The trolley took off half of my car. I spun around and when I looked back, my back seat was basically gone. I was milliseconds away from possible death. I was in shock. I was overseas, and I didn't know what to do. I just sat in my half of a car in complete disbelief. I sat there in tears thanking God while cars drove past me staring. I couldn't control my emotions. I was bawling. I couldn't believe that I had almost lost my life driving in Belgium. I don't know how long I sat in the car crying until Biggs pulled over stunned, making sure I was OK. After seeing my friend, I regained my composure and drove what was left of my car to the side of the road. I got in to his car and we went to practice.

When we got to practice I told management what had happened. I assumed that they were happy I was alive, but they acted very nonchalantly about the whole thing. They actually told me that I would have to pay for the car. Did they think I cared about money or their car? Why were they telling me this now? Did they not understand that I had almost lost my life? I was livid but I held it all inside. I was definitely a little sensitive and emotional at the time but this incident made me lose respect for "management." I then knew, to them, I was simply another American there in Oostende, Belgium, to play ball. Who I was as a person, and whatever else I did off the court, wasn't very important to them.

A week after the accident I had a new car. I couldn't have cared less about a new car because I didn't drive for almost 2 months. I rode with Biggs everywhere. What he did, I did—forget that! I was too nervous to drive. I was thankful to be alive, and I prayed every day, thanking God for keeping me safe and for preserving my life. Understand, I lost half of my car and didn't have a scratch on me. God is good, and I can definitely say, ALL THE TIME. That car accident reassured my faith and belief that God was protecting me. I truly believe that He had so much more in store for my life. And not just as a basketball player, but as a child of His.

We weren't expected to have much success as a team that year, but I felt as if everyone might have written us off a little too soon. In a preseason game against Charleroi, the Belgium champions from the previous season, we were manhandled by 30 points. I didn't panic after the defeat. I thought it was a great learning experience to face such a good opponent before the season. It let us know where we were at presently and how far we needed to go to be considered a good team.

However, after the drubbing, the press and our fans thought our season was over. Many said we would be lucky just to stay in the 1st Division (that meant that if we ended up in last place during the regular season, our team would move down a Division the next season). I took all these remarks and negative comments personally. How could these people say all this after one preseason game? Charleroi was a team that had been together for a few years. They were a cohesive unit, playing against a starry-eyed, young team that had been together for less than a month. All this negative press was great motivation for Coach Lucien and our team; he would use this blowout game later in the season to keep us focused and humble. My season wouldn't start quite the way I wanted it to, but with no pressure from management and a coach who truly believed in my talent, I knew we had the potential to exceed everyone's expectations, including our own.

To kick off the season, we went on the road to play a game against a team called Ghent. If the first game of the season was any indication of the year I was going to have, then management would have sent me home after the first contest. I played HORRIBLY! I missed lay-ups, easy shots, and had turnovers; I just couldn't do anything right offensively. The good thing was that we won a close game, and Biggs played incredibly. I was a little down about my performance after the game, but I was sincerely happy for our team, and Biggs. A win is a win and starting the season with a victory is a team confidence booster.

After the game Coach Lucien, a big guy about 6' 4" and over 230 pounds, came over to me and wrapped his arms around me and said, "You're going to be great this year. I loved the way you played tonight, regardless of how you feel." I sat there staring at him like he was crazy. He continued, "You never quit, and you never slacked up on defense, no matter how many shots you missed, or how many bad plays you felt you made. That is the sign of a kid with heart (he touched his chest) and a kid who wants to win. You are my Little General; you never forget that." I never forgot his words. No coach, outside of my summer league coach Raj had ever believed in me the way Coach Lucien did. He calls me Little General to this day. He is one of the nicest men I have ever played for. His words gave me a lot of confidence, and I needed that at the time. I was young and searching for my own identity and role on the team. His words reassured me and allowed me to believe in my ability to succeed. I never looked back or doubted myself after that game. It was full steam ahead on my quest for a Belgium League championship.

Off the court, I partied like a rock star. My sidekick Biggs and I would go out after almost every game. We partied in both Belgium and Holland. Living in Oostende, we had to drive 35 minutes to 1 hour to party at the best spots, and 2 to 2.5 hours if we drove to Holland. We most often went to Ghent and Antwerp to party, and did Brussels and Mons occasionally. We also traveled to Holland 2 to 3 times a month to hit the famous nightclub MundyHall on Sunday nights. MundyHall was the spot on Sunday; people came from Holland, Amsterdam, Belgium, Germany, and even France to party there. That club was well known in those parts of the world.

Biggs and I got into a lot of good trouble that year. It was so much fun! I met German women, French women, women from Africa, women from the Caribbean, women from Holland, women from Morocco; it was just amazing to me that all these different ethnicities lived in such close proximity, and all were out partying, getting along, and having a good time. I flirted with many women who wanted to hang out and have a good time. This environment helped me understand women's traits. They may have been of different nationalities, spiritual backgrounds, or financial status, but they generally wanted and liked the same things—to be respected, to feel good, and to spend time with a "good" guy.

Talking to the women was the easy part—making sure they understood me was more difficult. Every guy wants to seem smooth but with most women in Belgium and Holland not understanding American slang, or even that versed in the American language, it was usually best to keep the conversation simple and sweet. Every woman and every experience was unique and I enjoyed them all. What really caught my attention was that they loved the same hip-hop and R&B music that we were vibing to in the States. Plus, these women could really dance! They had rhythm and a swagger similar to that of women in the States. It amazed me that I lived a world away from the States but felt right at home when out partying and having a good time.

The toughest part to all this fun and interaction with different people was that I had a girlfriend back home. I respected Nicole so much and I didn't want to lose her. So, most times I would keep my fun to a minimum but at other times, I would give in to my desires and feel guilty about it afterward. This was a real hang-up with having a woman back home and playing ball overseas. Nicole had been there for me and really helped me get through a tough year in Latvia. I couldn't just up and leave her. I believed I loved her. However, was love enough? Did she know what I was doing? I seriously doubt it. Make no mistake—Nicole was on top of her game. She knew that I was a wide-eyed, young man trying to find his way. She gave me that leeway to grow and that, in many ways, made me love her that much more. I know she wasn't always happy about our relationship but she was always there for me and supported me through the good and the bad—this time and beyond.

That season in the European competition we played in the Korac Cup. We fared well but didn't do anything special. We competed hard and showed that we could contend with the big boys. I believe the Korac Cup helped prepare us for battle in the Belgian League.

In the Belgian League we were the young, energetic team that truly believed we could beat anyone. We gained this swagger early in the season by defeating the same team that beat us in the preseason by 30 points— the powerful Charleroi. This early season clash was on the road in their home gym. Most people predicted we would get pummeled. However, I thought we were a different and better team than the one they hammered a month or so ago. To everyone's surprise, my analysis was right. We went in there and shocked everyone by defeating Charleroi at their place by 2 points. I played well that night with 21 points on 8 of 15 shooting, and 4 assists. Tomas VanderSpiegel, our center, hit 2 free throws with 0.8 seconds left to win it for us. We had battled and defeated the defending champions on their home court. The team that everyone had said was unbeatable at home had been overwhelmed. We hadn't won the war yet, but this victory gave us the confidence and belief that we could defeat any team in Belgium.

We began steamrolling opponents one after another and Biggs and I started this funny little dance after every victory called the "O-Train" dance. The "O" stood for our team name Oostende and the train meant that you better get on board and roll with us because once it got going, there was no stopping it. Simply, it was a wild and entertaining dance that Biggs and I made up. It was great having a young teammate from America, of the same race and age, who loved to play the game. It gave me a sense of comfort and camaraderie that I hadn't felt or had the previous season. In any case, we were a nightmare match-up for teams—2 young guys who played the game with no limits and no fear. We took great pleasure in playing with each other. It was a perfect match. At that place and time, I felt as if I could have played with that team and Biggs forever.

The team that had our number that season was the runner-up team from the year before, Antwerp. Our kryptonite that season was Antwerp's 2 Americans, Mike Huger and Louis Rowe (James Madison University). This first-rate team and these 2 players were our nemesis all season long. They somehow always found a way to beat us when it mattered most. Our first big defeat by Antwerp came in the Belgium Cup Finals. When it mattered most in the 4th quarter of the Cup Finals, we could not make a play offensively or get a stop defensively. Their point guard, Mike Huger, flawlessly controlled his team and the game down the stretch to defeat us. How did I let this game slip away from me? I couldn't make a play or hit a shot when we needed it most. I had failed to push my team over the top. It was disheartening, but I knew we would possibly face them again in the Belgium League Finals.

We made it to the league finals to face the heavily favored Antwerp. It was a best-of-5 series and they had home court advantage. Game 1 was a wake-up call that let us know we had never been here before. They came out aggressive and beat us handily. We didn't realize that it was the finals until the 2nd quarter. By then, the game was over. By Game 2 we were ready and determined to go back home with the series tied at 1. In spite of our determination and will to win Game 2, they escaped with a win. A few questionable calls late in the game by the referees and a desperation shot that miraculously found its way in the basket sealed the victory for Antwerp. Dejected but refusing to give up, we knew that we still had a chance to win the series.

Game 3 was all about us. We had come too far not to battle to the end. In Game 3 we spanked Antwerp. It felt as if they were already celebrating. They played flat and now our confidence was sky high. We also knew that if we won Game 4, the pressure would be on them in the 5th and final game. It appeared as if we were going back to Antwerp for a deciding game the way we controlled the first 30 minutes of Game 4. Then, just like that, Antwerp was back in the game and we were fighting for our lives. We had our chances to put them away but we went dry and couldn't score for a few minutes. Still, clinging to a 1-point lead with 5 seconds left in the game, this was our test to see if we had the heart, intensity, fire, and desire to play good defense one more time in order to win a championship.

Like true champions, we buckled down and played great defense. The offensive player shot an air ball (the ball didn't hit the rim or backboard). But, the unthinkable happened. Herbert Baert was standing right under the rim, caught the ball and put it in the basket. Season Over!!! Antwerp was the Belgian League Champions. I stood there in shock. Dazed and stunned all I remember was giving Mike a hug and saying, "Congratulations, man, you earned this one."

I was sick to my stomach as I watched them celebrate on our home floor. I hate to lose, and losing was 10 times worse watching Antwerp celebrate in our gym. I never feel like I should be the one to lose. I am that passionate about winning. In sports, I've learned that champions know how to lose; that is what makes them champions. They know how to lose, but they never accept it. Losing pushes a winner to get better, work harder, and do whatever it takes to win. A winner is able to look in the mirror and know that he did all he could to help the team win. Everyone can be a winner, but only a few can be a champion. As for me, I yearned for my team to be the champions of Belgium, and I knew that my work in Oostende wasn't quite finished!

As I packed to go home for the summer, I didn't have any idea what I would be doing or where I would be playing next season. I wanted to come back to Oostende but I wasn't sure what management was thinking. Before I could finish packing my bags, they called and said they wanted me back. I didn't have an agent at the time, so I just went into the office, sat down for a meeting, and listened to their offer of $75,000 for the next season. Without hesitation I accepted. I had some unfinished business to complete in Belgium. I could not leave Oostende without a championship. Plus, the money was great for me. I was more than happy to play ball for that type of money. I left the office and Belgium for the summer with a smile on my face. I would be back in August to a place that I loved and that I hoped loved me.

VI | Getting Settled

THE SUMMER OF 2000 was a blur. I tried to do everything that I could possibly do in the 2 or 3 months I was home. I traveled to New York to see my nemesis and new good friend, Mike Huger. I spent time with my family and I also started spending "quality" time with a young woman I had known for a few years named Toya. I really liked this young woman. I can't quite pinpoint why, I just did. That summer we had our first intimate encounter. Although we both truly enjoyed our time together, we knew that my current situation (my then girlfriend Nicole and I were struggling) on top of my playing ball overseas would be too much to overcome. So, instead of fooling ourselves into doing something that would inevitably fail, we decided to continue to grow as friends. In spite of all these social things, I worked continuously on my game. I was determined to win a championship in Belgium and I knew that hard work and dedication would help me accomplish my goal.

Coming into the new season we were very confident as a team. We added 1 or 2 players, but for the most part we were the same team. Lithuanian Virginius Praskivicios was a new addition. He came from the Minnesota Timberwolves of the NBA. He was just what we needed at the power forward position. Also, he was a great locker room guy—very down to earth and just a pleasure to be around. We were a close-knit team, and we knew coming into the season that anything short of a championship was a failure.

We got off to a fast start. We were rolling right along when it was time to face our first early test—an improved Charleroi team at their place. They had supposedly regained their championship status with the addition of 2 very good Americans, Mike Batiste and Lenny Brown. We knew it would be a tough game and a good test at this point in the new season.

We started the game like we were playing another average Belgium team. We played with little emotion and no sense of urgency. We soon picked up our level of play as the game went back and forth for 4 quarters. Both teams stood toe-to-toe with about 8 seconds left. I had the ball in my hands with the game on the line. I knew I could get a good shot off but I wanted to make a good strong move and possibly draw a foul. With the defender backing off a little, I decided to try and get to one of my favorite spots on the court to take a rhythm shot. It seemed like everything slowed down and in an instant, I was right at my sweet spot. I rose up and shot the ball, swish! They missed a Hail Mary shot at the buzzer. It was a huge victory for our team and for a few seconds, I temporarily lost control of my emotions.

I had just made my first game-winning shot overseas. I couldn't stop what I was feeling inside. I ran over and jumped on the scorer's table and put my arms up high in the air. It was like saying, "How do you like me now?" It was my way of declaring that we were the team to beat this season. I didn't have a great game shooting, but the last shot was the biggest one. This is one of the rare times in my career that I let the intensity of the game get the best of my emotions.

The O-train was rolling that season when we hit a sudden and unexpected slide. Not only had we just lost 2 games in a row in late January, but we hadn't played well in a couple of weeks. I am not sure why we weren't playing well but we weren't playing with the energy, passion, and concentration that we had in the past.

The 2nd loss, a blowout defeat at home against a very good team from France got our coach fired. They didn't fire him right away but there was gossip. I didn't believe any of it because Coach Lucien had done an amazing job with supposedly less talent and definitely less money than previous seasons. How could management forget this so soon? We were supposed to be just average last season and Coach Lucien had us playing in 2 finals (Belgium Cup and Belgium League). Was management crazy? We had just finished winning a Belgium League game on the road when the gossip became reality. On the bus ride home, Coach Lucien informed the team that management had decided to fire him and bring in another coach. I sat at the back of the bus speechless and heartbroken. I felt terrible for him. I loved Coach Lucien. He cared about me as a player and a person. He would sit and talk to me for hours about various topics. Our conversations were mostly about basketball but they were also about life—my future. He truly believed in my ability to do great things. It hurt me to see someone so supportive, genuine, and caring released so nonchalantly. I felt like I had let him down. Would I ever get another coach who believed in me like he did? Coach Lucien was a genuine man. He was a teacher who truly believed in and tried to get the most out of his students. I knew I would miss him. Matter of fact—we would all miss him.

A few days after the firing, Coach Aarron McCarthy arrived. Coach McCarthy (Mac, as we would call him) won a lot of us over at the first meeting. He was an American. I knew there weren't many American head coaches overseas. He must have been pretty good to coach us. I also liked his father, Neil McCarthy, and his teams at New Mexico State. Still, I was very cautious because Coach Lucien was my guy. In any case, at our first meeting he told us that he was here to make us a better team. He wasn't here to change a lot but he said from this point on everyone would dedicate themselves to defense. Coach Mac was up-front and honest from day one and eventually won every player over.

Coach Mac was not only a good coach, but also a great man. I have a great deal of respect and admiration for him and his passion for life, his family, and the game of basketball. But that respect and admiration came with some head-butting as well.

During one game, I committed a silly turnover. I was trying to hit the home run instead of the single, and I knew it. Sometimes I have the tendency to make the game harder than it is by trying to do too much. To my surprise, Coach Mac subbed me out of the game. I didn't think that my mistake deserved for me to be substituted. I was pissed and walked off the court, giving Coach Mac a look that read, F★★★ you!

Then I went on to mumble under my breath, "Why are you taking me out the damn game?" Coach Mac stared right back at me and said, "Sit your ass down and relax." Instantly, I recognized that he was the new sheriff in town. I smiled and nodded to him to let him know I understood and respected what he was doing. We never had another incident. I wasn't perfect, but he knew he had my respect, and that I would do whatever I could to try and help our team win.

Playing in the Super League (top European competition, now called the Euroleague) that year, we knew the competition would be stiff and that we weren't expected to do very well. This was because we were a small unknown basketball club playing against top European teams with big budgets and a history of success throughout Europe. I didn't know much about other European teams so I couldn't care less about their successful history. I just wanted to play ball against the best.

Our first opponent in the Super League was a powerhouse from Instanbul, Turkey, called Efes Pilsen. Their team was stacked. They had 1 of the top-5 point guards in Europe at the time, Damir Mulamerovich. They also had Mirsad Turkan (NBA), Huseyn Besok, Predrag Drobnjak (Seattle Supersonics, LA Clippers) and Mehmet Okur (Detroit Pistons, Utah Jazz), to name a few of their talented, highly paid players. One player on their team made a million dollars; that was more than our whole team's salaries combined. So, when they came to Belgium to open the Super League season they figured the game would be a cakewalk. However, we had something else in mind.

We started the game in attack mode and never let up. We ended up defeating one of the top European teams with more talented and bigger-name players. In addition to a great win, both Biggs and I played well. I ended the game with 20 points, 4 assists, 3 rebounds, and 1 turnover. The best part of this victory was the stunned look on the faces of the Efes Pilsen players when the final buzzer sounded. You could sense they were in shock. This was a stunning upset that made other top European teams take notice of our no-name, low-budget team. This win gave us even more confidence that we could defeat any team in Europe when we were playing at home.

This theory held true for most teams that came to Belgium. But the one team with the talent, hunger, and confidence that defeated us was Maccabi, Tel Aviv. Nevertheless, we could be proud of playing them tough. They were the eventual champions of the Super League that season. That team had something special; you could tell from the first time we played them. They had a sense of togetherness and toughness about them that not many teams have.

As a personal victory, I played well in both games against them in losing causes. Their point guard at the time, Ariel McDonald, said something to me after our second defeat that stuck with me for years to come. He said, "Great game, nice show, but you LOST. A lot of players can score, but can you score and WIN! Winners make money overseas; scorers get stats, play for average teams, and make average money their whole careers. You're a good player. If you learn how to win, you'll be great." At first, I thought he was jealous of my game but that was just my ego talking. The fact is, Ariel was a darn good player himself and he didn't have to take the time to say those words to me. He must have seen something in me and I needed to be thankful for his guidance. Ariel, I am humbly thankful for your insight and I took heed to your words.

One of my best games that year in the Super League came in the top 16 against a team from Russia called CSKA Moscow. Their star player at the time was Andrei Kirilenko (Utah Jazz). He was a 6' 9" athletic forward on his way to play in the NBA the following year. In the game in Russia, I had 30 points, 4 rebounds, and 4 assists. I played superbly in a losing effort. What topped off this amazing experience were the fans; they cheered for both teams. The game felt like it was played at a neutral site and not in Moscow. That was strange. It was as if the little team from Belgium had earned the fans' respect and support. The following week, CSKA came to Belgium and eliminated us from the Super League. It was a tough ending to our SL season but we could hold our heads high. We had a very good season and earned the respect of a lot of other teams, players, and coaches. Belgium isn't known as a top-tier league in Europe—what we did was a true feat. What I didn't know was that our play (winning games), my play in particular, had opened the eyes of many agents and team managers looking for young talent.

The 2000–2001 season was also the first year my family was able to visit while I played overseas. This was the first time it was financially feasible to do so. So my mom and sister came to visit me in Belgium. They had no idea what to expect but they both loved it. Every few minutes my sister would come over and hug me and say, "I am in Belgium with my brother, this is crazy."

After one of my home games, while my mom and sister were there, I was introduced to a woman basketball player named Jackie Smith. I didn't know Jackie, and I had no idea she was playing ball in Belgium as well. I had no clue she played basketball because she didn't look like the basketball type. Yes, I am stereotyping here, but she was very feminine and gave off the vibe of more of a diva than a ballplayer. Anyway, after trying to shake her hand and say hello, my mom interrupted and said, "Don't just give Jackie a handshake; give her a hug." With both of us laughing, I gave Jackie a hug, thinking to myself, "I plan on getting a few more of these when my family leaves." Typical man, huh?

That night a few of us went out to dinner and a club; I wanted to show my sister the nightlife. As I tried to get Jackie's attention that night and flirt with her, she kept laughing at me because another female basketball player was hitting on me. The other woman was cool but I was interested in getting to know Jackie. By the end of the night, Jackie had warmed up to me and we exchanged telephone numbers. About 2 weeks later we got together. From that point until the end of the season, Jackie and I spent a lot of time together. We liked the same music, had similar tastes in movies, and really just had a good vibe. I never thought I would meet an American woman in Belgium who I would enjoy spending time with. I didn't think about it; I just lived in the moment. We both knew the end of the season would come and we both weren't looking forward to it. Going home was always a good thing—home is where the heart is—but we also knew that the special time we spent together would come to an end. Our time in Belgium ended but we remain the best of friends to this day. Jackie will always have a special place in my heart.

Surviving my trolley accident was a terrifying ordeal, but what happened this year just reinforced how truly blessed I was. One Sunday night while hanging out with Biggs in a city called Mons, Belgium, watching

I had just returned to Belgium after spending Christmas and New Year's in the States. It was my first year overseas playing ball and it was tough. A week after returning, an American from another team invited me to hang out with her and her friends for a day. I welcomed the opportunity. She mentioned that we would meet up with the family of one of the American men's players (who played in a city about an hour from me). We grabbed some lunch and then headed to the men's Super League game.

I learned so much information about J.R. before I ever met him. I could tell that he and his sister had a special bond. I learned that his mom was not shy about bragging how special her "baby" was. They had a great amount of pride in regards to J.R. It was a great day and his family immediately made me feel like I was back home.

After the game, we waited for J.R. to come out of the locker room. I definitely felt like the outsider because everyone else already had some type of connection with him and I was the "new girl." He kissed his family and the other American young lady. I didn't expect a kiss but his mom insisted on the infamous European greeting. We all ended up going out to a club after that game. That was the beginning of something special. We talked all night. I wasn't sure if he enjoyed the conversation as much as I did, but he brought a smile to my face when he texted me to make sure that I got home safely.

Over the next 4 months, J.R. and I formed a unique relationship. We both had crazy schedules with our teams but we spent as much time together as we could. He was my friend, my psychiatrist, my brother, my confidant, my love. He taught me how to be me and not to settle for anything less than what I deserved. We exchanged books, songs, movies, journals—anything that helped us express our thoughts, fears, and beliefs. We would talk for hours and laugh for days—it seemed like we were in our own little bubble. We danced in his apartment. We watched movies and sometimes simply just enjoyed each other's company by sitting in silence listening to music.

(Continued on page 250)

the NFL games, we decided to go see these 2 young ladies who lived about 45 minutes away from Mons. They were friends of ours living in Antwerp. We had stayed in Mons, watching a good NFL game and were late leaving. Pressed for time, we asked a friend the quickest route to Antwerp.

Unsure of this new route, we hit the rainy highway—speeding. Stupid! We drove separate cars and foolishly sped to see who would get to Antwerp first. Driving back and forth past each other, I noticed a slight turn fast approaching. I started to slow down hoping that Biggs would see the corner as well. After witnessing Biggs swerve out of control, I tapped my brakes. Before I knew it, I was swerving out of control as well. The car spun, hit the rail on the inside of the highway, and kept spinning until I was on the other side of the road. When the car came to a complete stop, I was not hurt and I prayed Biggs was OK. How could I tell someone's parents their son was hurt in a car accident because we were speeding foolishly in the rain rushing to go see some girls?

I took a deep breath and got out of my car. As soon as I got out, I could see Biggs outside of his car walking toward me. Thank God he was OK. I was so worried about him that I didn't realize that my car had been severely damaged. I could not drive it at all. Biggs, looking a little unsure of what just happened, asked me if I was OK. I told him that I had banged my knee but was otherwise fine. I asked him the same question and he said that he was straight. We gave each other a soul hug (a hug equivalent to the Obama fist bump) and started walking toward his car. We were both shaken by the accident. I was in a fog. I was thinking to myself, "What am I trying to do, kill myself?" Two serious accidents in 2 years.

We rode in mainly silence back to our apartments in Oostende. When we arrived, I got out of his car and we barely said goodnight. I don't know what Biggs thought, but I know what I felt. I was happy we were OK, and just happy to be alive and well. No injuries, no bruises. I learned 2 valuable lessons that night. First, never play around in a car—period. You have your life in your hands and your life is nothing to play with. Second, if you're late, you're late. Better to get there safe and explain, than to not get there at all.

In March of 2001, I received a phone call from my sister crying hysterically. I was nervous and anxious, not knowing why she was crying. When I finally calmed her down, she told me that my Uncle Marvin had passed. Shocked and hurt, I asked her how. I knew he had diabetes, but I didn't think that diabetes would lead to his death. She told me it was pneumonia. He had caught pneumonia and complications from pneumonia caused his death.

Always trying to be the calm, supportive, big brother, I asked her if she was OK. She said, "Yes," and that most of the family was at the house. I immediately asked her about Mom. Uncle Marvin was my mom's brother. She said Mom was doing OK under the circumstances. I then told my sister that I loved her and that I would call a little later to find out about the wake and funeral. Once we hung up, I slowly walked to my bedroom and cried. I couldn't believe my uncle was gone. I lay in the bed crying for about 30 minutes just recalling the memories. I had some great times with my uncle. He was the "fun" uncle. He taught me how to curse as a kid. He educated me about women as I got older. He kept me smiling and laughing. I had never seen my uncle sad or down. Even when he was in and out of the hospital, he stayed upbeat and vibrant. He always told me to protect my sister. He said, "You be the tough one, she is a princess. You take care of her and never let anything come in between you two." I live by his words.

Uncle Marvin was a big advocate of family unity. He taught me that family would always be there, through the good and the bad—if you're going to throw money away, throw it away on your family. "When you make it to the NBA, Booper, all I want is a ticket to the game," he said. "I don't want or need money; I just want to be at the game cheering my nephew." His words made me believe that one day I would make it to the NBA. I felt as if I had to make it to the NBA just for him. When he died, a piece of that NBA dream died with him. My only regret is not going to his funeral to say goodbye. What hurt most was not being there for my mom and sister. In a sense, I felt like I had let them down. Yet, I told myself that I could make it up to my family by being the best player that I could be. One day I would make enough money for my family to be able to enjoy the finer things in life. I knew now more than ever that death was inevitable and could sneak up on you. I knew that my biggest achievement in life would be giving my family a life that they had never dreamed of. God is good because now I can look at myself in the mirror and say, "I kept my promise and did my best to give my family the best life I could give them."

I had no idea that I had met the man who would become my agent in Belgrade, Serbia, earlier that season. We were playing a tough Partizan team in Belgrade when I bumped into an agent named Alexander Raskovic. I didn't know who he was or who he worked for, but as I walked into the InterContinental Hotel after the game, he asked if he could have a few minutes of my time. A little frustrated after a tough loss, I said OK with a hint of attitude in my voice. He introduced himself and then told me he liked the way I played the game. He told me that I would need an agent if I wanted to have a successful career overseas and that he would like to represent me. He spoke broken English with a European accent but I understood everything he was saying to me.

After a few minutes of conversation, I found that liked him. He had an aura about him—a confidence that made me hang on his every word. In spite of this, I couldn't make a spur-of-the-moment decision about my future. Honestly, he wasn't even asking me to. He told me that he would be in touch and to keep playing well. I didn't know whether to believe him or not, so I just said thanks and OK. I must admit, he was a man of his word.

By the end of the season I had interest from a few agents. They all knew that I didn't have one, and most thought I was searching for one. What they didn't know was that I was happy in Belgium. I didn't care about having an agent and all that extra stuff. I just wanted to play ball and make some good money. I spoke to Coach Mac about all these agents and the stuff they were saying to me. Actually, he was the first person to change my mind about hiring an agent. He told me that I had talent and the best way to move forward in my career was to hire a good agent. I seriously looked at 3 companies to represent me. The three agencies at the time were Courtside, SFX, and AIG (Advantage International Group). Courtside represented my teammate Ralph Biggs. However, they represented a lot of guards and I didn't feel like they liked me or wanted me any more than the next guard. This was discouraging and I didn't pick Courtside to represent me for this reason. I really liked Doug Neustadt from AIG. He was a great guy. I enjoyed all of our conversations; he was down to earth and a straight shooter. AIG had a lot of good players, like David Robinson, Charlie Ward, Sarunas Jasikevicius, and Boris Diaw. I was really leaning toward them because of their association with my friend Mike James. Neustadt was high on Mike, and that impressed me. What I was unsure of was what he meant when he said, "I can't promise you I will ever be able to get you $300,000, but I will do the best I can." I knew he couldn't promise me a dollar amount, but I felt like he was putting limitations on me, what I was worth, and my potential growth as a player. This dampened my feelings toward AIG.

Alexander Raskovic, who was a European agent working for SFX, thought that my potential was limitless. He talked about making big money in Europe and possibly trying my hand at the NBA in the future. He said my future was up to me—if I continued to play well and win, I could make some good money on European teams. This is what I wanted to hear, but I didn't know what to think or believe. Alex was such a smooth talker and exuded so much confidence, that at times he made me very unsure of him. When my mind couldn't take any more, I directed all the agents who wanted me as a client to speak to my then girlfriend, Nicole. Nicole loved Alex from the very beginning. I leaned toward Doug, and Nicole pushed for Alex. After much prayer and a little guidance from Nicole, I chose Alex and SFX. They had the biggest name and they represented the likes of Michael Jordan, Patrick Ewing, Elton Brand, Kobe Bryant, and Peja Stojakovic—to name a few. How could I pass up being represented by a company with client names like this? I didn't!

I accomplished this season what evaded me the year before. Our team won both the Belgium Cup and the Belgium League championship. Our nemeses the year before, Mike Huger and Louis Rowe could not defeat us this season. I think they celebrated a little too hard last year. They didn't seem as hungry this time round. The big bad wolf was a year older, and the young pups just got stronger, faster, and wiser from defeat the year before. It was our time, and we tried to punish every team that stepped on the court against us. We had that killer instinct and didn't let anyone get in the way of what we were trying to accomplish. We won both titles handily and proved that Oostende was the best team in Belgium that year, hands down!

After Game 4 of the Belgium League championship, we had a party at our gym that night to celebrate our victory. It was jam-packed; all the fans and management were there. We drank, partied, and just had a grand time. We had accomplished in 2 years what others deemed damn near impossible. We played well in the toughest European competition and then came back to Belgium and won both the Cup and League championship. We deserved to enjoy this night. In the middle of the celebration, Biggs, the outgoing one, got up on stage and grabbed the microphone. He said a few words and then told them to blast the music. He looked at me and said, "Let's do it one more time." Of course we did our O-train dance one more time for the fans. However, this time we had the whole team on stage doing it. I never knew that a team could be this close. I got special satisfaction playing with this group of guys. It was truly a one-for-all, all-for-one team mentality. Winning like this was unbelievable to me. I didn't want it to end. But I kept it all in perspective.

While everyone was celebrating, I walked into the locker room to be alone for a few minutes. I had dedicated the rest of the season to my Uncle Marvin and I knew he was in heaven smiling down on me. It was an emotional couple of minutes. I really wanted this team, this season, this moment to last forever. I was truly happy. From the firing of Coach Lucien, to the summer workouts, to not being with my family during tragedy, it felt good knowing that I had accomplished something special.

After a successful season, I hoped that management would want me back. I loved Belgium and I wanted to stay with Oostende. I was comfortable there. I liked the coach and my teammates, and I didn't see any reason to leave—except money! My new agent Alex told me that I had a few contract offers from teams in Greece, Italy, and Russia. That sounded good but I wanted him to exhaust my options with my current team first. I really felt that I could be a part of a dynasty if I stayed with Oostende. Yet, after a few weeks of negotiations, Oostende didn't want to pay me what my agent and I felt I deserved. My agent said I shouldn't go back for anything less than $150,000, but I would have gone back for a little less. Oostende wasn't even in the ballpark.

At this time, a team from Greece was looking to sign me for 2 years for bigger money than Oostende could offer. I thought to myself, "Wasn't Greece where Dominique Wilkins, Byron Scott, Ricky Pierce, Eddie Johnson, Cliff Levingston, and a legend in Europe, David Rivers, played?" They all played ball in Greece. Additionally, Alex told me this could be a big step for my career. If I could play in Greece and do well, I could play anywhere in Europe. This was very encouraging but I was still uncertain about leaving Belgium. I was wary of Alex; I didn't know him well enough to know if he was shooting 100 percent straight with me.

That summer while on vacation in Myrtle Beach with Nicole, my phone rang and Alex told me that I needed to get to a fax machine ASAP. I walked downstairs to the hotel fax machine and waited on Alex's fax to come through. After 5 minutes, a fax came through. I looked at the contract in disbelief, I read over it 3 times. I looked at the dollar amount again and again. I wanted to scream but instead I played it cool, walked back to the room, and handed it to Nicole. She read over it, started smiling, gave me a big hug and said, "Congratulations, baby, you deserve this." At that moment, I was good—no more worries. I could now take care of my family. Thirty minutes later I had signed a 2-year deal worth $450,000 to play for AEK, a team in Athens, Greece. I had no idea that what I had just signed was not ironclad—everything that glitters isn't always gold.

VII | Learning Life's Lessons

As I BOARDED the plane to Greece in August, I was relaxed about going overseas but was nervous about my ability to excel in the toughest league in Europe at the time. I knew I was headed to the big time as soon as I sat down on the plane. I was in first class! I had never sat in first class before. That was an experience in itself. I was treated like a king. The flight attendants were courteous, asking me every few minutes if I wanted or needed anything. They don't treat you half as well in coach class—believe me, I know! And the flight—I could have stayed on that plane for 2 days. The seat was comfortable—the area spacious—I could stretch out. I had my personal TV and a selection of 20 movies or so to watch—it was amazing. I enjoyed the flight so much that I haven't flown coach overseas since.

After a wonderful flight, I arrived in Athens but my luggage didn't. I waited in baggage claim—disappointed—for about an hour and a half before I gave up. I had no clothes, underwear, toothbrush—nothing. I walked out of the baggage claim area to look for someone from the team. The team manager introduced himself and immediately reassured me that my luggage would arrive in the next day or 2. He said not to worry, this happens all the time. I chuckled and said, "I wish you had told me this before I left America."

He laughed and said, "You'll know for next time." Despite his smart remark, he was very helpful. He filled out some paperwork and told me that my bags would get to me in 2 or 3 days. I thought, "Damn, I have to go shopping now." As we drove to my living quarters, we made small talk.

I'd stayed in apartments my first few years overseas, so I expected the same in Greece. When we pulled up to a big house, I thought whoa, I have really taken a step forward in my career. The flight, this house, the contract, the pressure was on me to produce—for real. I thought that the team manager would show me around the house, the city, and help me get situated—but to my surprise, he did none of this.

Basically, he abandoned me. He dropped me off, gave me the key to the house and the car out front, and said that someone from the team would call me about practice. To my dismay, he drove off. He knew that I didn't have any luggage. He didn't ask if I was hungry—if I needed to go to the store—anything. I was so blown that I had to take a seat on the couch and get my thoughts together. I have no idea how long I remained there before I heard the doorbell ring. My initial reaction was, "Thank goodness, he came back to help a brother out." To my surprise, I saw a big, 6' 10" white dude smiling at me through the peep hole. I opened the door and the fellow introduced himself as my team-mate, Geert Hammink.

Geert rescued me that day. I asked him what made him stop by to say hello and he said his family had not arrived yet; he figured that he would go say hello to the "new" guy. He had played for AEK the season before, so he was familiar with the city. We went shopping for clothes, to the grocery store, and grabbed a bite to eat. He did all this and he wouldn't let me spend a dime. I was at a loss for words. He was the nicest, most genuine, sincere, and helpful person I had met. He didn't know me from a can of paint and to take care of me like this touched my heart. It was as if he got great joy out of making me smile. His kindness was overwhelming. I couldn't stop telling him how grateful I was for all he did for me. The more I got to know him, the more I got to see that he was this way to everyone. Geert is a phenomenal person. He is an agent now, and I tell him every time we bump into each other—I owe him one, BIG TIME!

The preseason in Greece was unlike any other that I had encountered. We trained in Italy. I assumed that they wanted to isolate us and have us eat, sleep, and drink basketball every day for about 2 weeks. And isolation certainly brought us closer together as a team. The training was very difficult. I ran a lot. It was a good, productive camp, but I was happy when it was over. I was excited to get back to Greece and start playing games. To my surprise, by the end of camp, my playing days with Geert Hammink were over. They released him before the start of the season. He was under contract for the year but I had seen this before—that contract didn't mean anything. I was disappointed to see him leave. Player release is the nature of the business.

As the preseason came to a close, our chances of having a good season in the Greek League seemed possible. No egos, no superstars—just a team full of hard-working players with great potential. I liked what I saw in our team. I didn't know about other teams in Greece, but I knew that we had some talent. I was extremely excited about the season's first game. It was a big game for us because it was a Greek Cup game.

The Cup uses a single elimination system so we needed to win this first game, but with the pressure on us to win against a team called Panionis, we lost. And as if losing wasn't bad enough, I played horribly! I was totally out of my game and we were now out of the Cup. I knew management would not be happy, but I never thought that they would put me on the hot seat. After just 1 game, I was on the verge of being cut (sent home). The rumor was that I wasn't talented enough or physically gifted enough to play at the Greek League level. The rumor was probably true because I heard this information from my teammates. Management and the coaches had seen me practice and play all preseason. I couldn't believe they would cut me after one bad game. Needless to say, I couldn't let this chit-chat rattle me. One of the best teams in Greece would be our next opponent, and I knew I had to perform at a very high level if I wanted to remain in Greece.

The team we played next was Olympiakos. They have a great tradition and rich history in European basketball. Their team consisted of key players such as Alphonso Ford, one of the best shooting guards ever to play in Europe, James Forrest, a solid power forward who went to Georgia Tech and played for a year in the NBA with the Lakers, and Theodoros Papaloukas, a 6' 6" Greek point guard who NBA scouts were raving about. They had a very good team. People expected us to lose easily after the way we played in the Greek Cup game. In spite of all the hearsay, I went out and played an exceptional game against

Olympiakos. I controlled the game, made shots from all over the floor, and made a move down the stretch that some AEK fans still talk about. In the 2nd half of a fairly tight game, we were running a fast break. As I ran full speed toward the middle of the court, we got the rebound and our big man hit me with a pass. I got the ball around half court and took one dribble, made an in-and-out dribble, took one extra dribble, faked a bounce pass across my body to make the defender move, and then shot a lay-up for 2 points. The fans went crazy. All I did after the move was sprint back to get on defense. No time to celebrate—I was battling for my livelihood. It felt good to be playing well after all the critics and naysayers had been doubting and criticizing me. We ended up winning a big game against a very good team. I was proud of my performance and finished the game with 21 points. After the game, I just shook hands without even cracking a smile. I planned on staying in Greece with this team. With my performance, everyone else knew of my plans as well.

After the game, I decided to dine at Friday's restaurant with a few other American players. I didn't know that it was typical for the Americans to meet up on Saturday nights after games at this particular restaurant. That seemed pretty cool and I was all in. I was new to Greece and didn't know many people, so I saw this as an opportunity to mingle.

As we ate, I met a young woman named Nyree who was playing ball in Greece. She had played in Greece the year before, so she knew most of the players and knew her way around. At dinner, I was quiet. I wanted to get a feel for everyone. She noticed this and sparked up a conversation with me. She offered to show me around and help me get adjusted to my new surroundings. It surprised me, but I said, "Cool, that would be very nice of you." After dinner, most of us chose to continue hanging out and we went to a club. By the end of the night I had a new friend.

True to her word, Nyree and I connected a few days after the club. She showed me the city and we became close. She was a true friend. She helped make me comfortable in Greece and I truly appreciated her for that. She cooked me meals, we went to the movies, clubbed, shopped—all types of stuff. She met my friends and family when they came throughout the year and she treated them like her family and friends. We spent a lot of time together, and I enjoyed our conversations the most. We would talk about everything. She was always brutally honest and that made me laugh. She would call me out on stuff and say, "That's some b.s., J. I don't care what you say." Eventually I would concede and be like, "You're right, I am full of it." We developed a genuine friendship. I truly appreciated her kindness and friendship.

September 11, 2001, is a day that will forever be remembered around the world, but especially in the United States. On that day, my phone rang in the afternoon, during my nap time between practices. I thought to myself, "Who is calling me?" After the fifth or sixth ring, I decided to pick up. All I remember hearing was, "Turn to CNN, talk to you later" and then a dial tone. A little confused and not sure of what was going on, I slowly got out of my bed to turn on the television. As soon as I turned to CNN, my mouth opened wide and I was speechless. I was reading, hearing, and seeing the worst thing that I had ever witnessed in my lifetime. I was in total shock—my stomach turned; I started to feel sick. I could have never imagined that something this tragic would happen in the United States.

My country was being attacked and there was nothing that anyone could do to stop it. Four airplanes were hijacked and had crashed into 3 different places. Two of the planes crashed into the Twin Towers of the World Trade Center in New York City, one into the Pentagon, and the final plane crashed in Somerset County, Pennsylvania. That day was like a bad dream. I continued watching CNN for hours in disbelief and shock, with sadness in my heart.

As I watched this catastrophe on television, I called my family. I needed to hear my mom and sister's voice; I wanted to know that my family was OK. I asked them about other family members. To their knowledge, everyone was OK. I sat in a fog after I hung up. Innocent people were dying. It was tragic. I had always felt the United States was the safest country in the world, but on that day, my opinion changed.

With all the devastation that was going on back home, I turned to basketball to help me feel a little better about life. And focusing that energy was what I needed to do because this was the first year I got the chance to play in the Euroleague (the year before, it was the Super League). The Euroleague consisted of the best 32 teams from different countries competing for European supremacy. It was a tough league and I enjoyed every minute of every game. It was a solid season for me. My shooting percentages did not indicate the type of impact I had on every game. And my effect on the games was directly influenced by my coach.

I love to compete and Coach Dragon Sakota gave me the freedom to do just that. I was playing at the highest level in Europe and didn't have a big name, but that didn't influence Coach's decision to let me play my game. He didn't try to change me but helped me mesh my skills to help the team. He did this under immense pressure to win immediately and I will always admire and respect the fact that even under this pressure he simply let me play. Coach was replacing one of the best coaches in Europe, Dusan Ivkavich, who had coached AEK the previous season. Coach Sakota could have easily chosen a big-name player with NBA experience or tried to make me conform to a different style and system. Instead, he put pressure on me to produce and play well every game. He was patient, supportive, and positive with me all season. What I appreciated most was his honesty. If we lost a game because of me, he would say, "J, you killed us tonight, too many bad shots." On the other hand, if we won and I played well, he gave me the praise I deserved. He was a stand-up coach, and I liked him for that. We had a solid Euroleague season but were eliminated by the eventual Euroleague champions, Panathinaikos, another Greek team in the top 16.

I enjoyed life in Greece. The people were very warm and welcoming. Greece was a wonderful country and I saw myself playing there for a long time. It just had the feel of a place in which I could get the best of 3 worlds—basketball, money, and a social life.

The only setback I had playing in Greece was the financial situation with the team. The money was always very late. That made playing basketball very stressful. I don't mean 2 weeks late. I am talking 2 or 3 months late! I had never been in this predicament before. It was the worst—working hard every day trying to do your best to live up to your end of the contract, and management not living up to their end of the deal. I didn't quite understand, so I talked to my teammates about the situation. Most of them had experienced the same thing in years past, so they were used to it. They said, usually, things worked out and they got paid. This made me even more uncomfortable. Actually, it infuriated me—as if they were paying us late because they could. This was not what I signed up for and it weighed on me all season.

Unfortunately, I didn't have the name or money to just walk away from these circumstances so I tightened my boot straps and continued to work my tail off every day. This didn't happen without a few negative incidents. At one point, I was behind 3 months' salary and I didn't care much anymore. I was playing hard to win because I love the game but my heart wasn't in it. In my mind, I was playing for next season's contract with a new team. How could I care about this team when I was treated like this? How could I put my heart and body on the line game after game, if not respected as a player? When Coach Sakota sensed my ill feelings toward management—my focus on the game had started to wane—he sat me down and had a heart-to-heart with me. Our talk changed my season and my outlook on the situation.

First, he said that I played for a lot less money last year. He understood that I wanted the money that I had been promised contractually but he wanted me to see the big picture. He went on to say that at one point in my life I played this game for free. He wanted me to simply play my butt off and try and win—what better way to move on from here than to win and do your best. If not, then quit and go home. It didn't take me 5 minutes to realize that he was right. I had to push on and continue to do what I did best—play basketball. I had learned a huge lesson from this situation. I learned to always try and do the right thing, no matter what my predicament. If the situation was that bad, then I needed to get out of it; my character should never be in question. Furthermore, what I didn't know then was that management's lack of professionalism would help take my career to the next level.

Midway through the season, management decided that we should add another quality American player to the team. That class act came in the form of Chris Carr. Chris and I hit it off immediately. He had played for many years in the NBA, but he was coming off of knee surgery and wasn't as athletic and mobile as he was in the League. Conversely, he had become a better shooter than when he was in the NBA. Chris took me under his wing from the first day we met. He became my mentor. I would talk to him for hours about all kinds of stuff. He had so many stories to tell, and I was all ears. In addition, he was a comedian. He would have me laughing all the time. Overall, he was genuinely a good guy. He was what I would call a "no-pressure–no-stress" friend. Because he was married, I learned about the value of commitment and trust; I didn't have any pressure to go out and pursue women. I did that on my own and without his influence. No stress—because he had his own money and was overseas because he loved the game. All he wanted from me was for me to become a better player and person. That is what you call a real friend, and I cherish the time he spent with me and the influence he had on me as a young man.

Chris's stay in Greece wasn't all peaches and cream. He clashed with the coaches a few times. He was very knowledgeable about the game and because he could be outspoken, he very rarely held his tongue. I believe those small disagreements caused them to treat him unfairly at the end of the season.

When it came to basketball, Chris was a positive influence. He had a zeal and enthusiasm for the game that was contagious. We would stay after practice and compete. We had a few fun battles of 1-on-1. He beat me a few times, but he knows I got the best of those battles. We also played shooting games—often for money. I hadn't done that before. That was even more fun. Upping the ante to shoot for money definitely caused me to focus more. I hated losing those games! He would laugh and crack jokes when he won. Unfortunately for me, Chris won most of those shooting games. I am a streaky shooter, and I would get hot and think I was going to win. He would just laugh and say, "Consistency, baby. That streaky stuff doesn't last." He consistently kicked my butt! He would take my money and just smile—and he had this infectious smile. No matter if you were pissed, upset, or whatever, if Chris smiled at you, you couldn't help but smile back or laugh. We didn't bet a lot of money, $50 here, a $100 there—nothing major. Oftentimes, he would beat me and then treat me to lunch or dinner—that was Chris—a kindhearted guy. I still remain in touch with him; he is a great friend. He taught me what it means to be a true professional both on and off the court.

Greek League basketball is like American football; the game is very physical. Also the supporters make the game much more intense and

My European experience was unbelievable. The experience really allowed me the opportunity to find my true gift—reaching out and helping people. I met a young guy by the name of J.R. Holden. He showed up at my Holiday Inn hotel room on my 2nd day there. I was sleep-deprived, but really wanted to take in all that Athens had to offer.

From our first dinner together at Appleby's, we connected. When J.R. and I first began having basketball talks, he wasn't overly talkative. He just listened a lot. One day, we were on the back of the bus going to the hotel for one of our annual "coffee breaks" and he pulled out a notebook and asked me, "What do I need to do to get better?" From that point, I knew he trusted me. I knew that I had just gained a valuable friend. We formed a friendship that would last a lifetime. Throughout the 6-month period that we played together, J.R. and I experienced a number of different highs and lows.

Not receiving our payments on time was a low point—one of our biggest frustrations. We played very well together—a high. We shopped together, ate together, but most important, we became very good friends. I think that J.R.'s recollection of our 1-on-1 games is a little skewed. I can say this, that little sucker was really fast!

I had partially torn the tendon in my left knee, which I later fully ruptured. That is why I am so thankful for the bond that I had with J.R. He helped me keep things in perspective. He made sure that I understood that it wasn't like being at home, and that I needed to change how I thought about things. Yes, I am somewhat opinionated when it comes to doing things right, but, I did adhere to his advice, which helped keep me sane.

The highlight of our season was winning the first round of the playoffs on a couple of last-second shots. In our first-round game in Greece, J.R. came off of a screen and hit a 3-point shot

(Continued on page 250)

passionate—fanatical! The Greeks love basketball and are some of the craziest fans in Europe. They did things that are inexplicable.

For instance, late in the season, we played a game against our rival, Panathinaikos. These games were usually wild, so there were 100 or so policemen around the gym and near the two team's benches. It was odd to warm up for a game and see police with their guns and shields on guard, as if someone might start shooting. During the 2nd half of a close game, a fan threw a plastic water bottle at me. Luckily, I saw it coming during a break in the action, and it only hit me in the leg. I couldn't believe it. I was infuriated. It's a freakin' basketball game, is it that serious? I just didn't understand the stupidity. Not thinking, I reacted; I picked up the water bottle and threw it back in the same direction. Stupid and wrong move!!! I was immediately ejected from the game. I didn't know the rules, but I knew what I did was wrong. I just put my head down and walked off the court. I was angry at myself for letting my team down; I didn't have to retaliate, but I let my emotions get the best of me.

When I got to the locker room, I vowed never to be that brainless again. I came to understand that fans in Greece take rooting for their team to the extreme. They throw coins, lighters, and anything they can get their hands on, if things aren't going their team's way. Supporting a team in this way was ridiculous I thought, but this is their culture and I had come to respect and appreciate their commitment.

Another incident occurred that I still can't wrap my mind around. This one happened at an away game in Thessaloniki. It was during the 4th quarter of a close game, and the ball went out of bounds. It was a small court so the fans sat close to the court. As my teammate stood out of bounds to send the ball to me to resume play, a fan (a nut case in my eyes) gathered as much saliva as humanly possible in his mouth, and spit right in my teammate's face. I mean you would have thought he was a llama, he spit so much! You could actually see the saliva running down the side of my teammate's face. Standing there as if nothing happened, he didn't turn to the side or speak a word to the fan—nothing—he simply wiped his face with his jersey and inbounded the ball. I was in total disbelief. Oh My God!!! The referee didn't say or do anything. He had to see it, because I saw it, and I was standing about 5 feet away. All I could think was, "My goodness, how could one person do that to another person?" This was a game, not life or death. Spitting in someone's face is the ultimate disrespect. Fans had to have some boundaries; this incident was simply outlandish. I admired my teammate's professionalism, and his ability to stay focused on the task at hand, but I don't know if I could have been that professional then—or now for that matter. I commended him for that and for his strength in that situation. These examples are just a minor look into the craziness that goes on at Greek games.

We had a phenomenal regular season and finished at the top of the Greek League. That meant we had home court advantage throughout the playoffs. It was an unpredictable season and there were doubts about whether we could win a Greek League championship (AEK hadn't won a championship in 35 years). We started the playoffs having a bye; so finishing in first place in the league allowed us to start the playoffs in the semi-finals. Our semi-final match-up was against a tough team from Thessaloniki, called Iraklis. They had 2 very good future Greek National Team players in Nikos Hatzivrettas and Dimitris Diamantidis, and a good young American point guard in Roderick (Moo Moo) Blakney.

We knew it would be a tough series because they were an exceptionally good home team, and the format of the Greek League playoffs gives the lower seed a good chance to pull off an upset. In a best-of-3 series, the home team starts off on the road and then comes home for the final two games. I didn't particularly like that format; it gave the weaker team the advantage. If they won the first game on their court, they had no pressure coming to your place for the next 2 games, and could possibly steal a game and win the series. I always liked to play from ahead, not behind. It was easier playing a game when you were up in a series 1–0 than down 0–1.

Others must have agreed with me about that format being unfair because it was changed the following season. Anyhow, we knew that Game 1 would be a dog-fight at their place. We lucked out and stole Game 1 on the road. After trailing most of the game, late in the 4th quarter an unlikely hero stepped up for our team—Chris Carr. He scored 3 consecutive 3-pointers down the stretch; the third 3-pointer was the game winner. We won by 1 point; no, actually we escaped by a single point. It was amazing to me how Chris was ready to perform under pressure when Coach called his number. Coach Sakota didn't give Chris many minutes that season, and when he did, they were erratic. So for Chris to be ready and confident under the circumstances was a credit to him and his work ethic. He saved the game that night for us and put us one win away from reaching the finals. Our next game was at home and we played well enough as a unit to win the game and the series 2–0. We were in the Greek League Finals.

You could feel our fans stirring and hoping for a championship. AEK hadn't won a championship in 35 years, so the fans were eager to capture one. In the finals, we would be facing a tough Olympiakos team. Olympiakos had defeated the European champions, Panathinaikos, in their semi-final match up. We knew this would be our toughest challenge of the year. It was AEK vs. Olympiakos, best of 5, for a Greek championship. The finals game format was a little better. The home team plays the first game at home, then you alternate games for the rest of the series.

Before Game 1, you could feel the anxiety in our locker room. All season long we had been a pretty loose bunch of guys. Players talking and laughing before the game was the personality of our team. However, before Game 1, the locker room was dead silent. We clearly felt the pressure of playing Game 1 at home.

We came out tight and struggled the entire game. I didn't play well, and I believe that is the reason we lost. Literally, I must have been tight because I pulled my groin during the game. As a result, not only did we lose Game 1 at home but I hobbled and was not sure if I would be ready to go for Game 2. I had never had an injury to my groin before, and I became worried that I could hurt myself even more by playing. Yet, I had come too far to throw in the towel now. My heart was all in, but mentally I was fragile.

I did everything I could to prepare for Game 2. I did therapy 2 or 3 times a day and was at 70 to 75 percent by the start of Game 2. I knew that if I played better we could beat Olympiakos. We all played a little better in Game 2 but not enough for us to beat this powerful team. Knowing that I was not at full strength, Chris took over some of the ball-handling responsibilities in Game 2. He did an adequate job, for the most part. Nevertheless, he had 2 crucial turnovers in the 4th quarter that helped Olympiakos seal the victory. Down 0–2 with everyone disappointed and frustrated at our start to the finals, management made a decision that was thoughtless, ridiculous, and just absurd. They released Chris from the team the day after the Game 2 defeat. I couldn't believe it. One day, he was the hero and the next day he was the goat. How could they release a player in the middle of the finals?

There was possibly only 1 game left in the season. We are down 0–2; 1 more loss and it would be over. Even worse, I felt responsible for Chris's departure. If I had been healthy, Chris would not have been in a situation to make those turnovers. He was trying to help the team and me. When the team heard the news about Chris everyone knew it was b.s., but they didn't have the time to worry about that. We were down 0–2 and trying hard not to get swept in the series.

Most people, including our fans, thought the series was over. Frustrated and not used to playing injured, I called the person I trusted most when it came to me and the game of basketball, my confidant, Darius Newsome. As I told him about my situation, I could almost feel him smiling over the phone. Before I could finish my spill he said, "Quit feeling sorry for yourself! You're a champion, you're a beast, no one knows what you have gone through to get where you're at. You keep pushing yourself, get that treatment and lay it all on the line out there. You gotta believe, Boop. All those doubters, all the people that never thought you could be a professional are still rooting against you. Be a fu★★★n' beast and call me when you win that championship. I'm gone." and immediately hung up the phone on me. I didn't fully understand why he spoke so sternly, or why he hung up, but I felt better. I know now what he was trying to say. I had come this far on my own. I didn't have someone looking over my shoulder or pushing me to excel. That person pushing, that person working, that person who wanted to be the best point guard in Europe was—ME!

I knew that Game 3 could be our last game and deep down I was OK with that. I asked God to give me strength and my team courage to keep pushing forward. We were a good team but we had not yet played to our ability. If we were going to lose, I had to push the team to give it our best shot. At the start of Game 3, we looked like a new team. We played with a sense of urgency and belief that we could win not only this game, but the series. We were phenomenal and captured our first win. Down 1–2 with Game 4 at Olympiakos's home court, we knew we had to play our best game of the year. We believed it was in us to win this series. We went into Olympiakos, focused and determined. I played the best game I had all series and we seized victory and momentum in the series. It was now 2–2 and we were going home for the 5th and final game. We went from a team undeserving of being in the finals to a team that could finish off a Cinderella season with a championship in a matter of 2 games. I was excited and happy to be a part of this, but my mind was also on my friend, Chris Carr. He had been a part of this journey and now he was gone. It appeared as if he was the reason we were possibly down 0–2, but I knew that wasn't the case. On the one hand, management looked like they had done the right thing by making an unethical decision. That bothered me, but I couldn't focus on that right now. I had a Greek League Championship to try and win.

In the locker room before Game 5, we were relaxed. Everyone was talking, laughing, and just being the team we had been all year. I felt very good about our chances. Running out for warm-ups with the arena filled to capacity (22,000 fans) and hearing all the cheering and Greek chants for both teams, the atmosphere was electric. It felt like I was dreaming. It was amazing, and I felt like a little kid playing his first basketball game in front of fans. I was so excited! This was a chance to show all those people watching TV and in the gym who had doubted me at the beginning of the season that they were wrong.

When that ball went up to start the game, I only thought about winning. I tried to be everywhere and do whatever it took to help my team win the game. I played great defense and patiently directed our offense. However, neither team could take control of the game. The game went back and forth for 35 minutes. The last 5 minutes of the game we made all the right plays. It felt as if we did everything right and they couldn't do anything to stop us. With the final seconds running down on the clock and the fans going crazy, I exhaled, said a silent prayer thanking God, then put my arms in the air with my forefinger pointing upward, signifying that we were #1. I can't even describe the happiness I felt inside.

From possibly getting cut to being an integral part of a championship team—who would have thought? All I could do was smile and enjoy the moment. I didn't think it could get any better than this moment. God is good. I'm not saying that because we won. I am saying that because my body held up. I got stronger as the series went on. HE gave me the strength to persevere and keep pushing. The result was AEK winning a Greek championship for the first time in 35 years. I played a major part in winning that championship, and I was overjoyed to be a part of AEK history.

Although it was a great season, I was ready to return home once it was officially over. I loved Greece, but it wasn't home. I missed the States, my friends and family, and just the overall feel of being on U.S. soil. What bothered me most as I left Greece was that I hadn't received a paycheck in 2 or 3 months. Imagine the irony of winning a championship and not getting any compensation in 3 months. It definitely made my moment bittersweet!

I had worked so hard to reach what many thought was unreachable. I felt underappreciated and disrespected. I had labored so hard. The way management treated me left a nasty taste in my mouth. All I wanted was what my contract said I would receive. I was very disappointed. In any case, what worried me most was that I had a 2-year contract. My agent said not to worry but I don't think he understood my point of view. If we could win a championship and be paid late or not at all, what would happen if we weren't winning? With that in mind, I packed up all my belongings, figuring I wouldn't be back for the following campaign.

When I landed in Pittsburgh, Pennsylvania, it was home sweet home! All the problems from the season, the financial situation, where I would play next year, all that stuff was in the back of mind for later. I was just happy to be home. I spent the first week or so exhaling, and spent time with my family and friends. However, that relaxation would end all too soon. The phone rang and it was my agent. The conversation went something like this:

Alex: They promised me they will send all your money soon.
Me: I don't care; I'm not going back to AEK next season.

Alex: No J.R., you gotta go back.

Me: No man, I can't play for a team that wins a championship and doesn't pay their players.

Alex: They love you there, and they promise to get better and do everything different next year.

Me: You told me that this year, Alex. I'm not going back, sorry.

Alex: I'll call you in a week or so, and see how you feel about it then.

Me: OK, nothing will change, but OK.

A week or so later, Alex called me to ask how I felt about returning to AEK; I had just received my payments as checks. I believe I received the checks the day before he called. I told him that my feelings were the same. He then told me not to cash them. I thought he had lost his mind. I suppose I was going to the bank that day. I had earned those checks. Nevertheless, he said not to cash them because he had something in the works. Actually he told me only to cash the checks for the money they owed me for the season, but not to cash the bonus checks. I am not sure why I even listened to him but I did. I trusted him. He had helped further my career—financially—more in one year than most agents would in 5 or 6 years. So I listened to Alex and patiently waited to hear what he had up his sleeve.

Around the same time, my U.S. agent, David Bauman, wanted to know if I was interested in playing in an NBA Summer League. To me, that was a no-brainer. I had never played in an NBA Summer League, and I was excited about the opportunity to display my skills and ability in front of NBA personnel. My confidence was riding high after a great season in Greece, and I was ready to take the next step of my career. David said that next step would be playing for the Charlotte Hornets, in the Orlando Summer League. I would be playing for the son of head Coach Paul Silas, Steve Silas. I asked David about the situation on the team, and he said this situation was ideal for me. Charlotte, which became the New Orleans Hornets the following year, was only bringing 10 guys. He told me that everyone would get a chance to play, and that I would play around 20 minutes a game. All I could think was wow! This was the perfect situation and opportunity for me to make a team, or at the very least, impress a few NBA coaches and scouts.

As soon as I heard this news from David, I called my brother Darius. Darius loved basketball and knew the game so well, that I knew he could help me get ready for the upcoming NBA Summer League. I had about 2 full weeks before I had to be in Orlando. We immediately got to work, doing 2-a-day workouts. Our work was very focused on shooting a lot of shots, and fine-tuning the things I already did well. I didn't know that working with my brother would be as difficult as it was. He was very serious about getting me ready and instantly my goals became his goals. Matter of fact—he probably wanted more for me than I wanted for myself.

The work we did was all about the love. Darius worked with me at a game we equally loved for no other reason than he loved his little brother. At times, working out felt like we were 16 years old again and just hanging out. Some nights we would be in the gym until 2 or 3 A.M. just shooting free throws and talking. It was the first time we had worked together since we were teenagers. It was refreshing and gratifying to have someone in my corner who loved the game and knew the game as much as—even more than, I. At any rate, it was a bittersweet time when the 2 weeks ended for Darius. He had to get back to his life as a school teacher. He would have liked to come to Orlando to watch his little brother try and make an NBA team, but instead he had to resume his teaching summer school. This was the real world and that's how life went. When I walked out of his front door in Virginia Beach, we both knew in our hearts that I would be on an NBA team when I returned home to Pennsylvania after the summer league.

My expectations were high when I arrived in Orlando to play for the New Orleans Hornets Summer League Team. I had never played in an NBA Summer League before, and I was nervous. But, I was ready to perform. After meeting everyone, especially Coach Steve Silas, I immediately realized how laid back and nonchalant this summer league stuff was. I imagined it totally different. I had envisioned the players being ultra competitive knowing they were fighting for NBA jobs, and the coaches making sure everything was structured and running precisely—they could be in line for an NBA head coaching job some day. To my surprise, it was nothing like that—at least not in my experience. Everyone seemed very relaxed and happy simply to be spending a few days in Orlando. I didn't know what to think or how to feel so I just rolled with the punches. I took pleasure in staying in a single room in a 5-star hotel, receiving meal money, and hanging with players who, like me, had played ball overseas and wanted to see if they could land an NBA job back home.

I didn't know what to expect out of this summer league after our first practice. The first practice was so simple it alarmed me. There was no way NBA life was this easy. Our first practice went like this. We played street ball for 20 minutes, the coaches put in 2 or 3 plays, we played pick-up basketball with the plays, did some individual shooting, and went home. You have to understand—I was chasing a dream. I had no idea that the path to fulfill this dream would be this easy and simple. All the players on the 10-man team were cool and friendly. I had assumed that it would be 10 players killing each other to make an impression. Instead, it was a group of good guys just happy to be playing ball in an NBA Summer League. I had never run in this circuit, so I didn't know much of anything. The coaches already knew what they were looking for and what they were trying to get out of the summer league. They were trying to develop 2 players who were already signed to the team in Jerome Moiso (UCLA, drafted by Charlotte Hornets) and their recent draft pick Kirk Haston (Indiana University). Consequently, I was simply a pawn there to assist them in fulfilling their goals—improving as players for the Hornets. As far as I was concerned, I was there—I wanted to kick in the door and make my presence felt with or without the recognizable name and NBA contract.

I should have known I was in for a long week when Coach Steve Silas called the starting lineup for the first game and I wasn't in it. My heart sank a bit thinking what guard on this team is better than me? No disrespect to the guards who were in the starting lineup, but I felt I was better than both of them. I tried not to get too down on myself because I knew there was nothing I could do but be ready to play when Coach Silas called my name. I figured that I would play 20 to 25 minutes a game, anyway. To my surprise, my name wasn't called much and we got blasted in Game 1 by the Pistons. I played about 10 minutes and I don't think I scored a point. Not a good start, if I was playing for an NBA contract or attention from other NBA teams. I didn't understand why I played so little but I figured that tomorrow would be a new day. Two other players on the team didn't share my sentiments and left the team after a few games.

Then, it happened—my opportunity to play. In the 3rd game against the Milwaukee Bucks, our starting guard got in foul trouble. This forced Coach Silas to put one of the guards from the bench in the game. There were two of us. After pondering his decision, he called my number. I played very well, scoring 18 points and helped us win our first and only game of the week.

After the game, I immediately called Darius, telling him that I was about to get my opportunity to play and perform. I was excited, knowing that my fortune was changing, or so I thought. The very next game, I went back to the bench and played sparingly. This whole experience had been challenging and very disappointing. I knew I could play this game, if given the chance. I was playing on an NBA Summer League team with 8 players and I was not getting much playing time. It was embarrassing.

We lost so badly against the Miami Heat Summer League team, the other guard who didn't play much turned to me on the bench and said, "We don't play, and we're on the worst team here. Most people probably think we are the worst two players at this summer league." I laughed because his remark was funny, but his statement stung! I was hurt, but as I never quit anything in my life, I stayed the whole week. In the end, I sat on the bench most of the time, feeling disrespected and insecure as a player. I sat there wondering how fast I went from being on top, winning a championship in one of the toughest leagues in Europe, to rock bottom, not playing on a losing 8-man team in an NBA Summer League. When it was all over and I was on the flight back home, I promised myself I would never play in another NBA Summer League—EVER!

VIII | New Beginnings

WHEN ONE DOOR closes, another opens. Unsure of where my career was headed after the summer league debacle and my steadfast decision not to return to AEK, I had no idea what was next for me. Just when I thought things weren't going my way, my agent called about 2 teams in Europe for next season. One team was Partizan, a prestigious European club in Belgrade, Serbia. The other club was CSKA, a highly celebrated team in Moscow, Russia. Partizan was my first choice because of part-owner, Vlade Divac. He was an NBA veteran, a European legend and it was an honor that he wanted me as a player. On the other hand, CSKA was being led by a new, young, and vibrant vice president named Sergei Kushchenko. I had never heard of Mr. Sergei Kushchenko, but Alex told me he was a good man, and he wanted to win. That sounded good, but my major concern was would I get my money? I did not want to go through another season like the one I had at AEK. Alex told me not to worry. CSKA had a rich tradition—money would not be an issue.

This was great news and having options made me feel good as a player. Now I was unsure of where I wanted to play. Both organizations sounded good—places that I could win and succeed at—both individually and as a team. I was a little hesitant about Belgrade though. A Serbian player who played for Partizan was killed outside the gym the season before. My agent heard that he was killed about money, a gambling situation or something to that effect. Still, that made me nervous. They had killed a man outside of the gym—to me that was serious. On the other hand, Russia seemed like a place I didn't want to be. I had already played in Latvia and it was a part of the old Soviet Union, so I assumed things wouldn't be too much different in Russia. Latvia was a tough year for me, and I didn't want to go back to that situation. So, I told my agent to give me a few more days and I would let him know where I wanted to play next season. After much prayer and a few talks with Nicole and my U.S. agent David Bauman, I decided to sign a 3-year contract worth $1.5 million net to play basketball in Moscow, Russia. Had I made the right decision? How would I survive living in Russia? Is money worth the possibility of unhappiness for 9 months a year? I would soon find the answers to all these questions and more. But, I had made it, right? I was going to make over a million dollars over 3 years. Does money equal success? Were my basketball skills worth this amount of money? I didn't have all the answers but I was more than happy with my contract.

Now, my focus was to put in the extra time and work to prove to myself that I was worth even more than what the contract revealed financially. Make no mistake about it, working hard is in my natural genetic makeup, but this was different. For the first time in my career overseas, I believed in my heart that a team was investing in me. Not just now, but for the next 3 years. I wanted to prove to them that I was going to be more of an asset than they were anticipating. I was determined for them to see that Jon-Robert Holden would not only be an investment that they could be proud of, but my mind was set on leaving my name in the history book of CSKA! This wasn't just a big payday; I knew that I had to raise the bar. I was well aware of the fact that "To whom much is given, much is required."

Touching down in Russia immediately brought back memories of Latvia. The scenery and surroundings were déjà vu. My stomach churned thinking back to the Latvian days. I took a deep breath and thought to myself that this was a new beginning.

When I arrived at my apartment in Moscow, it had the feel of New York City projects I had visited. There were a few high-rise buildings close together that all looked really old. I had never been to Russia, or in a bad neighborhood in Russia, but where I was living had the feel of being a rough and tough area. I took another deep breath and said to myself, "This is a new start for a lot of money—get your mind right and let's do this." As I walked back and forth from the elevator to the car to get all my bags, there were a few residents walking into the building, pausing at the entrance to stare at me. None of them said a word, but the looks on their faces read, "What the hell is this black man doing here?" I smiled and acted very nonchalant by nodding my head at most of them. You know, the "Hey, what's up?" nod. When I finally got all my bags into my new place, I felt as if everything was going to be OK. God never gives us more than we can handle.

Soon after my arrival in Russia, I had a meeting with the team's new Vice President, Sergei Kushchenko. I was a little nervous about meeting him. I never had to meet the big boss on the first day of the job. I didn't know what to expect or what type of man he was. However, as soon as Darius Songaila and I walked into his office, I could feel his positive energy. He was very upbeat. He threw no punches and told us of his 3-year plan. At the time, his English wasn't that good so he had his right-hand assistant with him, Ms. Vera. Vera did all the translating for him. He went on to tell us that this was a new regime and he planned on winning and winning immediately. He didn't get into details but he said CSKA had lost its luster in the last few years—not only as an elite club in Europe but had also failed to win the Russian League championship. He said this was a fresh start and that he would be changing everything—from the environment of the offices to the culture of the team as a whole. I could actually see how serious he was because everything was under construction—the offices, the locker rooms—just about everything.

Mr. Kushchenko was playing no games and changes were in full effect. He went on to let us know that he was available 24 hours a day if we needed anything. He was 100 percent committed to the team and he expected the same from us. He gave us his personal cell phone number, shook both our hands, and gave us this smile that made me feel like a champion. That first meeting gave me the sense that this club was the one that I really wanted to represent, play, and win for.

In the 2001–2002 season, I got a chance to play for one of the best coaches ever in Europe, Dusan Ivkavich. It was an honor to be selected by this great coach to play for him. I didn't know how things would work between us but I was open and ready to learn as much as I could. There were rumors that Coach Ivkavich was one tough, mean leader. That didn't bother me much because he selected me. A coach of his magnitude who wanted me as a player gave me the confidence that I could lead his team. After meeting Coach, I knew he would be a pleasure to play for. He spoke very openly and honestly about what he expected from me. He asked me to work hard each day and if I did that, he would make me a better player. I digested his every word and now knew I had a chance to be one of the best point guards in Europe.

During the preseason, management added NBA veteran, Chris, to our team. Chris had played 12-plus seasons in the NBA, and Coach felt that his scoring ability could help us become a better team. I was excited about adding him to the team and having him as a teammate. To me, it was a privilege to be playing with a former NBA All-Star. I felt like I could learn so much from a player of his caliber. However, things didn't go very well between Chris and me. His off-the-court demeanor and mentality affected our friendship. On the court, he was a great teammate. Off of it, he was arrogant, self-centered and pompous. I guess my every-one-is-equal mentality didn't mesh well with his view on things. I don't have the answers, but I sure wish things had been better between us.

One incident early in the season changed my attitude toward him. Russians aren't accustomed to seeing blacks on a regular basis, especially not very successful ones. Chris decided to make himself feel as if he could fit in a little better in Moscow by publicly saying some things that offended me. He made these disturbing remarks in a Moscow newspaper printed in English called *The Exile*. He had made some statements to the effect that I would probably have a little tougher time in Moscow than he would because I was a darker-skinned black man. He went on to say that he could pass for Spanish or some other nationality because he had light skin. His remarks totally shocked me. Maybe what he was saying was correct—maybe not. I knew we were both black men from America, playing sports in Russia. I thought there would be more of a united front, being so far away from home. I didn't think that his light skin or my brown skin had anything to do with adjusting to life in Moscow. In my eyes we were black—plain and simple. I had been through enough racial stuff overseas to know that no matter what he thought he was, he was going to be viewed as black—whether he knew it or not. It made me feel uncomfortable and uneasy around him. I didn't know if he had my back or not, or because he was light-skinned, my problems or safety while we were out together were my issues, not his. The fact that a fellow brother from America would make a statement like that hurt me and turned me off.

The other incident that occurred was so silly, all I could do was say, "Man, this is a different dude." At a hip-hop club called Karma Bar, Chris and I were both relaxing, having a few drinks, when I caught the eye of a young lady staring at me. She stood near us and I assumed that Chris was feeling her. After about 20 minutes of just staring at each other, she came closer to me and said hello. I said "Hi" back and we started a casual conversation. Chris wanted her attention, so he interrupted our conversation to introduce himself. I didn't think anything of it. He tried to take over the conversation, but she wasn't feeling him so she kind of brushed him off and kept talking to me. He started to get belligerent, saying stupid stuff like, "You must not know me, I got money"; "I am a millionaire, you don't know what you're missing." I thought to myself, "This guy is a clown." But, when he got disrespectful I had to walk away. He told her, "Dude, he doesn't have money like me." I almost lost my cool. I wanted to hit this guy over the head with a bottle to let him know I was not with this b.s. He was acting as if I was Shawn Kemp and had made him part of several highlight reels! I just took the high road and walked away without a word.

I was not overseas to be friends with Chris or to start fights in clubs. I could handle our situation later and protect myself physically, if need be. This encounter let me know that our relationship was strictly on a business level! He was a teammate and nothing else to me. In spite of all this, at heart, I think Chris genuinely had good intentions. He would give you the shirt off his back if he was in the mood. It's as if he had two personalities. He treated me like a little brother on the one hand, and on the other, like a dude not worthy to be in his presence. I just did the best I could to maintain a respectful relationship with him. I was trying to make my own name and handle my business on the court. I didn't have the time or energy to put into nonsense off the court. I knew I was in Russia for one reason—to play some good basketball.

As we began playing and winning preseason games, there was a buzz in Europe that CSKA could be a surprise team this season in the Euroleague. During a preseason tournament in Serbia against Panathinaikos (the Greek team that had won the Euroleague championship the year before), I realized Darius Songaila was a beast. He and I could be a powerful one-two punch. That preseason game felt like a regular season game, because of the intensity of both teams. I knew Darius was a work horse, but I had no clue that he could talk trash too!

At one point in the 2nd half, Darius started taking over the game offensively. He scored a few baskets in a row against a top American player named Mike Batiste. At one point, Darius started talking trash while he was scoring. He said, "J, come to me every time, he can't stop me." I was shocked. He was playing with such intensity and fire during a preseason game, wow! In the end, I was happy we won the game but what impressed me most was Darius's desire and love for the game. I knew then that he was a true competitor, and I would go to war with him any time. We left that tournament a confident team—a team headed into the regular season, knowing that we had the potential to do big things.

The season started well for us in both the Euroleague and the Russian League. The tough Euroleague games prepared us to pretty much dominate the Russian League teams. We were rolling right along when we encountered our first hiccup that November. In Italy, facing an inconsistent Virtus Bolgna team, Darius injured himself during the second quarter. When he went down, you could feel the shock among my teammates. Darius was our key player, possibly our best, and no one knew how we would play without him. In this game, we responded well. We kept our composure and played with poise. In the end, we won a close, hard-fought game by 1 point. Chris stepped up big for us, and had a double-double (meaning he had at least 10 points and at least 10 rebounds). I played a solid game with 21 points (7–19 field goals [fg]) and 5 assists. What's more, we kept on rolling without a blemish right into Thanksgiving break.

We had continued to play inspired basketball without our leading scorer Darius Songaila when we experienced a shocking move made by management. Chris had been playing well and averaging a double-double in Darius's absence. When management decided to let him go, I was stunned. I thought he had been playing well and the team chemistry was good. Nevertheless, CSKA had something brewing behind closed doors. They were going to release Chris and add a savvy veteran with a lot of NBA and overseas experience. I may not have been a big fan of Chris off the court but he was playing well and he was helping us win. I didn't know the new guy and wasn't sure if he would have a negative effect on our team chemistry. But I believed in management and Coach Ivkavich, and I felt that they knew what they were doing, so I stayed focused on playing ball.

As soon as Victor Alexander (Big Vic) joined the team, we were instantly a better ball club; he was that good. He could post up, shoot the mid-range jump shot, defend in the post, and defend pick and rolls—he was the total package. We still missed Songaila, but Big Vic was so good and such a dominant force that we didn't miss a beat. We kept rolling and winning games. With the addition of Big Vic, I became the second scoring punch. Big Vic was our first option on offense and he led the team in scoring. Having Big Vic as a teammate was very enjoyable. We connected off the court. Like me, he didn't say much if he didn't know you. He was from Detroit, "The D," and had an edge to him. He didn't play any b.s. and was a stand-up guy. As your friend, he would ride with you to the end. Big Vic was more like a big brother to me. He taught me the ropes to the overseas game. He mentored me on how to act, what to say, all in all on how to handle myself in the cutthroat business of playing ball overseas. He was a true blessing to me and my future. His friendship was vital to my growth as a player but more importantly as a man. That season, CSKA gained a great player, and I gained a life-long friend.

During a break in the season, my agent and I decided to go and watch the Russian National Team (NT) play a qualification game for the European championships. At the time, I knew very little about the Russian NT but had heard that for the past few years they had been struggling. That didn't matter or mean anything to me, I just wanted to relax, watch a good game of basketball and show some support for my fellow Russian teammates. I didn't care what they had done in the past or what they would do in the future—or so I thought. They may have been struggling, but the team I watched had talent. Although Russian NBA superstar Andrei Kirilenko was missing from the team, the skill level was apparent. CSKA V.P., Mr. Kushchenko, thought the NT needed a point guard. He even suggested that I play for the Russian National Team. I merely thought he was joking around. To show appreciation, I simply smiled and said it would be a privilege to play for the Russian National Team. He smiled and then gave me a serious look, saying, "Let me work on that, and next year you might be out there helping us win some games." There was nothing I could really say, so all I did was nod my head up and down. I didn't think in a million years that would actually happen.

Two incidents in my first year in Moscow had a major effect on my feelings and impression of Russia. The first occurred near my apartment. Every day I walked about 5 minutes to a parking garage where my car had to stay overnight. Earlier that year, someone had stolen the whole front bumper from my car—headlights included. I had seen people steal hubcaps or even emblems from the front hood of cars, but the whole front bumper? That was a first for me! The car was a BMW so I understood why CSKA decided to buy a parking spot at the nearest garage.

The walk from my apartment to the garage was not very safe. I only say this because it was through a park in the projects. Plus I was a foreigner. I was never fearful of the walk, just not at ease with it. As I walked to the garage one afternoon, 5 white young men approached me. I didn't think much of it because I was walking through a path in a park. As they got closer, I realized a few of them had bald-heads and one was twirling a chain. The chain frightened me because it had a ball on the end of it with spikes sticking out. As we crossed paths they stared at me while speaking Russian. Not knowing the language, I had no clue what they were talking about, but my radar went up to be on guard. As their voices grew louder, I realized they were surrounding me. I put my hand in my gym bag. What they didn't know was that I carried a shank (a long, sharp knife) with me every day. Big Vic had encouraged me to carry one because of the possible dangers of living in Russia. Big Vic lived by the mantra that "you never know who or what is out there." He used to say, "I'd rather be judged by 12 than carried by 6." He was right, and his words influenced me to carry a knife at all times.

Surrounded and knowing that I had to show no fear, I did two things. First, I pulled out my shank to let them know I was capable of hurting at least one of them, and second, I called Big Vic on my cell phone. Two of the 5 didn't seem interested in hurting me but I wasn't sure. In any case, I kept my eyes on the loudest one, possibly the leader, the one with the twirling chain. As I started to back away, the loudest one started twirling the chain faster and faster yelling something. I crouched down in a football stance—eyes watering ready to charge—when they all took off laughing and running. As they ran off, I heard them say in English one of the few words they probably knew—nigger. Relieved, I didn't care what they were screaming. I just thought to myself, "There will not be a next time for something like this." I never turned my back on them as I started backpedaling fast to my car and out of their sight. I felt my phone buzz. It was Big Vic who had tried to call me 3 times. I told him why I had called and what had just happened. He asked me if I was OK and said, "Man, you gotta be careful out here in these streets." I told him I knew that, and thank goodness, I had that knife with me. He started laughing and said, "I told you boy, you always gotta be ready." He was right, and thank goodness I was ready. I knew there was racism in Russia, there is racism all over the world, but until it's up close and in front of you, you never realize just how serious a situation can get. I also know that I could have been in the wrong place at the wrong time. It happens—it's just nice when you're ready for it.

The second incident caused Mr. Kushchenko to insist on me having a driver for the rest of the season—a driver that CSKA would indeed pay for. One early morning, as I drove home from a casino, I was pulled over by the police. I had been watching the American Football games played on television late on Sunday nights. The policeman pulled me over and immediately started questioning me in Russian. Not understanding a word, I turned over the paperwork to the car and immediately called the team manager. When the policeman came back to the car with my paperwork I handed him the phone. He took the phone and started speaking with the team manager. A minute or so later, he handed me the phone.

The team manager asked me if I had had any drinks? I told the truth and said I had 2 Bailey's on ice over a 4-hour span. He said the police officer would probably give me a hassle if I didn't give him any money so just give him $50 and go home. I wanted to ask him why, but I didn't. I was tired and just wanted to go home. I hung up with the team manager, gave the police officer $50, and was on my way home when suddenly, not 5 minutes later, I was pulled over by another police officer. This police officer walked up to the car and said, "$50 PLEASE!" This was no freakin' coincidence. This was a damn setup. I tried to explain to him that I had just paid his friend $50 and I wasn't paying him. I also noticed he was alone. In Russia, most policemen ride in two's.

I hadn't done anything wrong, why should I have to pay more money? I don't think he understood what I was saying because after I got finished talking, again he said, "$50 PLEASE!" I didn't say a word. I just sat there in my car. Agitated and frustrated he reached into the car and tried to take the keys out of the ignition. A little terrified, I pulled off, almost taking his arm with me. Scared, I drove directly to the Aerostar hotel. I knew that they spoke English at the hotel and I would be safer there. As I pulled up to the hotel, the police officer was in his car right on my tail. I jumped out and sprinted to the hotel. The officer gets out and chases me to the hotel entrance. The security guard on duty asked me what was wrong? I start to explain what had happened. He gave me a bewildered look and slowly walked out to talk to the policeman. I called the team manager to tell him what was going on. I hoped he could clear this situation up. I looked at the security guard as he tried to talk to the police, but the officer was not talking to him. He had his back to the security guard and was sitting on my car as if he would wait as long as he had to. The security guard walked back to the hotel and in broken English said, "He is a bad man; you may want to stay here for some time." I just shook my head thinking to myself, "What the hell have I gotten myself into?"

I had crazy thoughts. This was a policeman—who knows what he could do to me at a later date. He knew my car and license plate number. This could happen every time I go out. I was thinking all this when my thoughts were abruptly interrupted. The security guard came up to me and said, "You should be OK soon, he is leaving." I waited another 45 minutes before I left to go home. What a night!

The next morning after practice, Mr. Kushchenko insisted that I get a driver for the remainder of the season. He was worried about my safety, and didn't want any more incidents. He even used his resources to try and find the police officer who tried to harass me. This show of support meant a lot. Mr. Kushchenko cared about J.R. Holden the person. This show of support pushed me even more to give him everything I had on the court plus more. He made me feel like a part of his family. His kindness, thoughtfulness, and willingness to go above and beyond was something that I will always remember and forever be grateful for.

That year I played in the Euroleague Final Four, the Russian Cup Finals and the Russian League Finals. All three were different but important to win. What management thought would take us 2 to 3 years to accomplish, we achieved in our first year playing together; we reached the Euroleague Final Four (FF) in Barcelona, Spain.

At the Euroleague FF in Spain, I was like a kid at Christmas time. I wanted to experience and do everything. This was my first trip to the Euroleague Final Four. I just wanted to take it all in. Reaching the Final Four was a huge accomplishment for the team and management. The organization was ecstatic about us making our 1st Final Four. Coach Ivkavich had been to a few Final Fours and so had Victor Alexander. This was business as usual for them, but for the rest of us, this was uncharted territory.

For Darius Songaila and me, this was an opportunity to show the world that we were 2 young talented players on the rise in Europe. Our team mindset going into the Final Four was to do what we had done all year and win this thing. In spite of everything we had accomplished that season, many expected us to lose and lose easy at the Final Four. This was mostly because we were facing the home team in the first game—Barcelona. They had a very good team starting with Sarunas Jasikevicius (2 years—Indiana Pacers, Euroleague championships) at the point guard position, Juan Carlos Navarro (NBA, Memphis Grizzlies), Dejan Bodiroga (a legend overseas with a few European titles), and Gregor Fucka to name a few. The names and the hype didn't faze us one bit. We didn't have any pressure and were a serious underdog. My mentality was—let's shock the world.

In the locker room moments before we were to hit the floor for warm-ups, an incredible feeling came over me. It felt as if the world had stopped for a moment just to tell me—you're here, have fun, and enjoy the ride. As I ran through the tunnel to start warming up for the game, a chill ran over my body when my feet touched the court. Millions of people around the world would be watching a no-name kid from Wilkinsburg play basketball at the highest level in Europe. Knowing that no one in the arena thought we would win this game pumped me up even more. I was ready and this was our chance to shock the world.

When the game kicked off, the early momentum and flow of the game was in our favor. To my surprise, our young team was loose and confident. We set a very good tone for the game by being aggressive. We knew Barcelona was a solid, defensive, half-court team, so we needed to run and try and get some easy baskets. We accomplished this and played a good game for the first 25 minutes. As the game wore on, and many fouls were called against us, the game became half court. This was to Barcelona's advantage because we weren't having a great shooting night. Then again, they weren't shooting the ball that well either. Still, we tried to pick up the pace of the game by attempting to run after they made a basket or foul shot. We could not overcome the crucial plays they made down the stretch. Our team played our hearts out, but ended up losing 76–71. We were 2 plays (and a few crucial foul calls that went against us), away from making it to the finals of the Euroleague Final Four. This was the quote I gave after the game, "It was a game played hard, but both teams played well. We missed some important shots down the stretch, and that's what it comes down to in the end. I think we played aggressively, and that's how you play in a Final Four game. When you get 26 points from the line, you can't ask more than that. But that's how it is when you play against the home team. It's part of the game."

They scored 76 points and got 26 of them from the free throw line. I didn't feel like we were cheated, but I do feel like the game would have been officiated differently if played on a neutral court. Nevertheless, they were the home team and that's why they call it home court advantage.

When the game was over and we were in the locker room I was very emotional. I knew we were so close to being victorious that night— I could taste it. I cried with my head in my jersey for 10 minutes after the game. I knew this was a special team, and that there were no guarantees that I would ever get back to this stage again. I knew that I had just missed my opportunity to win a Euroleague title and it hurt. I didn't go out quietly, finishing 8–19 fg in the game with 21 points, 2 assists, 3 steals, and 4 turnovers. The stats reveal how much heart I played that game with. I left it all out there, and knew that my family and friends back home would be proud of me. The journey was sweet, and although we didn't finish it off, it was one of my best seasons overseas. This team had been a joy to be around, and we were accomplishing things on a high level. The players fought together as a unified group to win a championship. We were young, exuberant, and naive about what we set out to accomplish. It was a flat-out joy to play on that team.

Losing the Russian Cup that year was disappointing but what made matters worse was how we lost it and what went on after we lost the game. We lost the Russian Cup on a shot by Petr Somoylenko with less than 15 seconds left in the game. Petr was the point guard for the opposing Russian team, Unics Kazan. He wasn't much of a shooter, but somehow with no one to pass to, he maneuvered a shot from his pivot foot when no one, including myself, thought he would shoot the ball. This lucky shot went in and was the dagger that broke our hearts in the cup finals. Petr rarely scored or even shot the ball for his team. However, because his shot went in and we missed a shot at the buzzer, Unics Kazan won the Russian Cup that season.

Although we didn't play well, we thought we would find a way to win that game. We usually always did. We were the better team, but without our full attention on defense, we allowed them to gain confidence and find their shooting rhythm early in the game. We tried to pick up our defensive intensity later in the game, but it was too late; they had gained their confidence. The hungrier team won the game. I tip my hat to them. The loss had everyone upset, especially management. The week after the game, Coach called me into a meeting with Mr. Kushchenko. I had rarely ever met with the coach and the VP of the club at the same time. When

I sat down, Coach asked me about the final shot of the Cup game and why I didn't body up on the point guard when he shot the ball. I was in disbelief. All I could think was, "What kind of question is this?" He could not be serious. For one, why would he ask me this a week later and in front of Mr. Kushchenko? Is his job on the line or what? Is he blaming me for the loss? All this stuff ran through my mind as I sat there quietly. When I opened my mouth, I said, "I played good defense on Petr. When he picked up the ball, I just kept my hands up and didn't want to bail him out by potentially fouling him by bodying up. He is not a scorer and to my knowledge hadn't hit a jump shot that entire game up until the last shot." I just looked at him stone-faced and said, "Is that it?" I was pissed. Coach went on to say that I should have bodied up when Petr picked up the ball. I actually cracked a smile and said, "Next time." I was heated and really disturbed because I felt as if Coach needed someone to blame for the loss, and I was the scapegoat. I really couldn't pinpoint why I met with him and the VP of CSKA. Coach Dusan was a great coach, and he definitely gave me the freedom and confidence to play my game, but I didn't know how to feel about that situation. I wanted to win just as much or even more than anyone else I know. This caught me off guard and took me by total surprise. But this is the life of playing ball overseas. When you win, the team wins, but when you lose, watch out, the finger could be pointed at YOU.

In the Russian League Finals, we played Ural Great from Perm, Russia. They had beaten us once during the regular season at their place. In that game their point guard, Eddie Shannon, made every play down the stretch in the 4th quarter to beat us. He was the first player in Europe to outplay me, outwork me, and get a victory over my team. Many players have played well against me, but he dominated the pivotal part of the game. I was disappointed with my performance, and I knew I had to come out with guns blazing the next time we played Eddie and his team. Eddie Shannon was a great player who had overcome a major setback to have a phenomenal career. He was a true testament to perseverance and self-belief. He had overcome blindness in one eye to have a successful college and professional career. He had a great year statistically that season with Ural Great. He was a major reason they were facing us in the finals of the Russian League. In any case, the Russian League Finals was pretty much a breeze for us. We defeated Ural Great in a best-of-7 series, 4–1. We dominated the series, and I capped off a great season by being named the MVP of the finals. It was a wonderful ending to my first season in Russia.

As much fun as I had on the court that season, I was happy the season was over and I was ready to be back stateside. It had been a long year. I hadn't gone home in 10 months—not even for Christmas. That was tough for me, especially mentally. I missed home, my family, and friends. As soon as the last game of the finals ended, the very next day I was on a plane back to the United States. Management, coaches, and my teammates understood why I was rushing to get home. Because I was coming back to CSKA next season, no one said a word about me leaving so abruptly. They just said have a safe trip and a great summer—they'd see me soon.

When I got home, time was precious. I tried and did everything under the sun in a 2- to 3-month span. It was impossible to do everything in such a short amount time, but my goodness, I tried. This summer was a little different for me because for the first time in my professional career, I was coming home with some real money. I wanted to make plans for the future and one of them was to buy my own place. I was tired of coming home and staying with family and friends. It was time for me to have a place to call my own—to call home.

I didn't know where I wanted to set up shop. I was thinking either Virginia Beach, Virginia or Atlanta, Georgia. These were the two places that I had family or a friend who loved the city where they lived. My brother Darius and his long-time girlfriend Becky lived in Virginia Beach. I thought it would be nice to live close to my brother and near the beach—a nice beach-front place where I could completely relax and take in the simple things of life, after a season playing ball. I kept thinking about quiet, late night walks on the beach. All this, plus I knew Darius wanted to train me during the summer. I figured it could be a great benefit to my summer workout regimen, if I were closer to someone who wanted to help me work on my game. On the other hand, my teammate, mentor and good friend Victor Alexander lived in and loved Atlanta—also known as the Atl. The Atl had everything a young brother could need or want; I could party if I wanted to, go to plays, visit the MLK center downtown, or take in free outdoor concerts at Piedmont Park. There was a plethora of entertainment, and being single with a few dollars, it could be a nice place to settle down for a few years. There were a lot of affluent blacks in Atlanta. I figured that would help me with networking connections for life after basketball. Knowing all this about both cities, I decided to spend a few weeks in both places. By the end of the summer, I had purchased my first place I could call home, a penthouse condo in downtown Atlanta.

That summer, I decided to have a little fun for the 4th of July, so I traveled to New Orleans, Louisiana to attend the Essence Festival. On my flight to New Orleans, I bumped into an acquaintance named Jon whom I met while playing in Greece. He told me he was going to New Orleans for business. We ended up chatting for a minute and decided to grab a bite to eat before we went our separate ways. We decided to dine at a soul-food spot in New Orleans called Mother's. At Mother's, you stand in line to get your food, no matter if you're eating in or taking out. After waiting in line, getting our food, and finding a decent place to sit, in walked a rather tall, fine woman. As soon as she stepped foot in Mother's, she caught my attention. She was with another young lady, a friend I suppose, but the woman who had my attention was stunning. She was tall compared to the average woman, with a nice body and the sexiest smile! She was radiant; she just looked so happy.

I couldn't take my eyes off her from the moment I saw her until the time I left the restaurant; I followed her every move. She sat down with her food and was on the phone most of the time. I attempted to get her attention. I didn't want to go overboard or interrupt her dinner if she didn't want to be bothered, so I gave her a "Hey, how are you?" wave. Either she didn't see it, didn't want to say hi, or her phone conversation was good because she never even blinked at me. I didn't want to give up yet, so when I finished my meal, I purposely walked right by her to get her attention or at least get a closer look at that stunning young lady. She never raised an eyebrow, but I did get a closer look!

That weekend in New Orleans was a blast. I bumped into a few old friends—basketball players and college buddies. On the second or third day in New Orleans, while walking down Bourbon Street, I caught my college buddy talking to the striking woman I had seen at Mother's restaurant a few days earlier. I slowed my stroll to see if the conversation was intense and if he really knew the woman. I was a little jealous. I couldn't believe my college buddy knew this woman. Once they finished talking, I caught up with my buddy to try and get the scoop on her. I tried to play it cool, but I couldn't. I had to come right out and ask him about her. He told me that he really didn't know her, but that she was very nice. He finished by saying that he couldn't get her number because she told him that she didn't have a contact number. That sounded weird but funny to me. What woman in her mid-20s doesn't have a contact number?

I chuckled to myself, but the way he talked about this woman intrigued me even more. I got up the courage to go over and talk to her myself. As I approached her, her smile made me melt. I attempted to calm my nerves by starting a little small talk. As we conversed, I could feel she had a good spirit and I wanted to know more about her. However, she had just played my boy and I didn't want to get rejected as well. So, before I started to walk away I said, "I would ask you for your number, but my friend said you don't have a contact number." I knew that was lame, but I didn't know what else to say. I was happy with simply knowing her name at this point. She smiled and said, "Well, if you go off what your friend says, then that is on you." I chuckled and before we finished our conversation, she wrote her name and number on a piece of paper. Her name was Aireka. I knew she was special, but I had no clue how special this woman truly was. As I jumped for joy on the inside, I walked away from her, playing it cool but smiling from ear to ear.

That evening in New Orleans, I ended up partying with a good friend, from back home in Pittsburgh, who was at the Essence as well—Mike Todd. We partied hard until the wee hours of the morning. After having too many drinks and a morning hangover, I decided it was time to either leave New Orleans or try and spend the day with Aireka. I was having a great time but it was time to slow it down. That morning I decided to ring Aireka. When she picked up the phone I could hear she was busy so I offered to call her back. She sounded sweet and innocent. She told me she was packing up her stuff; she was leaving New Orleans today. I told her I had planned on staying another day for the old school concert and that maybe we could hang out. She said that was sweet of me but she had to go. Without hesitation, I said, "You know what, if I can change my ticket, can I meet you at the airport?

She said, "Sure" and told me it would be nice to meet with me before she left to go back home to Detroit. I threw my clothes in my suitcase and made the call to change my ticket while on the way to the airport.

I arrived at the airport, immediately checked in, and started looking for the fine young woman I couldn't take my mind off of. Wandering around a little, I finally saw her sitting down in an eatery. She looked even better than she did when I saw her at Mother's and I thought she was gorgeous then! She looked so at peace and at ease with life. Whatever she had going on in her life, I sure wanted to be a part of it. That was how tranquil she looked. I walked over and greeted her with a kiss on the cheek and ordered something to eat. I was starving. We chatted about different things over an early lunch, before she had to catch her flight home. I told her I truly enjoyed our conversation and that I would be in touch real soon. I could have spent the whole day sitting in that eatery conversing with her. She was a special young lady. That day changed my life for the better, and we have been connected somehow—some way—ever since.

Coming back to CSKA for the 2003–2004 season, there were a few major changes to the team. We added a prolific scorer in Marcus Brown, one of the top rebounders in Europe; Mirsad Turkan; and a few other Europeans who would definitely contribute that season. On the flip side, we lost 2 of our best players in Darius Songaila (to the NBA) and Victor Alexander (to a team called Unicaja in Spain). We would definitely feel the loss of both players. Yet, we knew that with the additions to the team and a good preseason, expectations would be high.

On a personal level, I officially broke up with my then long-time girlfriend Nicole. We had been distant for about a year or two; it was just a matter of time before we made it official. Still, this was a very tough decision for me. She had been very influential and supportive of me and my career. She had been there for me from the beginning. We had made some tough decisions together and that meant a lot to me.

My girlfriend called me up and said that her friend was going to the New Orleans Essence Jazz festival and that he wanted her to come. She asked me to go with her because everyone else had to work and could not get vacation on such short notice. As I was unemployed at the time, I told her that I would not be able to go, but she practically begged me because she didn't want to go alone. She told me that I didn't have to worry about air transportation or a hotel because her job was paying for it all (she had business in New Orleans that week); all I needed was spending money. Reluctantly, I went with her to the jazz festival.

Our first night in New Orleans was a chill night; there were all types of people up and down Bourbon Street having fun, drinking, eating, and socializing. We decided to dine at a soul food restaurant called "Mother's," where the food was so delicious.

I noticed this guy staring at me. I happened to look in his direction again and he waved and smiled. I waved back abruptly, smiled, and continued my conversation on the phone. My friend and I finished our food and continued on with our night's activities.

The next day we met my girlfriend's friend and he introduced us to the 2 guys who accompanied him. One of his friends was interested in me. He asked for my name and phone number; I was polite and told him that I didn't have a contact number. He followed me another 2 blocks because he was determined to get to know me. I kept reiterating that I did not have a contact number. Finally, we reached the 3rd block and he looked across the street and said, "Oh, that's my man." He then crossed the street and started talking to a clean cut, well-put-together guy, dressed in a red polo shirt and denim shorts. After a few minutes, the guy in the red polo shirt started crossing the street.

He came up to me and said, "Hi, how are you?"

I replied "I'm fine."

He said "I'm J.R., what's your name?"

(Continued on page 251)

On the one hand, I wasn't the man she deserved. Nevertheless, she was an amazing woman who I was scared to let go. I knew that her love was real—authentic. She wasn't with me because of basketball. My basketball career was icing on the cake for her. She genuinely loved me for me. She was my woman, my friend, and my advisor. She was everything a young man trying to find his way in this crazy world and business of professional sports could dream of having in his corner. I didn't quite know how to tell her that I loved her but that I couldn't be with her anymore. It took me a long time to get the courage to say, "It's over." When I did get the courage, I was overseas and had to do it over the phone. It wasn't ideal, but I had to do it. I was emotionally and mentally fatigued. I was fighting with myself every day trying to figure out what to say and what to do. Eventually I called her and told her my feelings. She knew we both weren't happy but she was willing to fight for what we built together. I knew I couldn't make her happy anymore and that hurt my heart. We talked for hours but in the end, we both got off the phone sad, hurt, and disappointed. After not speaking for 6 months, Nicole and I spoke again. She sounded great and I knew she was happy again. I could hear it in her voice. I could now take a deep breath, knowing I did the right thing months ago. We would both love each other for life; it would now just be as great friends.

Early in the season, the president of Russia, Vladimir Putin and VP of CSKA, Sergei Kushchenko, would change my career and life forever. No black American athlete had ever received a Russian passport. Because of Mr. Kushchenko's relationship with President Putin, I was to obtain a Russian passport. President Putin cited "Special Circumstances" as the reason. The process for me was simple. I arrived at the Russian Embassy, took a head shot, and 5 minutes later I walked out with a Russian passport in my hand. It was that easy. I didn't know that receiving the passport would create so much buzz so quickly around Russia. Right away, there was a lot of positive and negative press. Many Russian citizens felt that I didn't deserve it. They didn't feel that I would respect and love their country as they did. I didn't take any of this personally—the good or the bad. Everyone is entitled to their opinion. I just wanted to play basketball and do everything I could to help CSKA be the best team possible. I didn't expect anything "special" to happen to me because of this. I can honestly say, it was gratifying to have a man of Mr. Kushchenko's stature take a special interest me. I knew his intentions were pure. He wanted to help CSKA become a stronger team, and with the Euroleague rule (only 2 Americans permitted on the team) at the time, management could now go get another American player to help the team become stronger.

Within days of receiving the Russian passport, management brought back last year's leading scorer and my good friend, Victor Alexander. I am not sure how they pulled it off but I was happy to have my friend back on the team. I believed that he was the missing piece to us potentially winning a Euroleague championship.

There are times when being the nice guy is not the best way to handle a situation—especially in a foreign land when leadership may not understand how tough it is to be away from home for so many months. Sometimes you have to demand what you want instead of accepting what they give you. For example, the previous season the entire team spent Christmas in Serbia. I didn't feel as if I needed to spend Christmas in Europe if we weren't playing official games. So, in the off-season I told Mr. Kushchenko that I wanted to spend Christmas at home with my family. As Americans, if we had time off, we should be given the opportunity to spend it in the States. Mr. Kushchenko was OK with it but unfortunately, Coach Ivkavich wasn't. Right before Christmas break, I spoke with Coach. He said he would find another time throughout the 2nd half of the season for all the Americans to go back home. He simply didn't want us all to go home at the same time—and not for Christmas.

I wasn't missing my opportunity to go home because if we happened to lose a few games or started playing badly, none of us would get the chance to go home after Christmas. For this reason all 3 Americans went to talk to Coach. He finally gave in and said we could go home. The trick was we could only go home for 2 days. Now this had to be a joke. Two days for Christmas was absurd. Nevertheless, I kept my mouth shut and just thought, "Whatever. Once I get home, it's on me when I return." I wouldn't do anything outlandish, but going home for 2 days was unrealistic.

After 3 days at home for Christmas, Marcus and I returned to Moscow. When we arrived, management was OK with our tardiness, but

Coach was furious. He felt as if we had betrayed him. In addition to all this, Big Vic came back 3 days after we did. I knew this incident would blow over quickly if we won our first few games after the holidays. However, Coach was the angriest at me, and I think it was because he felt I was the ringleader or something. After a few weeks of the silent treatment and some looks of disdain, Coach and I were fine (good terms) again. We both had one goal in mind and 5 months to accomplish it.

After another very successful Euroleague season, we were once again at the Final Four. Like the year before, we would be facing the host team in the semi-final game. This year it was European powerhouse Maccabi, Tel Aviv. A year older and more mature, I knew what to expect and was more focused this time round. I knew we had an uphill battle in defeating Maccabi but I liked our chances. The Euroleague write-up went as follows:

"Maccabi's individual talents are overwhelming, but CSKA is the team least likely to be intimidated. CSKA has the depth to match Maccabi. Beginning in the back court, CSKA's duo J.R. Holden and Marcus Brown have been the driving force behind CSKA's success and spectacular play on both ends of the court. Both players can play at either guard spot, as Holden takes advantage of his ball handling and shooting skills, especially off the dribble, while Brown is the team's top gun, scoring in double digits in all games this season and averaging 18 points per game on 60.1% two-pointers and 87.2% from the free throw line, also dishing 4.1 assists per game and showing he is more than a pure scorer. Theo Papaloukas is ready to come off the bench and provide intensity and defensive skills, playing a key role for this team. CSKA's young duo of small forwards, Victor Khryapa and Sergey Monya create mismatches with their size and athletic ability. No-one in Europe rebounds and defends at the power forward spot better than Mirsad Turkcan. Turkcan will likely start along with big man Victor Alexander, who has been one of the premiere big men in the Euroleague over the past two seasons and can score in the paint or with his jumper from the perimeter. CSKA's deep front line also includes veteran Dragan Tarlac, Sergei Panov, who is the team captain, Alexander Bashminov and Aleksey Savrasenko."

There were no gimmicks or ploys. We knew we had to play a great game and contain their top two guns, Anthony Parker and Sarunas Jasikev-icius, if we wanted a chance to win. I love a challenge, and I knew my match-up with Sarunas was an important one. He was their leader and ultimate competitor. Still, I felt very comfortable facing him; I had faced him the season before at the Final Four, when he played for Barcelona. I have a lot of respect for Sarunas. He played with heart—a killer instinct—and a desire to succeed that few players have. He brought out the best in me every time we matched up against each other. I won the head-to-head match-up statistically last season, but he won the game and the Euroleague championship. This time round, it was my turn to win the game and take the hardware back to Moscow.

The semi-final game started well for us. We played loose and with supreme confidence while Maccabi started the game tight and tense. We hit a few shots against their match-up zone defense and it seemed to make them a little panicky. In an instance, the momentum of the game changed when Marcus Brown picked up an early 2nd foul. With our leading scorer passive and afraid to pick up a 3rd foul, we lost our advantage and Maccabi stormed back to take the lead. Still, the game went back and forth and seemed within our grasp heading into the 4th quarter. However, when they took the lead in the 4th quarter behind a spectacular performance from Anthony Parker and an unexpected hero, David Bluenthal, we couldn't recover. We lost 93–85. I didn't shoot the ball particularly well and, once again, my match-up with Sarunas was interesting. We had gotten into a small altercation during the game. It was nothing personal—just 2 ultimate competitors trying to will their teams to victory. Again, he got the win and I left the court, a semi-final loser. Would I ever win a Euroleague championship? Was I good enough to win a championship? Was I a championship-caliber leader? Was I that unlucky to face the host team in the semi-final game 2 years in a row? What was I doing wrong that I keep coming up short? These were just a few questions that crossed my mind while leaving Tel Aviv.

Overall, my second year in Moscow was a little more enjoyable than the first. I moved to a nicer apartment on a main street in Moscow—Leningradsky Prospect. That was a much needed change and helped me feel more safe and comfortable. Other than that, not much changed. I did enjoy the nightlife a little more. So, of course, I interacted with more people and that was pleasurable. I frequented a few clubs and had a good time. The good thing about living in Moscow was that it's a huge city. Most people didn't know who I was, so I was able to get out, relax, and enjoy myself without much of a hassle. I hung out mostly at Hip-Hop and R&B spots. Those places were the ones where I felt most comfortable. Most of the patrons in these places spoke English.

For the second year in a row we had lost the Russian Cup, and this time round, an incident occurred between Coach Ivkavich and me that would change our relationship for the rest of the season. In the Russian Cup Final, we played the home team in a small, fanatical basketball city called Perm. We were the superior team but this team was always very difficult to beat at their place. We couldn't find our rhythm offensively and Ural Great was playing like their team name, "Great." They made shots and out-hustled us early in the game. Right before the half, knowing that we were struggling offensively, I took a quick shot. It was a shot that you know that the team could do without but a shot that a leader had to take in the hope of sparking a fire under his team going into halftime. It was a one-on-one play and I would have to live with the coach's disapproval if I missed the shot—and I did miss it. So, we went into the half, trailing by 10 points.

Coach stormed into the locker room pissed and frustrated at our team play. He was ranting and raving when he decided to call me out on the last shot I had taken. I knew he was frustrated so I just kept my head down with a smirk on my face. I had been in this situation in the past; it was best to just let Coach get it off his chest. The shot I took didn't put us down 10 points but I understand it was fresh on his mind and he felt like he had to get on one of his leaders to push the team to play better in the 2nd half. I understood all of this. What I didn't appreciate was his response to the smirk on my face. As he finished his speech to the team, he walked toward me asking me what is so funny. I didn't say a word; I just shook my head back and forth—meaning "nothing." However, my response was not enough for him. He got in my face and put his hands on my shoulders as if he were trying to push me back. I instantly snapped. I was ready to fight him. I was not about to have Coach put his hands on me. Maybe I was overreacting but I had seen him literally smack a Russian player earlier in the season. That was not going to be me. This was a basketball game and I was playing my tail off. There was no need to take it to a physical altercation. I realize that in the heat of the moment, emotions can get the best of a person. Still, to what extent do you let a person go when their emotions or actions have a direct effect on you? I don't know the answer but thank goodness for my teammates Big Vic and Marcus.

I didn't even want to play basketball the 2nd half of the game. I was that affected by the incident. I didn't want Coach to have the satisfaction of me playing my heart out for him. I had now let my emotions get the best of me, and I wanted to go crazy on Coach. After I calmed down, Big Vic said that he wasn't sure if Coach was trying to push me or not but Coach Ivkavich still had no right to put his hands on me like that. In spite of this, I went out and played the 2nd half with a vengeance. I scored 20 points in the 2nd half, finishing the game with 25 points (10–21 fg) 5 rebounds, 3 assists, 2 steals, and 2 turnovers in a losing effort. We had fallen and lost the Russian Cup to Ural Great, a ball club we were much better than. Although Coach and I never had another altercation, our relationship was never quite the same. Years later, we both came to realize we had to let it go. Coach Ivkavich is one of the best coaches I have ever played for. He is a good man.

We won the Russian League championship. We defeated Unics Kazan 3–1 in a best-of-5 series. Nevertheless, there was trouble in paradise at halftime of Game 1 of the finals. We were losing and playing poorly at home. All season long, Coach Ivkavich had not been playing Big Vic. I don't know why but Big Vic was by far the best scoring big man on the team. He was arguably the best center in Europe. But game after game, Big Vic gathered more and more minutes on the bench. I assumed Big Vic snapped because he just had enough. After a terrible 1st half, Coach Ivkavich had an outburst on how bad the starters were playing. Yet, when Coach called out the starting lineup for the 2nd half, Big Vic was not in it. He immediately erupted. He threw a water bottle at the television, which broke the TV and went on to tell Coach Ivkavich f**k this, f**k him, and that he was done watching from the bench this season. I felt for Big Vic and I was surprised he had waited this long to lose his cool. He deserved to play and everyone on the team knew it. Vic had left his team in Spain at the beginning of the season to come back and try and help us win a Euroleague championship. He didn't get a chance to do that and that was disheartening to all the players, especially Vic. As a result of his flare-up at the half, the team woke up in the 2nd half and won the game and the series rather easily. Yet, it was depressing that the season had to end this way. We eventually won the series in a closeout game, in Kazan. The season was over and although we were back-to-back Russian League champions, I believe everyone was happy that this entertaining but draining season was over.

That summer was about one thing—hard work! The upcoming Euroleague Final Four was being held in Moscow. The last 2 Euroleague champions were the host team and I was not going to miss out on my opportunity to be the 3rd. I had to be ready to perform to the best of my ability. I yearned to be a champion and I was going to do whatever it took to try and win this thing. With that said, I called on my childhood friend, my brother Darius Newsome, the one person who knew my game best and would push me to the limit in training that summer. I didn't know how hard it would be until the first day he worked me out. The work was no joke—a real grind. Between the weight room and the basketball court, I never knew that I could accomplish some of the things he pushed me to do. Mike Ditka once said, "If you are determined enough and willing to pay the price, you can get it done." I lived by that motto every day that summer. The days started at 6 A.M. and ended most nights around 9 P.M. Darius was relentless and I hated every minute of it. I did every single thing he asked of me because failure next season was not an option. Anything less than a Euroleague championship was a failure. Darius knew this was how I felt, so his slogan all summer was "Whatever It Takes." If he ever felt I was slipping or not pushing myself, he would yell out, "WHATEVER IT TAKES!" As soon as he would yell those words out, I would take the workout to another level. Usually he would smile and then shout it out again, "WHATEVER IT TAKES!" That summer was great. The work I did was difficult, tiring—grueling—but I knew it would pay off. Mentally, I was sharper than I had been in years. I watched hours of video tape. Physically, I was bigger and stronger than I had ever been in my life. This was my year and my chance to call myself a Euroleague champion.

That summer CSKA management made a few key acquisitions to enhance our chances at winning a Euroleague title. CSKA signed a smooth, small forward from Detroit, Michigan named Antonio Granger (A.G.), and 3 big men, Martin Muursepp (NBA–Dallas), David Anderson (from Australia, drafted by the Atlanta Hawks), and Demos Dikoudis (Greek National Team). The media called us a European Dream Team. With the new acquisitions, the pressure would be immense this upcoming season. We had the most talent of any team in Europe and with that came the hype of winning a championship. Anything less next season would be considered a catastrophe.

By the time the preseason ended, I realized that our team might have too much talent. Yes, we were all unselfish players, yes we all wanted to win, but, we had 9 players that could start for any other team in Europe. That could spell disaster for a team. We all wanted to play, contribute, and win but I was unsure how long it would take for us all to grasp this concept. There were times when I was unsure of what to do and what not to do on the court because we were so talented. Then again, we had a famous veteran coach who was more than capable of handling this amount of talent. Or was he? We would soon find out.

Early in the season, I found that I disliked my new role on the team. I was splitting time with 6'6" phenom—Greek point guard, Theodoros Papaloukas. Paps and I had been together for 3 years now but with Coach gaining more confidence in his ability, that decreased my minutes and ability to have a major impact on the game. This was really difficult for me to adjust to. Coach felt like the team needed me to be more of a consummate point guard as we had so many scorers on the team. I was more of a scoring point guard who could do many things. As a result, I felt that Coach leaned more toward Paps to end games because he was less of a scorer than I was.

This was tough to accept also because I had never been in this predicament before. In spite of all this, I didn't whine or pout; I just played

163

This was the highlight of my year—probably of my life up to this point. To get in to the gym and work with a man trying to be the best player possible—was incredible. What really drove me to work with Booper was TRUST. Boop is his own man and he is big on accountability. If he loses, he doesn't want to look or point at anyone but HIMSELF. I also knew that he didn't want me living my basketball dreams through him. I respected that so much. I went out of my way to assure him that this work, this grind was about him. Once I got his confidence and the go ahead to do my thing, it was on. I had to make sure my agenda was on point and thoroughly thought out and planned because my best friend was putting his career in my hands.

My primary goal was to improve his conditioning. So I worked Boop as hard as I could. I wanted him to exercise skills on the basketball court, even when his body was under stress and fatigue. We worked twice a day and my guy gave me full control.

Boop knew how to play the game but I wanted to mentally take him to that next level with skill challenges. I also taught him patience and worked his tail off. We worked under the premise that greatness does not come without a price. There were times when he let his pride or ego get in the way because I was his brother and best friend. He didn't want me to get the better of him, even as his trainer.

But that was Boop and his competitive drive to win a championship. You could never read him and his feelings from the outside. I never knew that not being a Euroleague champion consumed him. He had won championships everywhere he played but I guess he felt like the Euroleague was the big prize. Boop would say that money, points, and recognition don't mean much if you don't win that big Chip. His drive to be a Euroleague champion subjugated him to do whatever it took that summer. By the end, I knew he had improved every facet of his game. He was ready to achieve whatever he put his heart and mind to.

my role and accepted the fact that we were winning games. Like Darius said all summer, "Whatever it takes!" The season we had was remarkable. We set a Euroleague record for the number of games won in the Euroleague and our domestic league. We won 50-plus games or so in a row. We were rolling right along oblivious to our wins. I didn't notice it myself until the latter part of the Euroleague season. We were winning games but we weren't improving. We were no longer blowing teams out but surviving games. Our wins were no longer impressive or decisive and that worried me. Had we gotten complacent? Had we gotten big heads and egos thinking no one could defeat us? This concerned me. What do I do when I am unsure of things? I get in the gym and start pushing myself to be the best player I can possibly be.

Eventually we lost our mojo and our first game of the season at home in the Top 16 against Barcelona. The loss hurt because we had a chance to do something great and we let it slip away. We weren't hungry enough to go undefeated. What disappointed me the most was that no one took the loss hard—not the team, not Coach, or even management. Mostly everyone took the loss in stride as if it had to happen at some point in the season. I didn't feel that way and looking back, I should have said something about our nonchalant acceptance of defeat. We bounced back after the loss to Barcelona and continued our winning ways. We breezed our way to our 3rd consecutive Final Four. We would be the host team, and everything seemed to be working in our favor.

For CSKA, reaching the Euroleague Final Four that season was a given—winning it was expected—but at the Final Four, the pressure was on us. When the 4 teams qualified for the Final Four, everyone was looking forward to a CSKA vs. Maccabi, Tel Aviv finals match-up. Yet, we both had to win our semi-final games to reach that dream match-up. First, our semi-final opponent Tau Ceramica, a team from Vitoria, Spain would not lie down and just let us win. We had faced them twice earlier in the season. We defeated them both times. Yet, we knew they were a dangerous team. Nevertheless, we were a confident group and knew we would defeat them at home in front of our fans. The Euroleague write-up before the game read like this:

"Both teams have deep, talented rosters that guarantee a collection of major stars on the court Friday at Olympiysky Arena. Tau has its own marquee playmaker in Jose Manuel Calderon, who is back on track after overcoming a muscle tear which had sidelined him for two weeks during the Top 16. Calderon is an athletic point guard with a unique combination of talent and jumping skills. Although Tau lost both Top 16 games that Calderon did not play, back-up Pablo Prigioni has also been key to the team's success. Prigioni is a defensive ace on the ball, and Coach Dusko Ivanovic doesn't hesitate to use both playmakers simultaneously. CSKA has its own stellar point guard tandem. J.R. Holden and Theodoros Papaloukas complement each other perfectly and are able to share minutes on court. Holden's quickness, ball handling and leadership are major plusses for CSKA. Papaloukas, named the Euroleague MVP of January, offers energy, aggressiveness and court sense off the bench. He was not the only monthly MVP from CSKA, however. Marcus Brown also received that award in April. Brown is arguably the biggest offensive threat for CSKA, not only because he is the leading scorer, but because he always gets the ball in crunch time due to his athleticism and shooting skills. He is able to create his own shot like few players in the competition. The starting small forward, Antonio Granger is an offensive specialist whose defense improved in the last year. Both his shooting range and driving skills will be required in this do-or-die situation. His back-up, young talent Sergey Monya, will be ready to step on court anytime and provide intensity and great defense, just as Sergei Panov will offer experience and solid overall skills while Zakhar Pashutin gives versatility at both guard spots. They will not have it easy against one of the best shooters in the world, Arvydas Macijauskas, who is virtually unstoppable when he catches fire. Small forward Travis Hansen has improved his overall performance after overcoming an adjustment period, while Sergi Vidal can play any perimeter spot and is having a career season, improving his shooting range and determination. The battle in the paint will also be interesting. Scola is one of the best low post scorers in the world and Kornel David is a blue-collar player with great work ethic and a deadly five-meter jumper. Both will get some help

off the bench from top prospect Tiago Splitter, who has already shown he might become a dominant player in years to come, while Andrew Betts will provide defense and occasional points in the paint. In CSKA's front court, David Andersen has stood out lately among a battery of fine players. Andersen has elevated his game to become a Euroleague star, becoming arguably the best mobile big man in the competition. Demos Dikoudis is an intense power forward with great shooting range and strength, Martin Muursepp is deadly from downtown as well as a good rebounder with good knowledge of the game, while Aleksey Savrasenko is CSKA's top defensive center, with good timing to block shots. Above all, both teams are in extremely good shape, so sit back and get ready to enjoy one of the finest matchups that can be witnessed on a basketball court."

Playing the Final Four at home would be an amazing experience. Those feelings surfaced when I ran out for warm-ups and saw the sea of red—screaming fans in the arena. We were at home and it was our time to take advantage of home court. A little anxious and excited, we started the game intensely but sloppily. Tau, on the other hand, started the game well and played with poise, patience, and confidence. This caught our team by surprise and I noticed the pressure of playing at home having a negative effect on us. Instead of stepping up and playing like gangbusters, it seemed as if we were starting to crumble. In such times, I do what I do best—step up and try and lead by example. I started scoring, passing, and playing pressure defense to bring some life to our team. Early on it worked. As the game wore on, however, Tau gained more confidence and we were in for our toughest battle of the season. With 7 minutes remaining in the game, trailing by a few points, I could see the panic and desperation on my teammates' faces. I remained calm and told my teammates that we were OK; we would win this game. With 3 minutes left, Tau believed more than we did. It was over. Tau looked better and stronger. We looked hesitant, passive, and bewildered at how good they played. As the final seconds ticked away, Tau pulled off one of the biggest upsets in Euroleague history. I was sick to my stomach, my heart ached. I was mystified knowing that our season was coming to a dreadful end. The only thing going through my mind was the hard work, the sacrificing—everything I went through from the summer until this point. It was all for nothing. We lost the game 85–78. I did what I could, finishing the game 6–18 fg for 20 points, with 1 assist and no turnovers.

As great as our team was that season, I put the loss on me. I disliked my role that season, and never quite got into the groove that I wanted—but no excuses. I will never point the finger at anyone but myself. Once again, I didn't make enough plays to help my team win. Three years in the Final Four and 3 semi-final defeats. I sat at my locker after the game doubting myself for the first time in my career. I didn't know if I was good enough to win a Euroleague championship. What more could I do to win? I accepted a role I didn't want, did things that past summer that I hated doing, but I assumed that winning a championship took sacrifice, and sacrifice is what I had done. This defeat had taken the steam out of me. I sat there for 20 minutes until I found the strength to pray, shower, and get myself dressed before I went to see my family and friends outside the locker room. As soon as I saw them the weight of the world came off of my shoulders. I could tell from their watery eyes that my girlfriend and sister had shed tears for me already. I kissed my girlfriend Aireka and gave my sister a big hug letting them both know that I was OK. I made my rounds giving everyone a hug. Lastly, I got to my dad. He kissed me on the cheek and said, "You make me the proudest father in the world." My father had been on this journey with me from day 1, and my goals became his goals and dreams. He was proud of me but I couldn't stop this journey to bring us a Euroleague championship.

I experienced an incident in a Russian nightclub that season that was dreadful. I learned that I needed to always be watchful and careful about the company that I keep. On this particular evening in Moscow, I decided to hang out with the 3 Americans from the other team we had just faced. I knew 2 of the 3 Americans from seasons past, so I decided to take them to dinner and then to a hip-hop spot later that night. This was nothing new to me. I hung out regularly with Americans from other teams.

At the nightclub, Danny (one of the 3 Americans from the other team) and I were talking, having a soda while his teammates were behind us, at the bar—just chilling. As an attractive woman walked in between us, one of his teammates reached out to get her attention. I really couldn't see where he touched her, but she was with her boyfriend and he took offense. I am sure Danny's teammate didn't know that she was with her boyfriend, who said something in Russian to him. The teammate snapped back, "F★★k you, dude. F★★k you." I didn't think much of it but I didn't know why Danny's teammate said anything at all. It was not as if any of us spoke Russian. We had no clue what the woman's boyfriend was saying. The boyfriend walked away. No harm done. Right? Anyhow, Danny and I started talking again. Out of nowhere, the boyfriend came back and slashed Danny's face with a broken beer bottle. None of us saw it coming. The boyfriend took off running with Danny's teammates in tow. I was left behind to make sure Danny was OK and looked for my Russian teammates in the club. All the while I thought, why did he go after Danny? Why didn't I see it coming? Why didn't his teammates see it coming? Obviously, he attacked the wrong person. Danny's face was bleeding uncontrollably. I had to get him to a hospital and I had to make sure my Russian teammates handled this situation.

After 10 minutes of mass confusion, my Russian teammates told me the guy was in VIP and the son of some high official in Moscow. If anyone laid a hand on him, they would face serious consequences. I was in shock. What the hell was going on? Danny remained calm, but his face bled nonstop. I needed to get him medical attention immediately. On the way to the American hospital, I stopped at the first hospital I saw, but it was closed. We got to the American hospital and they said they had no one on duty to handle such a serious injury. We rode around for almost 20 minutes looking for another hospital until we reached a Russian hospital that would help us. They took Danny immediately to the emergency room, and an hour later he appeared looking like a mummy. They had done a poor job of doctoring him up. Danny knew it and said he was going to the United States to get the proper medical attention. I felt for him and was thankful they had stopped the bleeding regardless of the poor wrap-up job.

In the end, Danny ended up with 40 to 50 stitches in his face in the shape of an S. He didn't deserve this. He was at the wrong place at the wrong time. He was nothing but an innocent bystander. He didn't have anything to do with the situation. It was still very unclear to me why that Russian guy chose to come back and attack Danny. Danny is my height—6 feet tall. His teammate was 6' 5". Danny had cornrows. His teammate had a regular, low, even haircut. They were not even close to looking like each other. The only thing Danny and his teammate had in common physically was their complexion—both light-brown skinned. I can only assume that the Russian dude was drunk and didn't care who he hurt. What was scary was that it could have very easily been me. Even worse, that guy could do that to somebody with no repercussions. No matter how long I was here, or what passport I may have been given, I was not Russian. I didn't speak the language and, in public, I needed to be aware of who I was with and what was going on at all times.

Although I hadn't won the Euroleague championship, we did win the Russian Cup for the first time in 3 years by defeating Unics Kazan. I played a solid game with 17 points (6–15 fg), 5 assists, and 0 turnovers. It felt good to finally win the Cup. It had eluded us for 2 years, now it was ours. Coach did a good job of preparing us and we executed the game plan with poise and precision.

Winning the Russian League Finals would be no easy task this season. This year we would face our country rival, Dynamo Moscow, in the finals. They had a solid team that was expected to dethrone us as the two-time champions. The 3 American players they had were Ariel McDonald, a proven winner who mentored me while winning championships at Maccabi, Tel Aviv, Trajan Langdon (Duke alum, 3 years in the NBA and a Euroleague Final Four appearance with Benetton, Treviso in Italy), and Lynn Greer (Temple University) a top scorer in Italy the year before. We knew it would be a tough series but we had defeated them twice during the regular season and felt confident that we could win the series handily.

So much for confidence—we lost Game 1 at home. The organization was not pleased, and CSKA legendary coach and now president Alexander Gomelskiy came in after the defeat and said a few words to the team. He said he could deal with a loss or even losing a series but he was unhappy with our effort and the way we represented the club during Game 1. He told us we had better play with more pride and effort in Game 2, or he would insist our coach let the junior team play during the rest of the series. I thought the speech was a little harsh. I don't think we played that poorly. We came out flat, and I have to give Dynamo some credit, they played a very good game. Nevertheless, we heard his message loud and clear. We played with maximum effort and pride for the rest of the series. What's more, we won the next 3 games and the best-of-5 series 3-1. We celebrated our 3rd Russian League championship in a row by defeating Dynamo on their home court in Game 4. I had a very good Game 4 with 20 points (8–13 fg) and 4 assists. The season was finished. We had a very good season, but still incomplete and bittersweet without winning that Euroleague championship.

I didn't win a Euroleague championship that season, but I gave more of myself to the game than I ever had. It gave me a greater appreciation for all the players who had overcome defeat and huge hurdles to win a championship. The first 2 NBA greats that come to mind are Michael Jordan and Isaiah Thomas. Michael Jordan had to overcome the Pistons before he took over the NBA. Isaiah Thomas had also gotten so close to winning a championship for a few years before he finally got his championship ring. I knew I was knocking on the door to a championship win and had to keep plugging away and doing what I believed in my heart was the right thing. My time would come, and all I could do was make sure I was ready.

The great thing about this journey was that I was not alone. My brother, Darius, was speechless when I called him after the Final Four game against Tau. He was as emotional a few hours after the game, as I was when the final buzzer went off. He was almost in tears talking to me on the phone. Darius didn't say much about the game or the work we put in, but what I do remember him saying was, "I'm sorry." Those words struck me hard. Why was he sorry? He didn't do anything wrong. All he had done was prepare me to conquer the basketball world. It touched my heart that he was as hurt and dismayed about the loss as I was. I knew right then that he was just as invested as I was. However, knowing that didn't make the loss any easier to accept. I didn't know it yet, but that feeling of disappointment and the pressure I put on myself to win a Euroleague championship would put a strain on my workouts and relationship with Darius during the upcoming summer.

When the buzzer of the final game went off for our season, you could feel a sigh of relief from everyone—from management all the way down to the last player on the team. It had been a stressful season. Expectations were high and what the club wanted most was a Euroleague championship. By the end of the year, each person who worked or played for CSKA was mentally and emotionally exhausted.

Also, most people knew that major changes were going to be made for the next season. As soon as we lost the Final Four in Moscow, there was talk about Coach Ivkavich leaving (not resigning with CSKA), and a few players not returning. One of the players was my good friend, Antonio Granger. Rumblings about Marcus Brown were heard as well. I felt for Marcus Brown. This man had gone out there and busted his tail for 2 years. He was 1st or 2nd team All-Euroleague, 2 years in a row. He deserved a little slack. He was the man for our team, but not the only man. I really wish I could have helped him win a Euroleague championship, but I knew that he would probably be gone next season. I have a lot of respect for his game and what he accomplished at CSKA, but at the end of the day, basketball is a business. I felt at ease about my job security. I had a Russian passport, but I felt like I had played a pretty good season. Coach and I didn't always see eye-to-eye, but that is the nature of the business. Coach had a lot of pressure to win that season and I understood that with that came some very critical decisions.

Coach Ivkavich had, nevertheless, taken me to the promised land and showed me what it was like to be among the top teams in Europe. I thanked him for that, and I felt like I let him down in some ways by not getting us over the hump. It's a team game, but if you don't expect great results from yourself, how can you expect to achieve great results as a team? I believe that every man must play his part to the best of his ability, in order to win a championship—accepting the part that Coach gives you—that's the tricky part.

IX | Determined for Destiny

THE FIRST MAJOR change at CSKA was made early in the summer of 2005. CSKA hired a new coach—the famous Italian named Ettore Messina. I knew there would be changes but having been a major part of the team for 3 years, I wish I didn't have to hear about them from the media and friends. A friend read it online and immediately called me. I had mixed feelings about the situation because I didn't know if this new coach would like my style of play. It would have been nice to speak with him and understand my role on this new team. I didn't want to play for a coach who kept me just because I had a Russian passport. I had always played for coaches who really wanted me. I didn't want that to change. After my brief disappointment, I quit fooling myself. I was nothing but a pawn in a chess game. I was going back to CSKA and I would have to get in where I fit in, simple as that.

In addition to the coaching change, CSKA also added Alaskan sharp shooter Trajan Langdon (Duke, Cleveland Cavaliers), a do-it-all guard in David Vanterpool, and a good inside/outside Slovenian power forward in Matthias Smodis. Coach Messina and these 3 players were supposed to bring CSKA that highly coveted Euroleague championship.

Also that summer, I was invited by the Russian Basketball Federation to play for the Russian Men's Basketball National Team at the European Championships in Belgrade, Serbia. I thought it was an honor to be invited to play for the team but I didn't feel comfortable playing. I wasn't a "true" Russian and I didn't want to ruffle any feathers on the team. I had to talk to Mr. Kushchenko before I agreed to play and even then, I was uneasy about playing. I wanted to be sure that the players truly wanted me on the team. Also, I was a little paranoid about being the first black American to represent Russia on the National Team. I didn't want this experience to be dreadful and uncomfortable for me. Nevertheless, after talking to Mr. Kushchenko I agreed to play. After hearing everything he said, I realized that this was a great opportunity for Russian basketball and me.

The transition to the Russian National Team wasn't very difficult. I knew most of the players on the team already. For the most part, everyone accepted me with open arms. Still, I felt terrible when I arrived in Moscow to practice with the team and shortly after 2 beloved National Team players decided to retire. This made my transition a little tenuous. All I wanted to do was be an addition to the team; I didn't want the team to lose players they enjoyed playing with. Other than this, things went rather smoothly on the court. It was the "off-court" things that mentally got to me sometimes. For instance, I heard from my teammates that many Russian people didn't want me on the team; I was black and American, not Russian. The transition may have looked unproblematic, but it was far from it!

The one great thing about most fans is that if you win and help them feel good, they tend to like you a little more. The 2005 European championships started well for our team and that helped quiet a lot of critics. In the first game of the tournament, we defeated the Ukraine in Vrsac, Serbia 86–74. It was a sloppy game, but a win nonetheless. It was our first official game and I knew a lot of eyes would be on me. I felt an immense pressure to play well so that my teammates and supporters could be more comfortable with my participation on the Russian National Team. After a jittery start, I got myself under control and chipped in 16 points in the win. Andrei Kirilenko led the team with 22 points and 14 rebounds.

The 2nd game would be our true test. It would reveal whether I was worth all the hype. We were expected to beat Ukraine, but how would we fare against a good Italian National Team? We shocked everyone—including ourselves—when we blew out Italy 87–61. Kirilenko led us with 16 points, Victor Khryapa added 15 points and I contributed 15 points, 4 assists and 2 steals. This win had everyone talking about our team. The media were now saying that we were contenders for a medal. I didn't know much about the other teams but I knew we were off to a good start.

In our 3rd and final game in Vrsac, Serbia, we lost to Germany in a nail-biter 51–50. It was a game we definitely had a chance to win. Both teams shot the ball poorly but played great defense. My inability to speak Russian, I think, caused us to look out of sync down the stretch. There were a few times late in the game when I wasn't comfortable enough with the team to just take over the game. I didn't know what play to call or which player even wanted the ball. I say this not taking anything away from Germany and their win because they played a very good game. I just feel as if I had been more comfortable, my decision making late in the game would have been better. I led us with 13 points that night but Dirk Nowitzki (Dallas Mavericks, 2007 NBA MVP) stole the show by hitting a 3-pointer with 27 seconds left in the game to win it. It was a tough defeat for us.

The tournament in Vrsac, Serbia was a qualification and seeding tournament. Now we were on our way to Belgrade, Serbia to play the more important games. These games would determine if we would medal or qualify for the World Championship Games in 2006. Having played fairly well in Vrsac, the one question every reporter kept asking me was—if you qualify for the World Championships, will you play against the USA team? And I gave every reporter the same answer, NO!

Our first game in Belgrade was a crucial game. Defeating the Greek team would guarantee us a place in the 2006 World Championships. The Greek team was a tough, hard-nosed ball club. They were one of the best teams in the tournament. They played great team basketball. Yet, we felt we had a good chance to defeat them. We were better athletically and felt our length and speed could give them problems on both ends of the court. Early in the contest, it appeared that we would control the game. We jumped out to a 13–2 lead. From then on we fell apart. We committed too many turnovers and to make matters worse, we shot the ball poorly as a team. I blamed no one but myself for this game. I committed too many turnovers and didn't play with the poise needed to win a difficult game such as this. On the other hand, my teammate at CSKA, Theodoros Papaloukas, led the Greek team with 23 points and genuine leadership to defeat us 66–61.

I was brought to the Russian National Team to do what Paps did for the Greek team. It stung me hard knowing I had failed myself, the team, and the country of Russia. I never recovered from this loss against the Greeks and neither did our team. We lost the next two games and an opportunity to compete at the FIBA World Championships in Japan in 2006. I was disgusted with myself as the tournament came to an end. I didn't play with the heart, focus, and desire of a champion. I could lie and blame it on my ignorance of the format, the teams, the importance of each game, so on and so forth. However, none of that has ever mattered to me. When I step on the court, I give maximum effort and play with my heart. I didn't do that and that was very disappointing. These are the things that others may not see; I scored my fair share of points in this tournament. But, I didn't impact the game the way I know I should have and can. No excuses, I had failed.

Going into the new season at CSKA I was refocused and re-energized. I felt like this season was a season of redemption for me. I had taken my play in Serbia to heart and decided this season I had a lot to prove. Not wasting any time I got off to a fast start statistically but our team lost our first 2 Euroleague contests. I wasn't too worried, we were a new team and needed some time to gel and mesh together.

After our slow start, we ran off a few wins in a row when Coach Messina noticed something that he thought would make us a championship team. He decided to move Dave Vanterpool to the point guard position and move me off the ball onto the wing. He thought it would help us get more ball movement and more touches among all the players. I am a player and a winner; I didn't think this change would affect me at all. I wanted to win so playing off the ball was cool with me. I just wanted different results at the end of this Euroleague season. Sometimes you have to check your ego at the door. That is what I did when Coach Messina talked to me about this change. All pride aside, as long as I could be myself, I would be willing to do what the team needed.

As the games progressed, I felt like I was being phased out of the offense. I didn't like this one bit. I realized that Coach moved me off the ball because he didn't trust my decision making. I could accept changing positions, but not feeling a part of the offense was another thing. Not given the chance to make plays was a tough pill to swallow. I worked my tail off to be the best player I could be and I had to slowly comprehend that it would not be enough to satisfy Coach Messina. Nonetheless, the team pushed ahead and kept progressing. Before we knew it, we were again in the Euroleague Final Four. This was CSKA's 4th straight Final Four appearance, but the team's first under Coach Ettore Messina. Coach Messina had won Euroleague championships before, so he knew the work that had to be done in order to win it all. I had never won it. I was eager to listen and learn from a championship coach. I had sacrificed this much—might as well finish it off with a title.

Off the court that season, I was in a life-threatening car accident. Christmas break is always a great time of the year for me. I got to go home and spend a few days with family. I always needed this break to get refreshed for the 2nd half of the season. I decided to fly into Atlanta for a day before heading to Pittsburgh to spend Christmas with my significant other and family. I needed to drop a few things off at my place and grab a few new things before I flew back overseas. I landed in Atlanta excited and ready to hang out with my good friend Laroyd for a night.

Laroyd (L) had worked me out that past summer and our friendship had grown over the years. In any case, L picked me up and we were on our way to my place to drop off my bags before we headed to Barley's (a bar/pool hall) for a drink. As Laroyd drove, I talked to Aireka on the phone telling her that I had made it safely and that I would see her the following evening. L was driving under the speed limit laughing about how he drove slowly with a superstar in the car. Suddenly, a big camper sped up and hit the tail end of our vehicle causing L's truck to spiral out of control across 3 lanes of oncoming traffic. I dropped my phone and braced myself against the dashboard. After the vehicle came to a stop, we looked at each other in shock. The back window on my side was shattered but we were OK. As we got out of the truck, the camper that hit us had pulled over further down the highway. When the driver saw that we were alive, he sped away. They were too far down the road for us to get their license plate number. Laroyd immediately called the police. As we sat there waiting, which felt like forever, L asked me a few more times if I was OK. I felt OK; my jaw was aching and I was bleeding a little from my face but I was thankful to be alive.

As we sat there waiting for the police in the middle of a 5-lane high-way, cars rolled slowly past us, but no one stopped until a kind-hearted brother stopped to ask us if we needed assistance. Laroyd explained to him what had happened and that we were waiting for the police. The brother saw my face bleeding and offered to take me to the nearest emergency room. I accepted his offer and thanked him for his kindness. Laroyd told me that he would call me once he got everything sorted out with the police and that he was OK to just wait. When I arrived at the hospital everything went smoothly. I saw a doctor rather quickly, was given a few stitches, and told that I had a badly bruised jaw. The doctor said I would be OK in a few weeks but for now eating solid food would be difficult.

I was happy to be alive, and his news was icing on the cake for me. By the time Laroyd and I reconnected, my evening was ruined but we were truly blessed and both of us knew it. The reality was this—we survived a fatal accident with barely any scratches or marks on us. His truck was totaled but that was a small price to pay to still be breathing.

I did spend Christmas with my family in Pittsburgh. I didn't give them the details of the accident because they would have been wor-ried. Instead, I just enjoyed being at home. What worried me was how I would stay healthy when I got back to Russia. I couldn't eat solid foods and wanted someone there to help me adjust. I didn't want the team finding out about the accident. I didn't know what they would say or do if they found out. Aireka said she would come to Russia with me and hold me down, no questions. I am so thankful she came. Her visit would change my life forever. She became pregnant—amazing how things happen in life. In one moment, I am scared I could lose my life, then in the next, my significant other and I are creating one. God works in mysterious ways.

On the court, we were going to our 4th straight Final Four. This year it was in Prague, a neutral site for all the teams. Unlike last year, or maybe because of last year, there was a lot of uncertainty about how we would perform. Having got to this stage in 3 previous seasons, management was on edge about the possibility of finally getting that semi-final monkey off our backs. I was very relaxed this time round. I know that the games have to be won on the court. Coach Messina had been here before and he had instilled in us a certain level of discipline and poise that took a lot of pressure off us. The whole team seemed relaxed during the Final Four preparation practices.

In spite of all this, Coach Messina experienced a setback right before the Final Four games. His son became very sick. Coach was a basketball fanatic but his family came first; he would not let anything come between him and his son—not even a Euroleague Final Four. Coach would spend all day and night at the hospital with his wife and son. The only time he wasn't with them was when he was with us—for 2 hours at practice. He didn't ride the team bus to practice, or attend team dinners; his focus was on his family, and he handled that to the best of his ability. I can only imagine how stressful a time it was for him. It was amazing how he was able to focus and prepare us for such a big game while his mind and heart was with his ill son. Coach was the most competitive coach I have ever played for. His will to succeed was second to none.

Our semi-final game was a match-up between two European powerhouses, CSKA and F.C. Barcelona from Spain. This was the Euroleague write up before the game:

"CSKA arguably has the most versatile backcourt in the competition, as Coach Messina tends to use David Vanterpool and Theodoros Papaloukas at the point guard spot, with J.R. Holden at the off-guard position. Papaloukas, an All-Euroleague nominee, comes off the bench to provide size, experience and superb defensive and passing skills. Meanwhile, Vanterpool is a do-it-all swingman who can either shut down any opponent on defense or take his man to the low post on offense. Above all, both are consummate team players. Holden is virtually unguardable when he heats up. Trajan Langdon rounds the CSKA backcourt with outstanding

shooting skills that led him to be chosen Euroleague MVP for April and
an All-Euroleague nominee. Energetic combo guard Zakhar Pashutin and
top prospect Vasiliy Zavourev rarely see much playing time, but might be
needed in case of foul trouble. Barcelona seems to have enough firepower
with which to answer. Shammond Williams is shining in his first Euroleague
season, becoming a fan favorite because of his long-range shots and excit-
ing transition game. Juan Carlos Navarro, the Euroleague MVP of January,
is a scoring machine who can create his own shot or come off a screen to
hit the bomb. Gianluca Basile provides deep range and experience at both
wing spots, while Bootsy Thornton always steps up in big games. Rodrigo
De La Fuente is Barcelona's top defensive stopper, while Roger Grimau
is in top form and can contribute at both guard spots. Michalis Kakiouzis
has become a top performer in the Barcelona frontcourt due to his speed
and baseline game. Denis Marconato provides rebounds and know-how at
the center spot, while the ultimate mismatch, Gregor Fucka, blends speed,
experience and ambidextrous hands to create advantages inside. Jordi Trias
and Marc Gasol complete Barcelona's battery of big men, which will have
the mission of trying to slow down Matjaz Smodis, who has been pacing
CSKA since Andersen got hurt. Smodis has the complete package: strength,
experience, size, speed and deep shooting range. His perfect complements
are Van den Spiegel and Aleksey Savrasenko, who are great defensive play-
ers and also provide occasional help on offense. Messina and Ivanovic
know each other quite well, so expect intense defense and few surprises.
Barcelona's depth will be one of its strong points, while the compact and
versatile CSKA lineup is adaptable to almost any situation it might face.
Expect focus and determination to decide this do-or-die battle for a spot in
the Euroleague Final!"

The game was everything a semi–final game is supposed to be. Barcelona started the game well and got their confidence early. We started
slowly and I picked up 2 early fouls that affected my rhythm early in
the game. As I sat on the bench because of the 2 fouls, Barcelona controlled the game. Shammond Williams was playing well and their team
was doing all the little things it takes to win a Final Four game. By the
half, we were down double digit points and looked as if we were headed

to our 4th consecutive semi-final defeat. In the locker room at the half, the atmosphere was as if we had already lost. The look on my teammates' faces was one of confusion and disarray. Coach must have seen what I saw because he gave a calm and positive speech. He said that we were fine and that we had to fight minute-by-minute. We were the better team and that once we started playing our basketball we could change the momentum of the game. I am not sure how the team felt but I felt a resurgence of energy and faith. I truly believed that we would win this game. I also knew that I had to be aggressive in the 2nd half. My early foul trouble made me hesitant, but it was time to step up. I live for the big moments and the moment doesn't get any bigger than this. I was tired of coming up short. It was now or never for me. I was going to go out there and leave it all on the floor.

Barcelona began the 2nd half in the same way as they started the game. They were controlling the tempo and the score, ahead by 11 points. Suddenly, a switch went off in my mind. It was as if I had been in this situation before. All the nights watching film with Darius talking about different situations and what to do when down 5, when down 10, when down 15—it all just came to me. It was my time to attack or I would be on the losing side of another Final Four. Mentally I went to another level and the physical part took care of itself.

I became extremely aggressive hitting three, 3-pointers in a small time frame and just like that—it was a new ball game. The score was tied up and the momentum was in our favor. Our confidence had skyrocketed and now back-up point guard Papaloukas was in a good rhythm. We were finally taking control of the game. We played with poise and patience throughout the 4th quarter and went on to defeat Barcelona 84–75. I was exhausted, but inside I was the happiest ballplayer on the planet. I was finally playing in a Euroleague Finals game. We got the 3-year monkey off of our backs. As I walked off the court with my head down, I thought, "God is good all the time." HE had prepared me for that moment. HE gave me the mental fortitude to keep pushing, no matter how bleak it may have seemed. Through HIM all things were possible. I finished the game with 19 points on 7–11 shooting. I was going to the Euroleague Finals. Yes, how sweet it was!

There was a day off between the semi-final and final game. On that day off, I relaxed and spent time with my friends and family who had come to Prague to support me. They were all excited about the championship game. That was all they talked about—that, and how well I had played in the semi-final game. They kept reiterating how we could beat Maccabi, easily the finals favorite, if we just played harder. It was cool that they were so supportive but it got a little nerve-racking. I needed a break.

I went to the lobby for some fresh air. As I looked for a quiet place to sit down, I spotted a quiet corner where a young lady sat on a couch alone. It appeared as if she were waiting for someone. It didn't matter to me, I just wanted to sit down, get off my feet and have a few minutes to myself. As I sat down, she smiled, said hello, and wished me good luck in the finals. I said thank you and before you knew it, we were chatting. It was just what I needed. The conversation had nothing to do with basketball and it helped me relax and enjoy the moment. I needed a mental break from the hype of the final game. She talked about her life and her first trip to Prague. After conversing for a minute, I stood up to leave and thanked her for chatting with me. She said that it was a pleasure. Some Maccabi players, she said, were real cocky so I was to kick their ass the next day. I chuckled and said, "We'll try." We hugged and I gave her the European kiss on the cheek goodbye. And even though I enjoyed the brief conversation, as soon as we departed, my thoughts went right back to the game tomorrow. I felt like this was our time—our year to win it all. We had come too far and were too close not to take this title back to Russia. So much for not thinking about the game!

When I awoke the morning of the championship game, I didn't have any idea how the day would go. What I did know was that I felt good. I was playing in the Euroleague final that evening and that was a blessing. I felt like the day would last forever. I wanted to play as soon as I woke up. I was that excited about the game. However, I had a full day in front of me. On the bus to team shoot-around that morning, my teammates wore smiles, which gave me a sense of calm and peace. I knew if we were relaxed our confidence was high. Our confidence, at least Dave

Vanterpool's confidence, was more than high. As we got off the team bus to walk into the gym, Maccabi was finishing up their practice and all you could hear was my teammate DV saying, "THE CHAMPS ARE HERE, THE CHAMPS ARE HERE!" It caught me off-guard but gave me even more confidence. I thought to myself, you're right DV, the champs are here!

By game time, I was so enthused about playing, I didn't know how to get rid of all my nervous energy. I was excited and ready. When the ball went up, I was prepared to go to war. Yet, Maccabi started the game well and appeared to be the superior team. They took an early lead and seemed to make everything look easy. We looked over-anxious and were a little amazed at how they were executing. Then, Coach Messina called time-out. I thought he was going to scream and yell and tell us how bad we were playing, but he didn't. He peacefully looked in everyone's eyes and said that we were the better team tonight. If we calmed down and executed, we could win this title. His words immediately reassured us and by the time we left the bench, we were a new team.

From the first minutes after the time-out until the last seconds ticked away on the clock, we controlled the tempo of the game. We played team basketball. We shared the ball. We played team defense and in the end, we played with a purpose that was to shock the European world. We had won the Euroleague title. As the final seconds ticked away, I was ecstatic. I can't even describe the feelings I had inside. When I looked over at my dad sitting courtside, I pointed at him with a smile on my face, letting him know this was for him—all the games he traveled to in both high school and college, all the disappointments, letdowns and failures I had—he was right by my side. He could finally smile and know that his son was happy and had finally achieved one of his main goals. We were Euroleague champions!

As the buzzer sounded, I ran over and jumped on the scorer's table. I pointed to my family and friends who had made the trip. Then I strolled over to my dad and gave him a huge hug. That hug was so tight that it released all the hurt and pain that we had ever suffered throughout my basketball career.

When we let go, I saw that my dad was crying. It was the first time I had ever seen him cry. They were tears of happiness. That moment will be near and dear to my heart for the rest of my life. I cried just thinking about it a month after it happened. Darius's tears after the game also made me realize how much this victory meant to him as well. We had been through a lot of struggles the past few summers. We had argued, bickered, tussled and almost killed each other trying to get to this place. Now that we were here, we looked each other square in the eyes knowing that all the hassles were worth it. We had finally acquired that elusive championship. Our embrace was one of respect, gratitude, perseverance, and most importantly, LOVE. I thought about my whole family. I thought about my mom, sister, Aireka and our baby inside of her—just everyone who had helped and supported me on this journey.

It was a special time for my family and me. When I looked at the final score, 73–69, before I walked off the court in Prague, all I could do was smile and say to myself, Jon-Robert Holden, you're a Euroleague champion!

When I finally got to the locker room, the first thing I did was call my sister. She had been my heart since we were kids. When others didn't believe, she did. When I needed support, she was right by my side. I wanted her to know how much I loved and appreciated her. She screamed from the time she picked up the phone until we hung up. That was my beautiful sister—my rock. Then, I called my sweetheart, Aireka. She had been the most understanding companion a man could ask for. She never questioned why, where, or what I wanted to accomplish when it came to basketball. She always gave me the space and freedom to chase my goals and do what I felt I needed to do to be successful. I knew it wasn't easy for her. I was always away. When I was there, I worked out a few hours every day, and watched film for another couple of hours. She could have nagged me or pushed me away. Instead, she embraced me and my love for my profession. I wanted her to know that I noticed and appreciated everything that she was and would be to me. I loved her dearly. Aireka and our baby would one day enjoy the fruits of my labor. Finally, I talked to reporters. I am a family-first guy and I couldn't care less about getting any media attention. I wanted my inner circle to know that their support and encouragement on this journey was recognized and cherished. Without them, I would not have been standing as a Euroleague champion!

While most players went to Disney World after they became champions, I went back to Russia to try and complete the Triple Crown. The Triple Crown was winning the Russian Cup, the Euroleague championship, and the Russian League Championship all in the same year. We had already won 2 of the 3 at this point. We had beaten Khimki earlier that season to win back-to-back Russian Cups. Next, we defeated Maccabi in the Euroleague Finals. Now, we would be facing Khimki again in the Russian League Finals to try and complete the Triple Crown. Khimki was a good team, but we were better. If we played hard and with focus, we knew we could defeat them handily. That is what we did. We defeated them easily, 3–0 in the finals.

The best player of the series was a seasoned veteran from our team, Zakhar Pashutin. Our team was so good that he didn't get many minutes all year. It wasn't because he was not talented. It had more to do with the talent and depth of our team. It was difficult for all players to get significant minutes. I admired and respected Zakhar because he stayed ready and when his time came, he played magnificently. I was happy for him and our team. That was my best year in Moscow. We started slowly but never doubted what we could do as a unit. I had my personal ups and downs because I changed positions, but I never lost sight of our team goals. No one ever told me that it would be easy. This was the most I had struggled with a coach and sacrificed with a team since I had begun playing overseas. I realized at that time that struggle and sacrifice weren't nearly as bitter when you were finally blessed with your rewards—and how sweet it was to have completed the Triple Crown!

Just when I thought my life could not get any more exciting, my sister threw me a surprise party that summer. A surprise party was one thing, but she found a way to get in touch with people I hadn't seen or contacted in years. She was able to do it without me ever finding out. It all began when she called me to explain that her husband Chris had been given an award and would be honored on July 21st, in Pittsburgh. It was supposed to be a community-service award honoring his efforts to help young black men and women achieve their goals and dreams. I thought that this was a wonderful achievement and accepted the invitation to support my brother-in-law. My sister gave me some excuse why she couldn't be there. Whatever the excuse was, I believed her. To my knowledge, she had never lied to me. I figured that she must have had something really important on her plate for her to miss such a special achievement. In any case, I told her I would be there. Actually, I was honored that my brother-in-law wanted me there.

I arrived in Pittsburgh for the banquet and was excited to be home. It was always nice to go back and spend time in the neighborhood I grew up in. I love my city, and I was back home for my brother-in-law. I was really excited for him; he was being recognized for his hard work and dedication. I knew this meant a lot to him.

"How does it feel to be receiving an award for all your hard work over the years?' I asked him. He looked over at me calm, cool, and collected, and said, "I love the kids, bro. All this is nice, but I truly love the work I do." I looked at him and smiled. I thought to myself, "I am in the presence of a special human being who will never quite get the recognition he deserves, but will continue to do great things."

Once we arrived at the hotel, I was anxious. It was as if I were receiving an award. I could not imagine having to get in front of a crowd of people to speak about how proud I was to receive an award. I was happy but nervous for him. Chris seemed cool all the way up until we got close to the door where the ceremony was being held. He looked at me and said, "Hold up, I have to go to the bathroom." Now, I was relaxed and chuckling because I thought, he must be nervous. So, I asked him, "Nervous, huh?"

He laughed it off and said, "Naw, just got to get myself together." After excusing himself, we walked toward the door where the banquet was being held. He asked me to go first. I looked at him and said, "Naw, this is your ceremony, you should go first." He then pushed me through the door and all I could hear was—SURPRISE!!! I saw ribbons, confetti, and a lot of familiar faces—some I hadn't seen in years. I was surprised. I couldn't believe what was happening. I turned to Chris and he put his hands on my shoulders and said "I love you brother, congratulations."

I was speechless. Everyone who knows me, especially my family, knows that I don't like a lot of attention and I hate surprises. This was different. This was all about love! I looked around the banquet hall, took a deep breath and just smiled as I made my way around the room to say thanks and hello.

It was unreal that family, friends, loved ones, and people I hadn't seen in more than 10 years were all gathered in one place to celebrate my career. The woman I loved was patiently waiting across the room with our baby inside of her, smiling from ear to ear knowing she had set me up too. I had left her that morning in Lansing, Michigan. All I could do was give her a kiss and let her know that I loved her. To this day, I am not sure she even realizes how much her presence there meant to me. I finally got to hug the woman who had pulled off this amazing night. My sister and I hugged both with tears in our eyes knowing how much we cherished our relationship. We have a true bond and she means the world to me.

After a nice dinner, the evening continued. A few people took to the stage. I am not sure how my sister decided who would talk, but everyone spoke kindly and said warm words about our relationships. It was very touching. I could feel the love in the room. To top it all off, the mayor of Wilkinsburg spoke. I didn't know him but it was an honor that he took the time from his busy schedule to attend my special evening. When he finished his speech, he offered me the key to the city, and proclaimed that from this day forward, July 21, would be known as Jon-Robert Holden Day. I didn't know what to think or say; it was surreal. I had grown up in Wilkinsburg, a skinny kid who just loved playing football and baseball. I had never imagined that in 20-plus years, I would be getting the key to the city. I couldn't fathom a day like this happening to me! It was as if I were dreaming. Next, it was my turn to speak.

I was nervous, in disbelief, and completely at a loss for words. When I scanned the room full of love—faces from Belgium to California—I finally broke down. I could contain myself no longer. No matter what I did athletically, I had done my family and the people who loved and cared about me the most—proud. I was truly grateful that they understood my journey, my generosity, my heart, my drive, my passion, and they knew that success was not only about me, but a reflection of them. All the time, love, and money they had invested in me throughout my young life was well worth it. That night will forever be etched in my heart. Thanks little sister for always loving me more than I loved myself.

As I enjoyed all the love shown off the court, I felt even more pressure to get prepared for the upcoming season. I wanted to push myself to the limit. Could I be a repeat Euroleague champion? I wasn't sure. I was aiming for greatness. I had watched Michael Jordan, Isaiah Thomas, and Magic Johnson repeat as NBA champions, and I dreamed of being in that class. No, I wasn't in the NBA, but that didn't stop me from trying to do my best.

That summer, my main focus was on working harder and smarter. I had to find a way to excel in Coach Messina's system and exceed his expectations. I was thinking about winning back-to-back Euroleague titles when the Russian National Team came knocking, asking for my assistance in helping them qualify for the European championships in Spain in 2007. I thankfully declined. I didn't have any desire to play in the qualifying games. After my experience in Serbia the summer before, I was OK with not playing. Yet, they persisted because their best Russian player, Andrei Kirilenko, said he would not play. He was 100 percent sure of his decision.

I was expecting my first child. I wasn't going to go play for the Russian National Team and miss the birth of my first born! There was no way I would do that to Aireka. She supported me and there was no way I would put basketball before my family. Nevertheless, they kept requesting that I play. They started calling even more when they hired a new coach, an American-Israeli named David Blatt. I thought his hiring was cool but that didn't have anything to do with me or my situation. I had just played 10 months as a two-guard, with restrictions and limitations under Coach Messina at CSKA, and wasn't very interested in playing and leading the Russian National Team as a point guard.

Playing for Coach Messina was mentally taxing. I was tired. I had other things on my plate with the pregnancy of my significant other.

It was like climbing Mount Everest, and shouting, "I Love You," and having it echo all the way around the world. This tribute to my brother Booper filled the Hyatt Regency ballroom with boundless love and appreciation. The bonds of friendship—old and new—were evident in the hugs, well wishes, and handshakes from our many guests.

I can't quite pinpoint when this special love between Boop and I first surfaced, but it has only grown stronger over the years. We have this thing—a game almost—I do something special for him and he tops it by doing something for me. This cycle has gone on for years and years.

I can never truly say enough about how much I love and appreciate my brother—words just don't capture it all—and yet this year, I really wanted him to know how much his sacrifice, hard work, and long days and nights, meant to us.

Hence a tribute to Boop was born. Of course, those closest to him said, "No, he doesn't like the spotlight to be on him." And they were right, but he needed to know it while he was alive—lives he has touched, the smiles he's contributed to, the relationships he's nurtured—how many blessings were answered from his prayers. He needed to see it for himself. Not doing it wasn't an option—we just now had to make it a surprise!

What was so touching was how many people wanted to come and share in this expression of love and celebration. The e-mails and phone calls came pouring in and the word spread like wild fire. I had to get a bigger space and then still had to cut the guest list. He had friends trying to come in from all over the world to express their gratitude. Those who couldn't make the event wrote wonderful letters to be shared at this celebration. Our family has always been very close, and as soon as the date was chosen, everyone played a part.

The night was filled with laughter and tears of joy filled the room when my brother stood before us. This wasn't a bad idea at all. God had blessed us.

(Continued on page 253)

After working out with Darius one day, I mentioned my circumstances concerning ball. I thought he would be the one person who understood my predicament. Instead he thought that I was making excuses about wanting to play with the National Team. In fact, he said he had been reading material over the Internet that said I had performed below par last year in Serbia, and with Andrei Kirilenko declining to play this summer, I would probably not want the pressure of trying to help Russia qualify for the Euro's in Spain.

This caught me totally off guard. I was shocked that he thought I was scared to play. Honestly, it pissed me off. He had never come at me this way about the game of basketball. He knew how hard I worked and how much I loved the game. After a few days of Darius banter, a call from Coach Blatt, and a long talk with my better half, Aireka, I decided to play. It wasn't until Aireka said, "Do it, go play, just get your butt home for our baby's birth," that I decided to play. I then called Coach Blatt and told him I would play as long as I could leave at the first sign of labor. He said, "No problem. You play your ass off and whenever you have to leave, get the hell out of here and enjoy the birth of your first child." Now, everything was a go. I was going to go over there and play my tail off. I wanted to shut up all the doubters, especially my brother Darius.

When I arrived in Russia to join the National Team, the atmosphere around the squad was welcoming. It seemed as if they truly wanted me there this time around and that made me feel good. I felt like one of the guys. I am not sure if it was something Coach Blatt had done or if I had been more open to communicating with my teammates but I fit in a lot better this year more so than the previous summer.

My comfortability enabled me to play some of my best basketball. I was there for 5 games and we went 4–1. I had averaged 24 points and 4 assists a game when I got the call. All I heard when the phone rang was, "Babe, it's time to come home." That was all Aireka had to say—I was on the next flight home. As for ball, my job was done. We had qualified for the European championships in Spain the following summer. I felt re-energized under Coach Blatt, and the team really pushed for me to play my game to help us win. I felt a new sense of pride representing Russia and it felt good, but at that particular time, the emotion of winning games played a distant second to the fact that I was about to be a father!

I must admit, when Aireka called me in Russia on the evening of September 13, telling me to come home, I thought it was a false alarm. She was nonchalant and calm over the phone. I thought a woman about to give birth could barely speak at a human decibel level. So much for what I knew! As we talked on the phone, I was excited about going home for the birth of our child. I didn't want to get off the phone with her but I had to book a flight home. I told my baby to wait for me—I was coming home.

I didn't sleep that night just thinking about getting home for the birth of our daughter (Aireka and I already knew it was a girl). I had to take flights from Perm to Moscow, Moscow to Atlanta, and Atlanta to Flint, Michigan to get home the next evening. It took forever. I ran from terminal to terminal as if the plane would take off earlier if I got there earlier. I had no such luck. Finally, when I landed in Atlanta, and called Aireka, her mom answered and told me that she had just minutes earlier given birth to our beautiful baby girl, Miyana Jade Holden. Aireka then got on the phone and told me that she tried to wait. I chuckled and told her it was OK; she did well. I told her I would be there soon.

When I hung up, I sat down in a chair and cried in the Atlanta airport. I was crying both happy and sad tears. I was happy because I had a healthy daughter and Aireka was doing well. I was sad because I had missed the birth of our first child. I could never get this day back. I hoped that Aireka would understand that I really wanted to be there. I still beat myself up about the decision I made to play for the Russian National Team that summer. When I finally arrived at the hospital and saw Aireka holding our daughter in her arms, I melted like butter. I was the happiest man in the world. I looked in our daughter's eyes and was overwhelmed with joy and happiness. I smiled at Aireka knowing she had just given me a true gift, a blessing from God that only she could give me. Our daughter was born September 14, 2006, at 3:10 P.M. and was 6 pounds 5 ounces. It was the happiest day of my life. I was a father—the happiest father alive.

God's plan is not always our plan, but when He blesses you with anything you embrace it. He always knows what is best for us. J.R. and my blessing arrived September 14, 2006, 6 pounds 5 ounces and 18" long. She had beautiful brown eyes with cute deep dimples in both of her cheeks. Picking her name was quite simple. Miyana is the one that J.R. liked. Miyana Jade Holden is what our little blessing would be called. Miyana means "Peaceful Temple of Grace" and Jade means "Jewel, Courageous, and Adoring."

J.R. had committed to play for the Russian National Team and planned on going back to Russia in August. Miyana was due on September 20, just when his season was scheduled to start. We had to attend a series of child birthing classes to make the delivery process go as smoothly as possible. J.R. attended the first 3 weeks of classes with me. My mother, Mardese, attended the remaining 3 weeks.

J.R. went overseas about two and a half weeks before Miyana's due date. He had planned to come home around September 18, a couple of days before she would be delivered. On September 13, 2006, as I shopped for last-minute baby things at Target, I spoke to J.R. again. I told him that I felt I was having contractions. I went back to my mother's house to take a nap. I realized that I had not felt Miyana move in my womb for a while. I called my mother at work and told her that I was going to drive myself to the hospital, so that they could listen to the baby's heart rate and make sure that everything was OK.

At the hospital, they examined me and heard our baby girl's heartbeat.

The nurse said, "Well, I am glad you came in because you are dilated to 2 cm."

I replied, "What!"

She said that I probably would go into labor in about 3 to 4 days. I called J.R. and told him. We decided that instead of waiting, he should make plans to come home after his game the next day. My mother and I packed my bag and were ready to go, just in case.

(Continued on page 254)

I have done some phenomenal things in my life but nothing compares with the birth of my daughter. Every day I wake up and tell Miyana that I love her, no matter where I am in the world.

After spending a few days with my newborn, it was time to get back to work. I would have loved to have spent more time with her, but I had to get to Italy. CSKA was already there for training camp and I joined them to get ready for the upcoming season. I was excited about the new season and extremely confident about having a breakout season statistically—winning back-to-back Euroleague titles. I had worked out hard all summer to get ready both mentally and physically for Coach Messina's coaching style.

We got off to a good start as far as wins and losses, but we weren't clicking as a team. My role was even more reduced than the year before; my confidence was starting to wane. I never felt that I couldn't play the game at a high level—I just wasn't sure of my decision making. I played passively, trying not to make mistakes because I knew that Coach didn't have a lot of confidence in me. This affected me mentally all season. For the first time in my career, I was the 6th or 7th option offensively. I believed that I deserved better than this, and I never fully accepted or embraced my role offensively.

When I thought things couldn't get any worse, Vanterpool got injured. He injured his back and the doctors said that he would be out indefinitely. With this, Theodoros Papaloukas moved into the starting lineup and Coach Messina decided to bring me off the bench. I embraced the idea. I figured it was less pressure on me and now I could play more like myself. For a while it worked. We won a few games in a row and I played much better. Then, suddenly Papaloukas wanted to revert back to his usual role of being a 6th man. He didn't like being a starter. Coach Messina didn't like this and I knew it. Papaloukas was forcing his hand. Coach had to put me back into the starting lineup. What Coach didn't know was that it was a pleasure coming off of the bench. He yelled at me less and let me play more of my game as a substitute than he did when I was a starter. So, when Coach put me back in the starting lineup as the point guard, I was disappointed. Instead of embracing my role as starting point guard, I remained frustrated and never quite found my groove. Did

I play badly? No, but I wasn't myself. I was playing to appease Coach and was over-thinking the game. I second-guessed almost everything I did on the court. Don't misunderstand me, this was not Coach Messina's fault. He was there to coach and do whatever it took to help the team win. He wasn't there to massage my ego or hold my hand.

We had a strong team and with European star Theodoros Papaloukas back in his groove as the back-up point guard, and Trajan Langdon playing some of his best basketball, we were once again back at the Final Four. We were going to Athens, Greece, the home of another Final Four team—Panathinaikos—with plans for another Euroleague title win.

Now that we had reached our 5th consecutive Final Four, I knew that all I had to do was be mentally tough and sharp for two games. This, I felt, was nothing for a player of my caliber. I had to let go of the past and focus on the present. I knew that the great players—the best of the best—they find a way to get it done—no excuses. What's more, I always played well in big games. I always found a way to play my best when the lights shone brightest. I figured this would be no different. I would learn the hard way that no matter how good you are physically, if you aren't on-point mentally for a big game, failure is almost inevitable.

The semi-final game was a match-up against a pesky but unheralded team from Spain—Unicaja Malaga. What made the game even more intriguing was the fact that former CSKA player Marcus Brown was the star of the Unicaja team. The game against Malaga was a tough one because they weren't expected to be at the Final Four. They were on a roll and had surprised everyone. This could work to their advantage. We had to be tough, confident, and poised to beat a team that was playing as well as Malaga was. The Euroleague write-up read like this for the game:

"Matjaz Smodis could also play a major role for CSKA. Jimenez and Pietrus will have an interesting matchup with David Andersen, who added a deadly three-point shot to his arsenal of offensive skills. Unicaja will also concern itself with Theodoros Papaloukas, CSKA's star sixth man and the MVP of last season's Final Four. Papaloukas is the cornerstone of a back-court featuring swingman Oscar Torres, combo guard J.R. Holden, and sharpshooter Trajan Langdon. Holden, one of the best on-the-ball defenders

in the competition, will try to stop Carlos Cabezas and Pepe Sanchez, a player made for big games like this. Langdon will test his skills against Marcus Brown, who made it to consecutive Final Fours with CSKA before Langdon. Unicaja is quite deep at both wings with Jiri Welsch and Marcus Faison. Unicaja coach Sergio Scariolo is famous for providing tactical surprises in big games, so expect the unexpected. In addition to speeding the tempo, Unicaja will try to bother Papaloukas and it has the right player to do it in Berni Rodriguez. CSKA must maintain its defensive intensity and get its big men involved to increase its chances. Ultimately, with two teams talented enough to reach the Final Four playing for a spot in the Euroleague final, anything can happen. So get ready for an intense battle and an exciting game like few others!"

The semi-final game started well for us. Although we did not shoot the ball well, we were playing with the poise and confidence of a defending champion. At the half, the score was close but we were controlling the tempo. Malaga seemed to be awestruck. The atmosphere of the Final Four seemed to have them in a daze throughout the 1st half. To our surprise, they appeared to be a different team as the 3rd quarter started. They were re-energized, and gained the control and momentum of the game. By the end of the 3rd quarter, we held on to a slim 2-point lead.

As I sat on the bench getting ready for the start of the 4th quarter, I sensed that our confidence was wavering. We had a sub-par 3rd quarter and appeared to be another victim of this hard-nosed, disciplined Spanish team. In any case, I decided to start the 4th quarter aggressively. We needed a spark and I felt that it was my responsibility to give us that push. I took 3 consecutive shots—all of which I missed, but my aggressiveness had a ripple effect. Suddenly, we were playing like a championship team again. We took control of the game and won an ugly, hard-fought game 62–50. It wasn't impressive but now we were one step away from accomplishing something I deemed impossible just a few years earlier—a chance to win back-to-back Euroleague titles.

The finals match-up against the home team Panathinaikos would be our toughest task of the season. They were a very good team with a lot of talent. The fact that they were playing at home made our mission that much harder to accomplish. In spite of this, we had been in this situation before and knew that we could win. It didn't get any better than this for a Euroleague final—the best two teams with the best two coaches squaring off for all the marbles. This was as good as it gets!

Panathinaikos started the game well and very aggressive. They forced the ball inside to create easy field goal attempts. This was no surprise. This is what we expected, knowing that their adrenaline would be high at the start of the contest. Our game plan was exactly the same. This game would be a chess match between the coaches. The players who made plays and executed would win this game. After the game went back and forth for the first 17 minutes, Panathinaikos gained control of the game right before halftime. We went into the locker room half-frustrated, knowing we had blown a few chances to cut their lead. I was very confident at halftime. I hadn't been aggressive enough and knew that my few mental mistakes would not happen in the 2nd half. I was upbeat and ready to do battle in the 2nd half. As Coach gave us our 2nd half assignments and game plan, he then named the starting 5 for the 2nd half.

My name was not called. I was shocked. I couldn't believe it. He was benching me in the finals. I was distraught. And for the first time in my career as a professional, I had been defeated mentally. I had lost my desire and spirit to push forward. All this mental anguish was happening in the middle of the biggest game of the season. I wanted to be out there, but in his eyes, I was not the player who deserved to be out there on the court. He probably made the right decision because we started the 2nd half like gangbusters and actually took a 2-point lead late in the 3rd quarter. I was on the bench cheering because I wanted to win, but inside, I was done—out of it. It looked as if we would take control of the game when both Trajan Langdon and Oscar Torres got into foul trouble. It seemed as if every time we made a run or looked like we could take the game, Panathinaikos had an answer and would turn the tide. Down the stretch, in the 4th quarter, I had a few chances to make plays to help us prevail. But, I didn't have it together mentally. I was playing not to hurt the team instead of to win the game. I didn't have the mental fortitude to look forward and see that my team would need me in this game. It seemed as if the mental frustration of the whole year came crashing down on me in the finals. I didn't do or have what it took to get us over the hump. I had let myself down and it hurt more than one could imagine. We lost our chance to win back-to-back titles and I believe I was a big reason for this. I finished the game scoring 11 points (4–6 fg), 1 steal, and 4 TURN-OVERS. Those 4 turnovers were my passive plays and those turnovers I believe cost us the game. I take nothing away from Panathinaikos, they played well and won a good game 93–91.

As a player, I know I cheated first, my team, and second, myself. The pain, hurt, and agony I felt inside when the final buzzer sounded was unbearable. At that moment, I felt as if my career was over at CSKA. I could no longer play for a coach who had no faith in my ability or talent. Also, I had to look within and do some soul searching when the season finally concluded. My performance was unacceptable, and I let down myself and the people who loved me the most. It was either time to leave CSKA, or step up and mentally take hold of my game and the way I played. No name, no blame. That finals loss was on me, and I promised myself to never let anything or anyone stop me from being the best me—ever again.

No one could quite understand what I was going through that year. Not my family, not my brother, and not my friends. They saw me as a basketball player who had a tough game or was hard on himself all year. But, that was not me at all. I had lost and not played great games many times in my career. Usually when that happened, I could pinpoint why or just deal with my not playing well and work that much harder to succeed. This year was different. I never was quite sure of myself. I didn't know why I was doing certain things. I would make a mistake and then ask myself—what was I doing? This happened so often that I quit asking myself that question. I hated basketball and hid that season—mostly at home. I didn't talk much and just kept to myself. The only person who helped me get through that year without killing someone was my teammate and good friend, Trajan Langdon. It was one of the worst seasons of my career, and I know I wouldn't have survived it without him.

So many times I wanted to quit, cuss someone out, vent my frustration at the coach, or hurt the team. Yet, Trajan would never allow me to do it. When I needed an ear and someone to be honest with me, he was there. We would talk for hours about ball, life, and anything worldly that came up. He was my saving grace that season, and I will never forget him for that. I am forever grateful for his friendship and kindness when things were at a low point for me. Basketball is a huge part of my life, and when it's not going well, my days are overcast. Through the talks and the time we spent hanging out together, Trajan helped me see the light at the end of the tunnel.

Winning the Russian Cup and the Russian League title that season were good consolation prizes. We defeated Unics, Kazan in the Russian Cup Final. I had 3 points (1–5 fg), 2 steals, and 2 assists in the game. It wasn't a bad game for me, but my stats described the type of season I was having. We were victorious against the same team in the Russian League finals. We swept the finals series 3–0. In Game 3 of the finals, I had 4 points (1–5 fg), 0 turnovers, and 0 assists. I didn't play badly, but again, my stats were indicative of my season. I was out there on the court playing the game I love but with no energy, hunger, drive, or life. I wasn't J.R. Holden. When the final buzzer sounded in the last game of the season, all the air came out of my body—like the air comes out of a basketball when you stick a sharp object into it. I was flat, finished, and ready to get home. I remember packing everything I had acquired over the 5 years I had been in Russia. My contract was up and I wasn't sure if I wanted to go back. On the other hand, I wasn't sure if they wanted me back. I wasn't going to make a rash decision. I was going to go home, take a long look within, talk to my loved ones and make a confident, well-thought-out decision about my basketball future.

In arriving stateside, my daughter revived the life within me. Seeing her smile and giving her a hug was the best feeling in the world to me. As I looked into her eyes, I knew that she loved me unconditionally and that made all my worries and problems seem like nothing. I just wanted to be Daddy and spend some time with my two girls. I would sit and hold her for hours just staring at her. She couldn't talk to me or understand what I was saying, but that didn't matter. I cherished our time together and had a true appreciation for the greatest gift God can give a man—a daughter. I was happy and blessed to have two women in my life who loved me dearly—Aireka and our daughter.

After just a few days at home, my phone rang. My agent called me every day about the teams interested in my services for next season. He said that the two teams with the best monetary offers were CSKA and their rival Dynamo Moscow. He pushed me to stay at CSKA, but I had to think. Maybe, I needed a change. Maybe I should take less money in another country. Maybe I should go to Dynamo. They had a new coach and I was sure that they wanted to beat CSKA. I just needed time. So, I asked him to give me a few weeks and told him that I would let him know.

I thought of a few things. First, I was unsure about making a lateral move in Russia. Dynamo had acquired a new and very good coach in Svetislav Pesic. That made it interesting for me, but I was unsure. I had heard rumors and I didn't want problems. Dynamo players were always complaining about being paid late or not at all. That was something I was not willing to deal with. Also, I contemplated going to Spain to play in the Spanish League. I just felt a change of scenery would do me some good. Finally, I could return to CSKA. I loved the fans and Moscow was like my second home. I was more than appreciative for the opportunity Sergei Kushchenko had afforded me years ago to become a top European point guard. It was going to be really tough to leave CSKA. My mind wanted out but my heart wanted in.

In the end, I chose to return to CSKA. I pondered the pro's and con's of staying or leaving but it was Darius who kept me at CSKA. He did this without even knowing it. After my dismal season, I felt that Coach Messina was pushing me out of CSKA. Throughout the season, my confidence wavered and Coach seemed to continually take shots at me. At times, I believe he didn't even realize he was doing it. I worked my tail off to be one of the best players in Europe, and now I believed I had a coach who didn't think I was one of the top 5 or 6 players on the team. That hurt, and it gave me the impression that he really didn't want me there. Messina was, and still is, a great coach. He rode me hard and in the end it made me a better player, but I didn't know this at the time.

I spoke with family and friends about my basketball future, including Darius. He gave it to me straight—no chaser. He said, "Is it the coach's fault if you make a bad pass? Is it the coach's fault if you don't play with heart and poise? Is it the coach's fault if you don't step up and be a better player each season? No, IT'S YOUR FAULT! Why let him run you out of CSKA? You work your ass off both mentally and physically this summer to be the best player you can be and focus on you and everything will work out on the court. No limits, and let's get this done TOGETHER! I am going to work you harder than ever before. Are you down or what? Think about it but don't make a dumb decision to leave CSKA because of your little pride or ego being hurt."

When he finished, I was speechless. It was an honest conversation with a true friend. He didn't spare my feelings for one minute, and I appreciated it more than he knew. I felt as if the weight of the world was off my shoulders. I knew the decision I had to make. I called my agent and told him my decision. He was elated by my choice and said he would take care of the rest. Within a few days, I was signing a 2-year multi-million-dollar deal. I was blessed and thankful to God for continuing to have favor over me and my career.

After I signed on for 2 more years, I was asked to play for the Russian National Team in the European championships in Spain. Without hesitation, I said I would do it. I wanted to play this year for personal reasons. I hadn't played to my potential in 2005 in Serbia. It was payback time. I wanted to do something special for Russia. I wanted to help Russia become one of the Top 5 teams in the European championships so that they could participate in the 2008 Summer Olympics. This was a daunting task, but I was up for the challenge. I was focused and ready to make sure that things would be different this time round. My motto was, "Why not us, why not now?" An excerpt from an interview for EuroBasket 2007 read as follows:

> *"Russia may have been drawn into group for the 2007 EuroBasket that includes defending champions Greece, but playmaker JR Holden isn't complaining. Russia will also take on Serbia and the team that wins the additional qualifying tournament and Holden is relishing the challenge.*

"I think it's a tough group, but that is what basketball is about, playing against the toughest teams and seeing where you stand as a team," Holden told PA Sport. "It's a great group, and we could be the surprise team if we just play well. We don't have to win the group. We just have to have a great showing playing good Russian basketball." Serbian basketball is in a rebuilding phase right now, but has a proud record, while Greece is right at the top of their game. "So much history, so much to prove, so much to gain (he said of Serbia) and a team that is at the top of Europe right now (Greece), what more could you ask for?" The Soviet Union won 15 EuroBasket titles, but Russia has only collected a 1993 silver medal and a bronze in 1997 since then. After finishing eighth in 2005 in Serbia and Montenegro, David Blatt was brought on as coach and has Holden leading an up-tempo, fast-breaking team with hopes of bringing glory back to Russia. "I think we have a solid chance to play well and surprise teams. I think we have the talent to compete with any team and this will be an opportunity to show and prove that. I like our chances," Holden said. "We are trying to get better and return Russian basketball to the status of the past." The American-born Holden, who led the EuroBasket qualification tournament with 23 points, will do his best to help Russia exact revenge against Greece, who beat them 66–61 in the quarter-finals of this competition in 2005. Furthermore, Holden will have another chance to face his CSKA Moscow team-mate Theodoros Papaloukas. "It's going to be fun. Me and Paps have a great relationship, and he is a legend right now. So facing him will be fun and a pleasure. This time there is no pressure on me but on him. He is on the hottest team, and they want to keep playing well and winning," Holden said. "They have a lot of good guards on their team, so me and Paps probably won't play man-on-man against each other, but just playing against Greece will be fun." Holden also talked about Serbia's desire to bounce back from their recent struggles, adding: "Serbia will be a tough team. They have great players and are hungry for success as well." Holden also said he's not worried about being in the group in which the winners of the additional qualification tournament will play. "As for the team that we don't know yet, I don't think it matters when we find out who it is. They have to win and then prepare to get ready to face a tough group so I don't think it matters at all. We just have to worry about our team and getting better."

Arriving in Russia to join the National Team, I felt a difference in the atmosphere. It wasn't like the summer before. The guys were relaxed and upbeat last summer. This summer, it felt as if the players weren't adjusting to Coach Blatt's system as easily and the pressure to qualify for the Olympics made the atmosphere a little more tense and stressful. Coach Blatt knew that he would have to make some changes to be successful. So, although everyone wasn't on-board with him early, he stuck to what he believed in and kept pushing the team to do what he felt was best.

Two guys who really struggled with Coach Blatt's adjustments were my CSKA teammate center Alexey Savrasenko and the star of the Russian National Team Utah Jazz wingman, Andrei Kirilenko (AK). Alexey didn't like the up-tempo style and wasn't satisfied with his touches (his opportunities to make plays or shoot the ball inside) in the paint. On the other hand, AK had not played last summer and just needed time. He was going to love Coach Blatt's system, he just needed time to adjust and fit in.

It appeared that Coach Blatt's system was too complicated when we got dismantled in a preparation game by 40 points. The French National Team destroyed us. I was disappointed of course but their team was strong. Their team consisted of then NBA Finals MVP Tony Parker, LA Lakers super sub Ronny Turiaf, Boris Diaw from the Phoenix Suns, and a few more very good players both in the NBA and in Europe. They were a strong team, but not 40 points better than us. I thought that this humiliating loss would tear us apart. However, it brought us closer together as a team. It seemed as if the loss woke us up. Every player started listening more and made an extra effort to understand what Coach Blatt was trying to implement. I could feel the new sense of camaraderie and togetherness among us. It was nice being a part of a team all fighting for one goal, together! I thought things were going great for us. But, I guess what I felt and what others saw were 2 different things.

Right before our first game in EuroBasket 2007, Mr. Tarakanov, the Russian National Team manager, asked my brother Darius if I was OK and feeling well. He mentioned that I wasn't scoring a lot of points and shooting the way I had the prior summer. Darius, not really knowing what to say, just smiled and told him that I was OK and that I was ready for the tournament. I had invited Darius to join me on my journey with the National Team. It was tough sometimes being the only black man on the team. In addition to that, I didn't understand or speak Russian. We had a fair amount of downtime and at times I felt alone and isolated playing with the NT. Having Darius there helped me enjoy the time. I wanted to be around someone else who could relate to me. Add to that, he loves the game. It was a huge plus for me both on and off the court.

As far as Tarakanov's inquiry, there was no need to worry. I was adjusting and feeling out the situation with the team as well. The summer before, I was asked to score and score a lot. My role would be different this summer as Kirilenko joined the team and Viktor Kyryapa would be healthy. There was no need for concern. I was focused and wanted to seize the opportunity to show and prove that I was a much better player and our team was a lot better than we showed in Serbia in 2005.

EuroBasket kicked off for us in Granada, Spain. We faced the Serbian National Team. We knew it was important for us to start the tournament with a win so we were focused and ready. We played a solid first game. Keyed by our defense and the sharing of the ball on offense, we controlled the game and prevailed 73–65. Our center, Savrasenko, played well by stopping NBA big man Darko Milicicic, and AK was fabulous, contributing 24 points and 12 rebounds. It was a good start to the tournament. But we started well in 2005 too; there was no need to get excited. We were in this for the long haul this time around. Coach Blatt talked repeatedly about staying focused, taking 1 game at a time, and staying the path.

Game 2 was against an underrated Israel team who had just played a tough game against Greece the night before. We came out focused and determined. We won handily 90–56. I led us with 18 points, 5 rebounds, 3 assists, and 3 steals. That win set us up for a key game against Greece, and it was a match-up that I was looking forward to. I kept thinking about how badly I had played in 2005 against Greece. They controlled us and I wanted revenge. Game 3 would be a dogfight. We started out smoking and pushed the lead to 10 points early in the 2nd quarter. However, Greece regained their composure and only trailed us by 3 at the half. We started the 2nd half well and played with poise throughout, winning a defensive battle 61–53. I led this game with 17 points. I was happy with our win but I knew there was no time to celebrate. The next round would take place in Madrid, Spain. That's where we were headed and the next round is when truly good teams excel.

The first game of the 2nd round was against a very familiar Portuguese squad that we had faced a few times during our preparation period. They played hard but we were the more talented team. We overpowered them and led by as many as 19 points in the 2nd half. The final score was 78–65. It was a good start to the second round but our next game would be our biggest challenge of the tournament; we had to face the home team, Spain. They were the favorite to win EuroBasket 2007. Then again, that is why you have to play the games. Our confidence rose and we felt we could play with any team in the tournament, including the favorite.

The game started well for us—a little too well. We were aggressive but we took a lot of 3-point shots. Sometimes, when you make a lot of 3-pointers early in a game, the team just ends up shooting 3-pointers all game. That is what happened to us and Spain capitalized on our lack of mental toughness. When I felt them starting to control the game, I started attacking with mid-range jump shots and lay-ups. But they were too good and too strong. They played smart and steady, led by their NBA point guard Jose Calderon. He played really well, and led with 17 points and 4 assists. The score ended 81–69, but the game was a lot closer than the score indicated.

It was our first loss of the tournament, and it was expected. That didn't matter to me. I didn't care what people expected, I expect to win every time I touch the court. As soon as I arrived back to the hotel after the game, I went up to Darius's room. I needed to vent and I knew he would listen without being judgmental or taking what I say too personally. As soon as he opened the door to his room, I went off. I was upset because I felt I could have taken over that game and given us an opportunity to win. I knew that we had let an opportunity to beat the best team in the tournament slip away. I had studied film over and over again mentally preparing for situations like the one that took place that evening. Seeing a situation or a predicament before it happens is a huge advantage in the game of basketball. I had failed and I didn't like failing.

What's more, I sensed maybe the team didn't have the same aspirations as I did. Trust me, I knew they wanted to win, but did we have the swagger, humility, toughness, and togetherness to beat a team as good as the Spanish National Team?

Darius and I stayed up half the night just laughing and talking. It was a blessing having him there, and that night I needed him more than he needed me. I knew while we were talking, his mind wasn't far from the game. He is obsessed with basketball but he genuinely loves me. When I said peace at 3 A.M., I had no idea he would stay up until 7 A.M. breaking down the Spain game for me. When I woke up the next morning, there was a note under my door that read, "Come to my room when you have time, we have some game film to watch."

Around noon that day we watched splices of the Spain game. He made a few comments, but mostly just pointed out different times and situations in the game where I should have been more aggressive. His final remark caught me by surprise and stuck with me for the rest of the tournament. He said, "Calderon is going to attack you, he has no fear and in his (Calderon's) eyes, he is better than you." He then gave me the DVD and said, "Keep it, you'll need it. You'll see Spain again."

As soon as I left Darius's room, I knew it was time to refocus and get ready for the next game. This is a tournament; it's not about one opponent or one loss—it's about winning enough games to qualify for the 2008 Olympics. The next game was the most important game. If we won it, we would move to the semi-finals. If we lost, our goal of qualifying for the Olympics that summer was over. Our next opponent was one of the teams we didn't want to face—the National Team of France. That same team had demoralized us by 40 points about 3 weeks earlier. They matched up well against us and had just as much or more talent than we did at every position. In spite of this, I felt confident. I knew our team wouldn't be confident, but to be successful, we had to overcome a major obstacle.

France was our obstacle and Tony Parker was the engine that made that team go. I knew that if I could slow him down a little bit, we would have a chance to win this game. Coach Blatt devised a magnificent game plan and he kept preaching to us every minute—attack and be the aggressor! We started the game just like Coach wanted us to—attacking.

We didn't take control of the game but we did set the tone. France controlled the game most of the way. Nevertheless, we kept fighting and clawed to stay close. It was a gutsy effort. Right when you thought we didn't have enough and would concede defeat, we gave a little more. In addition to our team effort, I stepped up big, late in the 2nd half after struggling most of the game. We ended up pulling off the upset, 75–71. What a WIN!!! I finished the game with 15 points and most of them came in the 4th quarter.

It was a great win for us, and an even bigger win for Russian basketball. It was the first time in 10 years that Russia had reached this level of the EuroBasket championships. As much as I wanted to celebrate and pat myself on the back, there was no time. I wanted to do something special. I could sense that the whole team wanted to do something extraordinary. With the win over France, now we had a chance to win a medal. Now, that would be truly amazing! We were a team that no one picked to finish in the top 8. Now we had an opportunity to potentially medal.

Our next opponent was a tough, talented team—the Lithuanian National Team. They were the real deal. They had a very talented team—filled with NBA players as well as a few other very good European players. What's more, the game was even more pressure packed because of the rivalry between the two countries. It has been a rivalry since Lithuania broke off from the Soviet Union. There was a lot of history involved in this rivalry, and I didn't know the half of it.

Truthfully, not knowing everything about the history of the rivalry, allowed me to focus and play this "big" game without being overly emotional. This was an opportunity to secure a medal by defeating Lithuania and that in itself was enough. The excitement and adrenaline worked in our favor early in the game. We had a day off between our French victory and this game. Lithuania played the day before and was not as fresh as we were.

We started the game aggressively and firing on all cylinders. We took an early lead with a score of 28–12. I knew Lithuania would make a run at us. Basketball is a game of runs so we had to weather the storm whenever they made their run at us. Lithuania made their runs and played their style of basketball knotting the score at 52 in the 3rd quarter. We stayed the path and played with poise. Our NBA star, Andrei Kirilenko, played a marvelous game, stepped up big—hitting a few shots and helping us regain our advantage at 58–52. We never relinquished our lead after this. I made a few plays down the stretch in the 4th quarter to secure the victory. We stunned the team that no one thought we had a chance of defeating with a final score of 86–74. Andrei Kirilenko led us with 29 points and 8 rebounds. I played his sidekick, scoring 18 points and gathering 6 rebounds. This was a true team effort. What's more, we had just shocked the European basketball world by making the EuroBasket Finals, clinching a spot in the 2008 Olympics and at the very least—obtaining a silver medal.

No one had given us a chance, and now we would face for the second time, the favorite of the tournament—Spain. I guess my brother was right—I would play Spain again. This was the match-up I wanted. In order to be the best, you have to beat the best. Now we would see if we were worthy of being called champions! Russia hadn't won a gold medal with the men's basketball team since they were the Soviet Union. That was a pretty long time ago and we were a game away from making history.

I saw our match-up against Spain as a tough one but not an impossible hurdle. Everyone else saw this contest as no contest at all. There was a lot at stake and most felt that they had the better team with better players. My thinking was, anything can happen when it's just 1 game. Yes, they were the better team. Yes, they had the better players, but in 1 game, anything is possible. Their roster was stacked. They had the likes of Pau Gasol (LA Lakers), Marc Gasol (Memphis Grizzlies), R. Fernandez (Portland Trail Blazers), J. Navarro (Memphis Grizzlies), J. Calderon and J. Garbajosa (Toronto Raptors) and a few other very good players who played in Europe and the NBA. From their roster, we didn't stand a chance. Yet, only 5 players can be on the court at one time. If we played our game, I think we had a chance—a small chance, but a chance nonetheless.

The night before the championship game, I was really relaxed. I stayed in my hotel room most of the day and night listening to music. I wasn't antsy, anxious, or anything. I kept playing the game over and over in my mind. I visualized myself making big plays in the 4th quarter. And of course, I saw us celebrating on their home court with 20,000 stunned

Spanish fans in attendance. There was no pressure on me at all. I thought to myself, "At the very least, I have helped this team reach their goal of qualifying for the Olympics. Making it this far was a bonus. I was helping bring back a silver medal." Then I would snap out of it and scream out loud, "You gotta get that gold Boop, you gotta get that gold!" This was not my usual routine the day before a big game. But this was different; I had a whole country with its eyes on me. I was the outcast and the chosen one all in the same breath. This was major!

On game day I was my usual self—calm and relaxed. I knew nothing could be done or accomplished until game time. I couldn't tell this day or game was any different from all the rest until I walked through the hotel to get to the team bus. Walking out the hotel, seeing thousands of Spanish fans screaming and booing let me know that this moment was special. I also saw hundreds of Russian fans waving their Russian flags with pride. The atmosphere was like nothing I had ever experienced before. The excitement surrounding the event rubbed off on everyone, including me.

By the time we arrived at the arena and went through our pregame routine, I was calm. I was ready to rock and roll. During warm-ups, I was able to scan the arena. To my surprise, my brother Darius sat in the front row. To this day, I don't know how he pulled that off. He didn't even have a ticket for the game. That is just how he operates. He will find a way to make it happen! I was happy he was there. I looked over at him and gave him the "I am ready to shock the world" look. He smiled as he held his fist (the black power fist) high in the air, yelling, "We here now baby, we here now!"

The game began like we didn't even belong in the same arena as the Spanish team. They jumped on us 16–4 before we even realized the game had started. Coach Blatt called a time-out and calmed us down. He kept reiterating, "Continue to play defense and believe. We got to believe."

After the time-out we regained our composure, but Spain held on to their sizeable lead and finished the 1st quarter ahead 22–11. When the quarter ended, I sensed that the whole team felt we had a chance to win. Everyone was talking, encouraging, and supporting each other. I just felt a change in our attitude. I read it right and we fought our tails off in the 2nd quarter. We went into halftime believing we could shock the world, only trailing the all-powerful Spanish team 34–31. We had disrupted their offensive flow with our match-up zone defense. They seemed frustrated and annoyed that they couldn't pull away from us. In spite of our encouraging 2nd quarter, the 3rd quarter began how the game started. They jumped on us and pushed their lead to 9, 40–31. We bent, but we didn't break. We kept battling and ended the 3rd quarter trailing by 3.

At this point, I could see the worry and concern on the Spanish players' faces. What they thought would be a blowout win, had turned into a war. They had to play some of their best basketball to pull away from us. This didn't happen and our fans went wild when we took our first lead in the game with 9 minutes to play. The game went back and forth for the next 7 minutes. With 1 minute and 48 seconds left in the contest, and Spain ahead by 5, I could feel the players of Spain smelling victory. We had to give one more big push. It was now or never. Kirilenko hit a big 3-point shot to cut their lead to 2 points. However, during the last 4-minute stretch, I couldn't buy a basket. I missed 4 very makeable shots. I knew that if we lost, I wanted the ball in my hands. During a time-out, trailing by 1 point with 43 seconds remaining, Coach Blatt yelled, "Get a stop, it's our time."

Jersey drenched in sweat, my mind raced to figure out what play Spain might run. As we walked back from the time-out, I thought that they would go to their best and most dominant player—Pau Gasol. We couldn't stop him 1-on-1. Just as I expected, the play developed and they went inside to their beast, Pau. When he caught the pass and started to make his move toward the basket, I didn't think he could see me. When he started to spin, I reached in for the steal, GOT IT! As soon as I got the ball, I took a deep breath and headed up court, thinking, "Wow! CAN IT GET ANY BETTER THAN THIS?"

With fans on their feet as the clock wound down, all I could think was, "Make the right play and don't settle for a 3-point shot." I calmly walked the ball over half court with a little less than 27 seconds left in the game. I took a quick look at Kirilenko on the baseline, waving for me to make something happen. I knew he had a big heart and I respected him so much as a player that I had to make sure he didn't want to take the last shot or make the last play. This was his team; it was his decision.

Our big man and me immediately ran a pick and roll together. Pau Gasol jumped out at me and double-teamed me so that I had to pass the ball. I passed it to Zakhar Pashutin. He smartly took 1 dribble and passed it back to me. Without hesitation, I caught it and took a few dribbles right, pump fake. The man guarding me, Jose Calderon, jumped in the air—I paused, squared up—and let him jump past me; I shot a 15-foot jump shot. On the release it felt good, but I had just missed 4 shots in a row and they all felt just as good. I bent my knees to WILL the ball in the basket. Time froze. Everything seemed to be in slow motion. The ball skimmed off the front of the rim as if it were going to bounce out. It hit the back of the rim and went up in the air. Everyone in the arena looked at it. As the 24-second shot buzzer sounded, it rolled into the basket—swish.

Everyone screamed and jumped—except me. I knew there were 2 seconds left in the game. The arena became silent again. We may have just pulled off one of the greatest upsets ever in European championship history. I remained calm and collected. There were 2 seconds left and Spain would inbound the ball from half court. I had seen some amazing shots over the course of my life, and I knew that 2 seconds was a lot of time. During the time-out, all I could think about was getting one more defensive stop. Our team was focused. I could feel their anxiety and giddiness for the game to end. I agreed with Coach Blatt's advice, "Don't fall asleep and make them take a contested jump shot." As Spain inbounded the ball, I saw Gasol go to the free throw line to catch it. I thought that he would make it. The inbounder threw Gasol a perfect pass. He caught it, turned to the basket, and shot a tough fade-away shot. When it left his hands, the ball was dead on. I could barely breathe; he was going to kill my dream! The arena fell silent. As I walked toward the sideline to damn near cry, the ball went in—and OUT! Game over, we WIN!

It was pandemonium when the ball missed. I walked up the sidelines with both hands raised, my index finger pointed in the air—we were #1. My brother Darius jumped up and down in the team circle with the other Russian players. I smiled from ear to ear—I was a part of history. I can't even explain how happy I was at that moment—all the hard work, all the hours in the gym, all the frustrations of playing badly during EuroBasket 2005—it all just came together at the right time.

I wasn't a native of Russia, and I didn't speak the language, but in the spirit of the game of basketball, none of that mattered. What felt even better was my will, determination, and the grace of God in a time of immense pressure. I held the fate of the country on my shoulders when I took that shot. I had previously missed 4 shots in a row before I made the game winner. I had the heart and the belief in myself that I could and should have taken all those shots. I couldn't help but hug and thank Kirilenko as we celebrated. He could have very easily been selfish. It was a testament to his character. The feeling of accomplishment was inexplicable. I would have never fathomed doing something this unique in my life. It was the best basketball moment of my life. The press write-up said:

"Russia edged in the final of EuroBasket 2007 host Spain 60–59. The hero of the game was definitely J.R. Holden, whose 2-pointer jump just 2.1 second before the end of the game saved the game for Russians. It was their first European championship title in history (as Russia, since Soviet Union team won previously 14 gold medals at EuroBasket). Pau Gasol still could switch the victory toward host team, but his buzzer shot went in…and out. That way Spain got their 6th silver medal at EuroBasket. The MVP of the tournament went to Russian Andrei Kirilenko (205-F-81), who was the leader of his team thru all competition games including the final one, where he got 17 points and 5 rebounds."

Coach David Blatt: "Khryapa was the secret of our success. Thank you first of all to my two great stars—Kirilenko and Khryapa. Both of them they are wonderful people as well as they are great players. We wanted to stay in the game the whole time. In the scouting we spoke about that first—stay close and make them feel the pressure. They felt the heat and we took advantage of it."

"This is an ultimate moment in the history for the Russian nation. It's the first championship of the new Russia. I'm very proud to be the person in charge of this historical journey. I feel very lucky to be part of history both in Russia and FIBA Europe basketball."

*"We did not want to double team Gasol a lot. We did doubling late after
two dribbles just not to allow him to go close to the basket, but we did
a great job against Calderon, and he didn't play as good as he did in the
last game against us. We played a lot of matchup zone and didn't allow
Gasol to get the ball close to the rim. We wanted to put him on the line
and it worked. Holden stopped in the last three days—Tony Parker, Sarunas
Jasikevicius and Jose Calderon and people should acknowledge that."*

After a wild celebration at the gymnasium, I arrived back at the hotel
happy and grateful for what had just occurred. In spite of this, I had missed
my daughter's 1st birthday playing in these EuroBasket games, and I suddenly became overwhelmed with sadness. All I kept thinking about was leaving Spain the next day to go see her. I loved basketball but my Princess was
my world. It would have been nice to go back to Russia with my teammates
and celebrate but I couldn't. My family was my strength and what held me
together in good and bad times. Getting back to see them was my priority.

When the dust settled, weeks later, I was recognized as a 1st-team
selection at the European championships—that was really special to me. It
was like, "Wow! My name was on the same list as Andrei Kirilenko, Tony
Parker, Pau Gaol, and Dirk Nowitzki." All of those players, at one time
or another, had been NBA All-Stars. It was so gratifying to know that all
the hard work had paid off, and NOT just in my eyes—but in the eyes of
others. Winning was and will always be my #1 priority. All the sacrifices,
all the times I didn't think I could keep going, all the pushing and trying
to be the best player I could be—it was all worth it. Peer recognition was
most important, but receiving it from the public, well, that was nice too!

When I landed in Lansing, Michigan, everything that had just happened seemed like a blur. Aireka beamed with pride and smiled as I
walked to the baggage claim. It warmed my heart. As soon as my daughter saw me, she screamed, "Daddy" and ran toward me. That gave me the
best feeling in the world—yes, even better than hitting the game-winning
shot for the gold at EuroBasket 2007. It melted my heart knowing that
this woman and little girl had changed my life. They had changed my life
forever, for the better. There is nothing like genuine love.

X | Chasing Greatness

I SPENT A few days with my family before it was time to get back to work. It's always refreshing to get home and spend quality time with them. It was never easy leaving, but I always felt better knowing that they were well taken care of.

It was time for my journey to begin—accomplishing my next goal—bringing another Euroleague title back to Moscow. The previous season had been a personal catastrophe and it was now time to bounce back. I felt good about our team, my situation, and Coach Messina. Coach was on the last year of his contract, and I knew that he had his own pressures and stresses to deal with.

Coach and I got off to a great start. I put my pride aside and did my best to embrace my role on the team. He realized this and he let up a little bit. What's more, I believed that our relationship was improving. This would help improve our team chemistry. The overall atmosphere was a little more uplifting and it showed on the court. We won games and although we did not blow teams out as in seasons past, we were battle-tested. Others didn't feel the way I felt. The media and even the organization felt as if we weren't as strong as we had been in previous years. This is the nature of the business. Such scrutiny comes with playing for a high-level team in Europe. If you win, but don't win big, it's a problem. If you lose, even if you're playing well, it could be your job. You could be sent home. We were a good team but we just needed more time to gel. We had added 3 new players in Nikos Zisis, Ramunas Siskauskas, and Marcus Goree, and they needed time to adjust. I had been through all this before. I know that patience and persistence were the keys to long-term success.

Hitting the winning shot at the EuroBasket had changed my status in Russia. Things that usually didn't happen were happening. For instance, early in the season I was asked to be on the front cover of two Russian magazines. One magazine was *Pro Sport* and the other was *Men's Health*. *Men's Health* was a really big deal because I was going to be the first black male and the first basketball player ever to grace the cover. We all knew this was granted because of the "shot." Nonetheless, it was nice to be recognized. It made me feel that all the hard work and dedication had not gone unnoticed. It also made me feel like people genuinely respected the way I played basketball for Russia. The color of my skin and my American nationality didn't matter. I felt good about the step I had taken to play for the Russian National Team. I was grateful for every opportunity, colleague, fan, and supporter had helped me on the journey to put Russian basketball back at the top. Needless to say, both magazine covers turned out great.

In late October or early November, players started dropping like flies. Three of our top players were injured. Siskauskas, Matjas Smodis and Theodoros Papaloukas were going to be out for a few games. When many believed that we would struggle and lose a few games, I considered it an opportunity to gel as a team. That is exactly what we did. Each player stepped their game up a notch to help us achieve success. What's more, I became a more vocal leader during this period. I guess the loss of our leaders forced me to speak up more. The one person who took notice and supported me 110 percent with my new leadership was Coach Messina. My speaking up allowed me to step up my play. Coach allowed me more freedom to play my style of basketball—the up-tempo game. With newfound freedom, I started playing better and in return, Coach started trusting me more. This boosted my confidence and enabled the team and my relationship with Coach to grow. In 2 weeks, we went from weaklings to darling overachievers.

As good as everything was on the court, off the court I experienced another death in the family. When my Uncle Johnny passed around Thanksgiving, a piece of my heart went with him. In my eyes, Uncle Johnny was a special man. He was a pillar of strength on my mom's side of the family. There was nothing that he couldn't do to make things better, or at least appear to seem better. I remember our last meeting. I was at our family reunion in Pittsburgh and he told me he had to talk to me. I recalled that he had looked weak—frail and just not himself physically. Mentally, he was as sharp as a tack. He said that he didn't need any money or anything like that but he just needed to tell me a few things.

He said, "You're the strength of this family now; you need to carry the torch."

I looked him square in his eyes and said, "OK, Unc, I got you, we will talk soon."

Before we parted ways—never to speak again—we both said, "I love you." It tears me up inside that I never had that talk with him. I had 24 months. I had 24 months to make that conversation happen but I didn't. I always found a way to seem too busy. I remember when my sister called me in the locker room minutes before I took the court for a game with the sad news. I knew when the phone rang that something was wrong. My sister never called me before a game. As soon as she said my name, I knew someone had passed. Saddened and in disbelief, I walked into the restroom to cry. I didn't want the team to see me crying. As I wept, all I could think about was my mom. She had lost both of her brothers. I knew she was hurting. There was nothing I could do to help. I felt for her. As I sat in the restroom stall, I thought to myself, "I must enjoy the quality time that I have with my loved ones because this time is priceless." I never know when it will be my last chance to speak with them or say, "I love you."

The year was full of surprises. In January I had the pleasure of meeting and playing in front of a legend, one of the NBA's 50 greatest—none other than Scottie Pippen. It was surreal meeting such a legend. No, he wasn't Michael Jordan but let's be real, who else is close to Jordan—except Michael Jordan? Pippen was a sincerely down to earth and humble person. I thought he would big-dog me and not pay me any mind. That was far from the truth. I probably had a 30- to 45-minute conversation with him after one of our practices. It was a pleasant surprise and a great thrill to be in the presence of "greatness." Seeing him at the game really gave me an extra boost. I was getting a chance to play in front of a man who had won 6 NBA championship rings, an Olympic Gold Medal, and had been places I could only dream of. I thought to myself, "Man, I get to play this big game in front of Scottie Pippen."

I played well as we defeated Spain's Tau Ceramica, 70–62. I finished the game with 19 points, 5 rebounds, and 4 assists. It was an unbelievable feeling to have one of the 50 greatest come up to me and say, "Good game kid, I like the way you play."

As the season wore on and we got back our injured players, we started struggling again as a team. Our chemistry and rhythm were a little off. Some players were passive, others were too aggressive. It was going to take more than a few games to get our cohesiveness back. We were at a point in the season when the games mattered a little more and we really wanted to win. Our first bump in the road came in the Russian Cup.

The Cup was being held in Kazan, Russia and we faced the home team in the semi-final game. Unics Kazan was always tough to beat at home. They played with more confidence and more heart in front of their fans at home. We were the better team but they were playing better basketball at the time. We were expected to win the Cup, so the pressure was on us. I don't know how we managed to pull it off but we survived the Unics game on a last-second 3-pointer that I made—to win 51–50. It was a big win for us but it was ugly. I was concerned because we were playing horribly and we faced an even hotter Khimki team the next day in the finals.

My concern was warranted; Khimki destroyed us the following night, 85–67. They were hungrier than us and it showed. They beat us to every loose ball, got every rebound, and they dismantled us. What stung me the worst in that defeat was their over-exuberant celebration. Their players were jumping on scoreboards, waving towels, and really just going overboard. I walked off the court thinking, "We are going to see them again, and they will pay." We would possibly face them in the Russian League Finals. They got that victory, a well-deserved one I might add, but I wouldn't forget that celebration.

That season, for the first time, I felt as if I was living up to Coach Messina's expectations. It felt good knowing that he was pushing me toward excellence. I hadn't felt this way in the past. He sang praises to the media, and this really took me by surprise. He told *Sports Illustrated* that season that he had a lot of respect for me and appreciated the hard work I had put in to help the team. I had no idea how he viewed me as a player before I read the article. In the article, Coach Messina said that I had become the best point guard in Europe after 6 years with CSKA. He was also quoted as saying, "He's very quiet, very reserved. I owe him a lot for the patience that he has, because sometimes in my rotation I am giving more attention to other players, and I took for granted this contribution from him. And I put him a little bit on the side in terms of attention [in the offense], and he never quit or never showed any sign of being angry or whatever. He managed to keep everything inside and still do his job. Honestly, I've learned a lot from him." I was speechless. I admired Coach Messina. I had never showed it because I was often disappointed. I wanted to please him but didn't know if I could. When I finally knew that he respected me as much as I respected him, I was reassured that our relationship was fine. Little did he know I would run through a wall for him.

The article further stated, "CSKA was on the verge of losing the semifinal when Holden nailed a jumper in the final seconds to steal the victory. As Holden walked into the team hotel an hour later, there was no telling from his expression whether he had made or missed the shot. 'Some people shy away from these situations,' Holden said. 'You have to be able to accept not being the hero. If I miss this shot, am I going to be able to take it? Some people can, and some people can't.'"

This was my attitude/demeanor in a nutshell when it came to the game. I was not afraid to fail. I knew that I worked hard and was prepared to succeed in all situations. If I failed, I could walk out of the gym with my head held high knowing that I would work smarter and harder. I would do whatever it took to be the best. I was once asked how good I wanted to be. I didn't answer honestly. The true answer is—I want to be the best American ever to play in Europe. I want to be remembered forever. I don't want to walk away from the game and in 2 years be forgotten. I want to win and win big. I want to be remembered as a pioneer. I want to pave the way for others to achieve much more than I have. When they think of who started this movement, I want them to think of me.

To reach my 6th consecutive Final Four, we had to defeat Olympiakos. They were a very talented team led by Lynn Greer (Temple University, Milwaukee Bucks), Jake Tsakalidis (NBA vet), Qyntel Woods (NBA vet), and Roderick Blakney. They reached the quarter-finals of the Euroleague on a winning streak, and were destined to reach the Final Four in Madrid, Spain. To reach Madrid, they had to defeat us.

At this point in the season, we were starting to find our rhythm. We had faced Olympiakos twice during the season and each team had won on their home courts, splitting our match-up. This was a best-of-3 series so we had one thing in our favor—home court advantage. Game 1 was a must-win game for us. We were shocked 76–74 on a buzzer-beater by Lynn Greer. It was a tough defeat and now our backs were up against the wall.

Down 0–1 and on the road facing elimination, it was time to step up or go fishing. If we went fishing that meant our Euroleague season was over. In Game 2 in Greece, we played our tails off. We played with the confidence and poise of a championship team. We took their best shot and passed with flying colors. We defeated Olympiakos with a final score of 83–73.

The series-clinching game would be at our place and there was no way we could lose on our home court. The arena rocked for Game 3. Our fans gave us all the boost we needed to annihilate our opponents 81–56, en route to a record-setting 6th consecutive Euroleague Final Four. The record was great but people remember champions, not Final Four participants. We were happy to get there, but we were going to Madrid to bring the title back.

Before our trip to Madrid, Coach Messina informed me that I had not been selected for any All-Euroleague teams. He felt my exclusion from both the 1st and 2nd teams was a shame. He thought it had been my best year and a disgrace that I wasn't selected. He believed I was the best point guard in Europe and deserved to be selected. I thanked him and told him not to worry. In my eyes, I had been getting slighted for most of my Euroleague career. I didn't think this season would be any different. My mindset was to head to Spain and play my ass off and win a championship. I couldn't care less about All-Euroleague teams.

Coach was just full of surprises that season. This was the second time he had left me speechless. His kind words touched my heart. I know how tough he was on players. Matter of fact, I know how tough he was on me, but he made me a better and stronger player. He helped my game mature and I will forever be thankful for that.

At the Final Four, we knew that our semi-final match-up with Tau would be a great contest. They were a tough team and they always played us well. Nevertheless, we were prepared and ready to do battle. The game started well for Tau. They took an early lead and appeared to be in total control. Add to that, Trajan and Siskauskas both picked up their 3rd fouls in the 1st half. We looked to be in serious trouble. As soon as I sensed Tau taking control of the game I became aggressive offensively. I hit a few shots but we still trailed at the half by 6 points. Trailing by this small margin was good for us considering how well Tau had played the first 20 minutes of the game. When we got into the locker room, Coach loudly voiced how disgusted he was with our play. His speech woke us up and we came out and played some inspired basketball in the 2nd half. We scrapped every possession and pulled out a close victory, 83–79. I played a great defensive game against Tau's best scorer and also contributed 15 points, 3 assists, and 2 steals. It was a gutsy win. We were moving on to the finals to face Maccabi, Tel Aviv. This was a rematch of the 2006 Euroleague Finals in Prague.

It was always a joy for me to compete against Maccabi, Tel Aviv. I believe they have the biggest following in Europe—their supporters are fanatical. They bleed their team colors—yellow and blue. Such huge followings always made for an electric atmosphere and a great environment in which to compete. This was no different—the excitement was at its max at the start of the game.

Maccabi started the game well and set an early tone. We responded quickly and Trajan got it going, making a few shots early and often. To offset our aggressive defense, their ultra-quick and athletic point guard Will Bynum put us in numerous pick and rolls, creating problems. He carried much of their offensive load in the 1st half. Even with our defensive difficulties, we carried a slim 1-point lead into the half, 42–41.

Like we had done all year, we came out on fire in the 2nd half. I came out and hit back-to-back 3-pointers to push the lead to 48–41. From there, we took total control of the game and never trailed. When the clock hit 2 minutes left to play, I knew we were on our way to our 2nd Euroleague championship in 3 years. It was an impressive feat and I was proud. As the final seconds ticked off the clock, I started looking for my family. When the buzzer sounded I strolled over to hug and kiss my girlfriend Aireka and our daughter. Aireka was in tears. This was the 1st Final Four that she attended that we had won. She had experienced 3 defeats, but now she was able to enjoy a victory. All I heard her say was, "We did it baby, we did it!" That made me smile. I felt as if we had accomplished this together, as a family. I was a proud man. Then I had to find all my family and friends who had made the trip to Spain. Seeing them all screaming, jumping up and down warmed my heart. I had a smile on my face a mile wide. I felt so blessed and thankful. God is so good. HE always gave me the strength, endurance, charisma, and focus to perform my best on the biggest stage. HE deserved all the Glory. I had 14 points, 3 assist and 2 steals in a 91–77 championship victory.

After the game, it was time to celebrate and spend time with my friends and family. I wanted to make sure to thank everyone for their support. It really moved me that so many people had come to show me love. Holding my smiling daughter kept me grounded and put what I was experiencing in perspective. She was my world. My mom and dad beamed with pride. As I embraced my sister with tears in her eyes, I smiled. That evening, that moment, everything just felt perfect.

I made my way around to all 25-plus friends and family. I even reconnected with a dear friend and college buddy whom I hadn't seen in 10 years. Who would have thought we would reconnect in Madrid, Spain? It warmed my heart to know that our love—our brotherhood—formed in college, really, would last forever. I saw another friend, Roland Jones, and realized that the love he and his wife, Delisha Milton-Jones (WNBA star, European star-2 Euroleague championships), had for me was incredible. I admired and looked up to Delisha. She had overcome so much to be the player she had become. Her story is amazing, and I love her. Roland had been a good friend from the day we met 6 years ago, in an airport in Russia. I had a lot of love for him. I spent the next few hours enjoying my family and friends. We talked, laughed, and partied until the wee hours. It was a Final Four I will never forget!—a champion on the court because of the love and support I had off of it.

When we got back to Russia the following evening, party time was over. We had to get back to work and try to win another Russian League championship. I hadn't forgotten what Khimki did to us in the Russian Cup. I wanted revenge and revenge is what I would get. We would face them in a best-of-5 series in the finals. However, the series lost a little hype when a key player from their team, Daniel Ewing, was suspended for 3 games for fighting in their previous playoff series. I didn't care. I wanted to win and win big.

Game 1 would be at our place and we easily defeated them 97–76. It was a tone-setting game for us. We knew that Game 2 would be a tougher contest, but we were up for the challenge. However, we came out flat, and Khimki jumped on us early and built a 10-point lead. Then, our home crowd got involved and gave us the energy to push forward and seek out a 74–66 victory. Now, we were 1 game away from a sweep. I wanted the sweep badly and we got it! We finished the series on their court defeating them 88–78. We had now won our 6th consecutive Russian League championship.

There's no rest for the weary, so once the season ended, I took about 7 days off before I started training to compete in the Olympics. Although I needed rest, I couldn't afford it. The Olympics is the biggest stage in the world; I couldn't be on that platform and not be prepared. I could not cheat myself. Going to the Olympics was never a dream of mine but now that I was blessed with this opportunity, I had to be ready.

Pat Riley once said, "There's no such thing as coulda', shoulda', or woulda'. If you coulda' and shoulda', you woulda' done it." This rang true for me. There was work to be done, and it was time to get to it. On the other hand, I knew that my family was my priority. The summer time is the only stretch of time that I was in the States and I had to spend quality time with them.

For me, there was no better feeling than coming home after a tough workout, and having my daughter jump into my arms. She just wanted to spend time with Daddy, and that made a huge difference in helping me keep everything in perspective. I knew this was a special time for me as a basketball player, but nothing was more important than my daughter. I love and adore her.

Since qualifying for the Olympics last summer, I yearned to compete and play well on this global stage. I knew I would never play ball again on a stage this grand, and I wanted to take full advantage of the opportunity. No regrets, no second guessing, no shoulda' or coulda', just giving it my all—playing ball.

The stuff that bothered me the most that summer was the media attention. All the phone calls and requests for interviews were a little much. The press asked me about being an American with a Russian passport. I found this attention silly because I had a Russian passport for 5 years. And to be totally honest, I hadn't gotten much attention in the United States. It's nice to be recognized for what you do, but I'd prefer that it be sincere. I believed that I was getting so much attention because of another elite, American-born basketball player playing for Russia that summer in the Olympics, Becky Hammon. She received a lot of publicity and backlash for her decision to play for the women's Russian National Team. As usual, I was an afterthought. I wouldn't have gotten nearly as much attention if it weren't for her. After much prayer and deep thought, I decided against doing many of the interviews and other requests. I have never been about pumping up my own ego. All the attention was nice and much appreciated, but God had and would continue to bless me as long as I stayed true to the man He had made me. I was grateful for any attention bestowed upon me for my accomplishments. It was an honor that people were interested in my Olympic journey. However, I didn't want to bring any more attention to myself. My focus was on excellence and to help the Russian team try and win a medal. All this was unfathomable a few years ago. I just wanted to enjoy and cherish the experience. I was going to play basketball at the 2008 Olympics in Beijing, China.

I arrived in Italy on July 11, to meet with the Russian National Team. We were getting together about a month before the start of the Olympics to prepare. We had a lot of work to do. Our primary goal was to develop a chemistry and sense of togetherness that we shared the summer before at the EuroBasket, in Spain. Also, Coach Blatt knew that getting everyone on the same page was imperative if we wanted to compete for a medal. So, he screamed and kept on our tails from the first day. His yelling was doing the team no good early on. Some players were out of shape and not ready to play at such a high level. In addition to this, I felt as if we weren't as hungry this time around. We weren't clicking and it seemed as if very few people really cared. It appeared to me as if everyone thought we would just magically start playing well once the Olympic games started. I knew better than this and so did Coach Blatt. We were in trouble and it instantly got me thinking. Were we good enough to medal at the Olympics? What role players would step up and help us in Beijing? Were we still hungry for more success, or were we content as a team with what we did at EuroBasket 2007? I didn't know the answers to these questions. What I did know was that hard work creates a little luck, and with that, anything is possible.

To get ready for the Olympics, Coach Blatt had scheduled a few pre-season games for us. The first one was against an average Portugal team. It would be a good first game for us. It would help build our confidence and team chemistry. Winning and playing well will do that for any team. Nevertheless, our 2nd preseason game would be a rematch of the 2007 EuroBasket Finals, Russia vs. Spain. This would be a tough, early test for us. We had not been together very long and knowing Spain, they would come out and play this game like an Olympic contest. Spain would have their home crowd pushing for sweet revenge. A pre-season victory would only be but so sweet, but a win is a win.

Shockingly, the game was over by the middle of the 2nd quarter. With the score 17–13 in the 1st quarter, I received a technical foul for overreacting to a phantom foul called against me. I did get emotional and didn't react like I normally would to a bad call. I was a little too excited and pumped up to play this game. I love a challenge and I knew this game would be a huge test for us. I was amped up and cost my team the game. My overreaction gave me 3 fouls and forced Coach Blatt to sit me on the bench for the next 8 to 10 minutes. The score went from 17–13 when I exited the game to 45–20 when I re-entered it. The game was basically over. This loss was on me. I knew how important a player I was to the team. I made a mistake. I knew as soon as it happened; it would never happen again. Lesson learned!

We would finish our early preparation games for the Olympics by playing a tournament in Moscow, in front of our home fans from July 25–27. The tournament was called the Michelle Cup and our first game was against Latvia. Playing at home, we came out strong and won easily, 84–63. Our next opponent was an inferior Ukraine team. We again came out strong and won handily 91–55. The final game would be against a strong, young Serbian team. They had the talent and toughness of teams we would be facing in the Olympics. This would be a good test for us.

Unlike the other 2 games, we started slowly. Serbia came out aggressively and was shooting the ball incredibly well early in the contest. They shot 70 percent in the 1st half, on their way to scoring 48 points. In spite of this, we were still only down by 6 points. The 2nd half started well for us. We came out rejuvenated and inspired in front of our home fans. I hit back-to-back 3-pointers to start the 2nd half to cut the lead to 2 points. From there, the game went back and forth, with neither team taking control of the contest until the middle of the 4th quarter. That is when Kirilenko came alive for us and started playing like his usual self. With the game in our grasp, and ahead by 4 points with 1 minute remaining, our young and inexperienced forward, Andrey Vorontsevich fouled a 3-point shooter. The Serbian player made all 3 foul shots. We failed to score the next possession while Serbia did and they took a 1-point lead. I hit a mid-range jump shot the next possession to take a 1-point lead. We then made a defensive stop and while trying to play keep away so we could run out the clock, they fouled our veteran guard Zakhar Pashutin with about 15 seconds left in the game.

Although I was the hot shooter on the team, at the time, I decided to pass the ball to my teammates knowing that whomever Serbia decided to foul had the ability to step to the free throw line and make both free throws. When they fouled Zakhar, I was confident he would make the free throws but I was second-guessing my decision to pass the ball to him because it's a lot of pressure to put on a player who has not taken many shots in the entire game—to walk to the free throw line and ice the game for the team.

With immense pressure on him, Zakhar missed both free throws—which was OK; the best players in the world miss crucial and key free throws. We were still clinging to a 1-point lead. Yet, on Zakhar's 2nd missed free throw, Kirilenko foolishly fouled their best shooter once he rebounded the ball. He had just made a crucial mental mistake, and the Serbian player made us pay for it by making both free throws. Coach Blatt then called a time-out and put the ball in my hands to make the right play to either win or lose the game. I would end up taking a shot that felt good leaving my hands, but it went long. My teammate Nakita Morganov captured the rebound and tried to put it back in the basket between 3 Serbian players. The ball rolled off the rim, GAME OVER, we lost by 1 point.

I cracked a smile as I walked off the court, knowing I live by the motto, "Never let 'em see you sweat," but believe me, I was pissed. We lost a game that we should have won. We made too many silly mental mistakes. What made it worse, I still had the ball in my hands to win the game, and I didn't. In any case, I finished the game with 20 points (3–8 2pt, 3–10 3pt), 4 assists, and 4 rebounds. Also, I received the MVP of the tournament and the Best Play Maker in the tournament as well. I would have given both of those awards back to have hit that winning shot. I wanted to be the #1 team. MVPs are forgotten, but champions are remembered forever.

Before reaching our final destination in Beijing, we would play our last 2 preparation games in Shanghai, China. In Shanghai—the vibe, the atmosphere—felt like something special was going on in China. The Olympics weren't in Shanghai, but you could not tell that from the number of security personnel, Olympic greeters, and well-wishers at the airport upon our arrival. By the time I grabbed my luggage and was on the bus, I had already seen a small city-worth of people. Forty-five minutes later we were at the exquisite, 5-star Portman Ritz-Carlton hotel. The hotel and the treatment we received were like nothing I had ever experienced—catered to—hand and foot. I had access to everything—all free!

We had a team lunch, which is a European team tradition. The spread for 20 people was incredible. The amount of food could have fed half the city of Pittsburgh. Everything about this trip to Shangai was first class.

One of our final games of preparation before the Olympics would be against the U.S.A. team. I was excited about this one—a chance to play against the U.S.A. team and the best players in the world. The team had been destroying all their opponents by an average of 30-plus points. Their dominance didn't worry me. Everyone knew that they were the best team at the Olympics. I just wanted our team to play well. I would have never imagined playing against this caliber of players. Now that I was here, I wanted to prove to myself that I could step on the court, compete, and play well against anyone in the world—including America's best.

I decided to go out to the court and shoot a few shots an hour or so before the game. I usually never do this before games. My normal routine is to sit in the locker room with my headphones on listening to my "Let's get it on" music. However, on this night, with so many butterflies in my stomach, I decided to get the blood flowing early. As I walked out onto the court I saw some of the best players in the world going through their pregame routines—Chris Paul, Deron Williams, Carmelo Anthony, and LeBron James all shooting together. I was about to play ball against the "Redeem Team."

As I stopped to watch for a second, there were no head nods, no what's up, no greetings at all—I felt as if I were a foreigner to my U.S. comrades. This didn't faze or disappoint me, all it did was give me the extra enthusiasm to play well. These guys weren't my friends. They would tear my head off, if I let them. As I finished my shooting and left the court, I heard the most thunderous applause I had ever heard in pregame warm-ups. When I turned to look, the cheers were for the best player on the planet—Kobe Bryant. For the next 5 minutes, all you could hear were chants of "Kobe, Kobe" and "M-V-P, M-V-P"—it was surreal. I had never seen anything like this before. All I did was smile and say, "Wow! This man is a mega-star, a global icon."

As I ran out for lay-up line with my team and looked across the court, I saw the other team wearing USA across their chests. A weird feeling came over me for a second. I was actually playing against my native country. It wasn't an eerie feeling—more of a reality-setting-in type of sentiment. It was one thing to play in Russia against other Americans playing for other European teams, but it was a whole other emotion to play against Americans—against your home country. I was moments away from playing against a country I loved. For the next 40 minutes, I would represent Russia and I would do everything I could to help "shock the world" and defeat the U.S.A. team.

When the jump ball began the game, all my butterflies, nervousness, and anxiousness were gone. I was here and ready to compete. In any case, none of this stopped me from shooting an air ball my first shot of the game. That didn't rattle me or deflate me. It got me loose and my mind right to make the next few shots. To my surprise, Kobe Bryant started the game by guarding me. I knew he always defended the best guards on the other team, but Kobe starting on me—letting me know the U.S.A. team was all business. Because he picked me up full court from minute 1, I knew this was not just another game.

When I got the first inbound pass from my teammate and saw Kobe in front of me, crouched in his defensive stance, icy glare looking me dead in my eyes, I said to myself, "Show me what you got Boop, it doesn't get any better than Kobe Bryant in front of you." The great thing about this moment was that I knew how great Kobe was. I had heard about and seen on television his heart, his swagger, his focus, and intensity, but seeing and playing against all that—live—really got me going.

Also, I got to match up against 2 of my favorite young point guards in the NBA, Chris Paul and Deron Williams. I am a huge fan of both of their games, so that was a lot of fun for me. Deron has a deceptive game. He is not exceptionally fast, but he can defend really well, and offensively can get to anywhere he wants to on the basketball floor. I remember him stealing the ball from me at mid-court on a careless spin move I had done. I also remember coming right back at him the next possession and scoring. On the other hand, Chris Paul was simply Chris Paul. He can just flat-out play the game of basketball. He makes everything look so easy and effortless. I love his game. All in all, it was a memorable experience for me. I got to compete and played well against the best players in the world.

There were a few moments throughout the U.S.A. game that are etched in my memory forever. First, I had 2 passing turnovers in the 3rd quarter when we were only trailing by 9 points. We probably wouldn't have won, but damn, that could have scared the hell out of them. Second, guarding Lebron James was memorable. Lebron is quite the physical specimen. You don't know how special he is until you're up close and personal. This man is 6' 8" tall, 270-plus pounds and he moves on the court like me. Plus, he has amazing skills. He truly could become one of the best to ever touch a basketball. Third, it was when I exchanged words with the best player on the planet. On a possession in the 2nd half, I hit a bank shot over Chris Bosh and smiled. Moments later, Kobe Bryant hit a 3-point bank shot and winked at me and said, "But, I called mine." Fourth, at the end of the game my teammate had just gotten fouled. While he shot his free throws Kobe asked me how I liked Russia. He said that I was a very good player and to simply enjoy the life I had created for myself. As the second free throw went through the net, he said, "Keep doing what you do, the whole world knows you can play now." I was stunned—the best player on the planet showing me love. It was an amazingly warm gesture from a phenomenal player. I had earned the respect from the greatest player on the planet.

Although we ended up losing the game by 21 points, I will remember it for the rest of my life. I played solidly but not great, finishing with 17 points, 7 rebounds, 1 assist, and 5 turnovers. I definitely could have played a little better, and I missed a few shots that I usually make, but that is the way the game is. You have to embrace every opportunity you get, regardless of the outcome. The U.S.A. team was the best in the world, no question. I could go on and on singing the praises of every player on that team; they were all that good. However, in 1 game, on 1 night, I truly believed anything could happen. It didn't happen for us on that night, but it was an amazing experience. I will probably never play in the NBA, but I got the chance to experience something more special than playing in any NBA game. I played against the best in the world on a single court, all at one time, in a pre-Olympic game in Shanghai. The Lord continues to bless me, and I am humbly grateful.

The experience was so gratifying. I was able to see my friend and brother of 20 years get on stage and perform against the best of the best. He was able to test his skills and measure his ability against the best in the world. I had a camcorder in my hand and tried to capture every moment of this event. I believe that is what kept me calm.

As Stuart Scott on ESPN would say, Boop was "cool as the other side of the pillow!" I knew he was feeling some type of emotions though. I don't care who you are, if you play basketball and you see LeBron, Kobe, D. Wade, Melo, Dwight Howard and a host of other bad (super-talented) dudes on the other end of the court warming up, YOU FEEL SOMETHING!

The game was pure excitement. The arena was packed and the fans were in their seats cheering during warm-ups. Those fans were ready to see the show. They didn't want to miss anything, including Kobe hitting 8 consecutive shots during warm-ups. All the U.S.A. players were showing AK–47 big love and looked right past J.R. AK is a part of the NBA fraternity; he plays for Utah Jazz.

The United States was blowing every team out by 40 points and exposing dudes' games and abilities in the process. They would try and squeeze the basketball life out of you for real—no competitor wants that. I had seen J.R. compete against NBA guys before so I knew he could play with them.

I knew he had to come with it—his best stuff. After Kobe knocked down a free throw to start the game, instead of running back on defense, he clutched his shorts and prepared to slide 94 feet with Boop. At that moment, I turned into a spectator eager to see how my guy would respond to this type of pressure. It is fair to say this is basketball and you don't know what somebody is going to do until they do it. I didn't focus on the match-up but it caught me off guard because I never expected Kobe to match-up against my guy. J.R. loves to play when the stakes are

(Continued on page 255)

The day after the game I was in for a special treat. On my way to eat at California Pizza Kitchen, I bumped into LeBron James. Not knowing if he felt like talking or being around a dude he didn't know, I ordered my pizza to go. To my surprise, he said, "What's up, J.R.? You wanna chill and eat?" I thought, "What, LeBron knows who I am? Is he crazy? I will sit and talk with you all day, my brother!"

He had 3 or 4 of his close friends with him but he wasn't surrounded by an entourage or anything. Actually, his friends were shopping for a camera and they had asked LeBron for his input. I was shocked that he remembered me, and of course, I took him up on his offer. I didn't want to impose, so I ate my pizza and enjoyed LeBron's company.

I would have never known that he would be so down to earth. He carries his superstardom and global icon image with such ease and grace, it's beyond comprehension. He is a regular (as regular as you can be to be LeBron James), young, intelligent man learning about and enjoying life— just like anyone else—except of course he is a multi-millionaire, and billions of people know who he is. At any rate, we laughed and talked about American football, music, and a myriad of other topics over lunch.

Being a music head, I had to ask him about his big homey Jay-Z and other hip-hop artists. He said Jay would be coming out with a new CD by Christmas, that Lil' Wayne's CD, *Tha Carter III* was solid, and that NAS's new CD, *NAS* was for grown folk and a beast CD. He went on to talk about the Dallas Cowboys as his favorite American football team, and that he would've been a nice NFL WR had he tried to play pro football. I just laughed and of course told him I couldn't roll with him and the Cowboys. I was from Pittsburgh, and the Steelers and the Cowboys were old-school rivals. We laughed and joked about a few more things before I finished my pizza and it was time for me to leave. I had enjoyed my time, wanted to stay, but I didn't want to overstay my welcome. I paid my bill, told him thanks for the conversation, good luck and bring home the Gold, if I didn't. He laughed and said, "Alright J.R., good luck and I holla at you man." When I stepped outside the restaurant, I just smiled and shook my head thinking to myself, "That is a good young brother. I just sat and ate in the company of greatness." Little did he know he did too!

Another high point of my time in Shanghai was the opportunity I got to meet 3 NBA greats—Dominique Wilkins, Willis Reed, and Sam Perkins. I met Dominique in the elevator while on his way to his room with his son. We got a chance to converse. It gave me a natural high when I introduced myself and he said he knew who I was. That was incredible. I knew who he was, no doubt about that. He was someone that I had watched battle Michael Jordan for many years in the Eastern Conference. I also knew him by his nickname, "The Human Highlight Reel." It was really cool meeting him. As for Willis Reed, I had already known a little about him through my godmother. They were good friends so I had spoken to him on the phone before but never met him in person. He was a legend whom I had seen on NBA TV and his heroic efforts in helping the NY Knicks win an NBA championship in the 1970s. He was a good man and someone I tried to emulate both on and off the court. Sam "Big Smooth" Perkins I had never met before. He was so laid back and congenial that I made fun of him right away about being in a magazine doing yoga. He laughed and said he had to keep his body right after ball. We laughed and held a casual conversation for about 20 minutes. He gave me his business card and told me to stay in touch. It was an immense pleasure meeting all 3 great men. They definitely had paved the way for someone like me, and I admired and respected them for that.

After our final, closed exhibition game against China (no fans were allowed to watch), a game we won, we were on our way to Beijing. If I thought that Shanghai had the feel of the Olympics, arriving in Beijing was like something out of a movie. A million people were seemingly at the airport. There were so many photographers, greeters, and people leading the way to baggage claim that I felt lost just standing in one spot. It was simply incredible how patient, kind and helpful everyone was. I don't even remember grabbing my bags off the baggage claim belt. It was as if I had my own personal assistant. I felt like royalty with such treatment.

Once everyone was gathered and on the bus, we had a 45-minute ride to the Olympic Village. Almost all the athletes stay there during the Olympics. There were a million more greeters and assistants trying to get us organized and settled once we arrived. Athletes and coaches were all given security passes with their picture and country name on it. It had to be scanned every time you entered and left the area. Outsiders without a pass were not allowed in. Security was extremely tight.

The Olympic Village was like a United Nations convention. There were numerous high-rise buildings with each country's flag on the outside. That was how you could tell where each country's athletes were staying. The more athletes a country had in the Olympics, the more buildings and flags that country had. The smaller countries, the countries with very few athletes in the Olympics, would share a building with another country. There were sometimes 3 or 4 countries' athletes in one building.

Although countries were separated as buildings, the feel of the Olympic Village was one of unity and togetherness. Every athlete was an Olympian—that was a unifying trait. We were all the best athletes in the world. In spite of this familial atmosphere, for security reasons, the buildings housing U.S. athletes had no flags. Many U.S. athletes didn't stay in the Village. They stayed in 5-star hotels in Beijing. I am not completely sure why but I expect privacy and star power were among their reasons.

As I walked inside my country's building, it felt weird. I represented Russia, but I didn't speak any Russian. I had earned the respect of the other athletes and it did not matter if I spoke the language. I respected and admired them as well. All the Russian Olympians made me feel very comfortable, and I truly appreciated this. In my country's building, each floor was separated by the sport you played. For instance, the 1st floor could be track, 2nd floor women's basketball, 3rd floor women's volleyball, and so on. Our men's basketball team was on the top floor. The floor was a long hallway, separated by 2 elevators in the middle. Each room was college dormitory style. Each player had a roommate, and there were no televisions. None of this mattered to me. Once inside, I just lay on my bed and thought, "Wow! I am at the Olympics."

A few days before our first Olympic game, the buzz around the city was electric. Everywhere I went in Beijing, I saw signs and billboards saying this and that about the Olympics. As the time grew closer to the first game, we started preparing for Iran, the team we would face first. During the Olympics, the basketball games are played at all different times throughout the morning, afternoon, and evening. So, everyone had to mentally and physically adjust their bodies to compete at these different times.

Our first official game was at 9 A.M., so 2 days before the game we tried to simulate game day as best as we could. We awoke at 6 A.M. and did everything we would do the day of the first game. Coach Blatt did a great job preparing us, and we had a very good practice at 9 A.M. on August 8. It felt weird getting ready to play a game so early in the morning. I hadn't played a game at 9 A.M. since high school. I didn't think I would have a problem getting my mind and body prepared for the first game. We all knew how important it was to start off the Olympic Games with a win if we wanted a chance to qualify for the next round.

The biggest event at the Olympics is the opening ceremony. I had never experienced an opening ceremony before so I had no idea what to expect. At first, I didn't even plan on attending the event. I figured I would stay low-key and watch it on television. I decided at the last minute to go. I figured I might as well take it all in and enjoy the entire Olympic experience. This was another example in which God is good all the time. Had I missed the opening ceremony, I would have missed a real treat and regretted not going for the rest of my life. I didn't know the significance of the opening ceremony. It was truly a special event.

I didn't know what was going on or happening when I got off the bus, dressed in my Russian opening-ceremony attire. I saw thousands of people walking into an arena—full of Olympians who wanted to participate. Olympians sat together by country in the arena. The arena was filled with 200-plus countries. There were 2 big screens in the arena. At some point, your country's name would show up on the big screen—it would be your country's turn to get together and head to the stadium. The stadium was for victory laps, from where you could wave at the thousands of fans and supporters in attendance, including the billions watching from home on their televisions.

Before my country, "Russia," was called, I took a lot of pictures with my countrymen and women. As the "black American-Russian," I probably appeared in more pictures than the average Olympian. It was cool though. For those few hours sitting in that incredibly hot arena I felt as if all the hard work, all the tears, all the heartache, all the obstacles were worth this one moment. To have my peers smiling, trying to speak to me in English, taking pictures, and just genuinely showing me love for my accomplishments was an astonishing feeling.

When I heard the word "Russia" over the sound system, there was a thunderous applause in the arena. Every Russian Olympian was yelling and clapping. I think everyone's applause was more of a thank goodness it's finally our turn than, yeah, we get to take that victory lap. It was our turn. I didn't know what was supposed to happen next so I just followed my teammates. We did a 30-minute walk from inside the arena to the stadium. I was excited to see what would happen next. I was anxious and nervous, not knowing what to expect.

As soon as my feet hit the track inside the stadium, I looked up and around. I was in awe. I gazed at the hundreds of thousands of people screaming and yelling in appreciation of all the hard work and dedication it took each athlete, team, and country to make it to the Olympics. The moment sent chills down my spine. With camcorder in hand to try and capture as much of the experience as I could, I started my walk around the track. My knees began to get weak as the lap ended. My legs weren't tired, but I wanted to collapse because of the magic of the moment. I thanked God for giving me the opportunity to experience something so special.

Settled inside the stadium, it was surreal seeing so many ethnicities greeting and embracing as Olympic athletes. It was astonishing to be surrounded by athletes from all over the world. I just couldn't fathom being one of them, but I was. The U.S.A. Olympians were right behind us, so I got to catch up with my good friend Delisha Milton-Jones. We laughed and took pictures like 18-year-old kids at a high school graduation. I mingled with a few other Olympians she knew, and took pictures with them as well. I got to chat and take pictures with Lisa Leslie, Carlos Boozer, Chris Paul, Dwight Howard, and Lindsay Davenport. Everyone was very cool and down to earth. It was a great time. The person I felt for a little bit was Kobe Bryant. This man couldn't move without 100 to 150 people moving with him. Everyone wanted a picture or an autograph. I just looked at him like, "Wow, am I glad I'm not him." I'm sure it has to be tough to be that famous. It must have its benefits as well, but seeing him in that atmosphere let me know that being a global icon has to be tough.

As I watched the fireworks and the last of the opening festivities, I exchanged pins with a runner from Libya, the United States, and Georgia. Yes, the country Georgia, not the state of Georgia. I had a wonderful time and was really glad I decided to attend the opening ceremony. Many say that was the best opening ceremony ever held at an Olympic games. I don't know if that is true or not, but what I attended and was a part of was something very special.

Now that the Olympics had officially kicked off, it was time to get down to business. What more could I ask for? On August 10, 2008, I was in Beijing getting ready to play Iran in an Olympic tournament game. How sweet was that? I wouldn't have guessed in a million years that I would be at the Olympics playing for Russia on my 32nd birthday. I was here and I wanted to win. Things went very well, and we blew out Iran 71–49. We didn't pull away until the 4th quarter, but we gave a solid performance for the first game. I had a good game with 19 points, 3 rebounds, 3 assists, and 5 steals in 36 minutes.

Following the game, I told my hometown newspaper, the *Pittsburgh Post-Gazette*, "I don't think I could have had a better birthday." Winning on my birthday was something special. It's a memory that will last a lifetime. What's more, the Russian Federation was very thoughtful and recognized my birthday by putting a sign up in our building saying "Happy Birthday J.R. Holden." Even a few Russian Olympians that I didn't know came up to me and wished me a Happy Birthday. It felt good knowing that the other athletes didn't see me as an outsider, but as one of them. Outside of that, I didn't do much on my birthday. We played games every other day, so my main focus was to rest and get ready for the next game. Besides, I didn't need to do anything special for my birthday—playing in the Olympics was special enough!

We had a very disappointing performance the very next game against Croatia. We lost by 7 points to a team we had beaten many times previously. Our game was lethargic and without enthusiasm. We got our tails handed to us. We definitely didn't play with a sense of urgency. Croatia played with fervor and deserved to win. I played very passively. I put too much responsibility on my teammates and I blame myself for the loss. I didn't play to the level that I needed to play to give our team a chance to win. However, I didn't have any time to harp on the loss. We were back at it in 2 days. I had to mentally stay focused on the goal at hand, which was qualifying for the medal round. Our road ahead wouldn't be easy, but I believed we could still win a few games.

I believe you can always learn from a loss. It has always been hard for me to watch myself play on film. After the game I called Darius so we could watch the Croatia game and get ready for the next contest. Darius is a tough critic so I knew watching the game with him would be a task. He analyzes and critiques my play with a fine-toothed comb. Since Darius couldn't get into the Olympic Village, we met at a hotel outside of the Olympic Village to watch the film. After 25 minutes of watching, he said, "You didn't play badly, but you didn't play aggressively." The aggressive player and the aggressive team will win the majority of times. He continued, "If you want a chance to win any more games at the Olympics you have to be aggressive, Boop."

The more film we watched, the more he recognized plays throughout the game where I wasn't attacking. By the end of the film session, some things were very clear; I had to take chances and be aggressive for us to have a chance at winning any more games. It was as simple as that. The competition level was too high for me to be passive offensively. I agreed with him without saying a word. This is a perfect example of how our relationship had grown over the years. I have so much respect for his basketball IQ and his willingness to look at a game and see what could help my team win—not just help me play well. That took a certain amount of trust, and Darius had earned that. I knew in my heart that we were fighting for the same goal, "Greatness." That alone put me at ease. As we got up to part ways, he said, "I love you Boop and it's all on you tomorrow." I smiled and said, "Yep, you're right, and Lithuania better be ready." He laughed and said, "They sure better be."

The morning of August 14, I felt like it was going to be a good day. I didn't have any doubts that we would win and I would play well against one of the toughest teams at the Olympics—Lithuania. We had faced this team in prior competitions throughout the past 4 years I had played with the Russian National Team. We knew they were a tough team, but we also knew they were beatable. There were no second chances—that night was a crucial game for us and winning was a must in my eyes.

When I ran out for warm-ups before the game, I waved and said hello to a familiar face, my college coach, Patrick Flannery. He had made the trip to China to support his former player. He had never seen me play live and professionally, and I couldn't think of a better time than at the Olympics.

He was excited to see me play, and I was excited about our upcoming game, just minutes away. The game started with Lithuania scoring quickly and often. However, I never stopped attacking and wouldn't let them pull away from us early in the game. I matched Lithuania's intensity and tried to make plays to help my team gain its confidence. The more aggressively I played, the more my teammates picked up their level of play. Yet, Lithuania led throughout the game. We stayed within striking distance most of the way. As long as the game remained close I knew we would win. I knew I had to play with all my heart with so much at stake. This win could qualify us for the medal round.

At the start the 4th quarter, I decided to guard Sarunas Jasikevicius, their point guard and best player thus far. I had battled with him many times and knew that I had to step it up in order to pull off the upset. With 4 minutes left in the game, I hit a jumper to tie the score at 77. Now, I could smell victory. They seemed to be faltering as we seemed to get stronger. And just like that—we hit a dry spell. We would only score 2 points the rest of the game. We could not score down the stretch, and eventually fell in defeat 86–79. I finished with 25 points on 8–14 shooting, 3–5(3pt), 6–10 (free throws), with 5 assists, and 3 rebounds. What hurt me the most was that I could have easily scored over 30 points and carried our team to victory. I missed a few very makeable shots, and I also missed 4 free throws. We killed ourselves that game by missing 14 free throws as a team. Small things like making free throws can come back to bite you in the end, and they did sting us on this night. This game really hurt because it was within our grasp. We played with a fierce intensity and a sense of urgency that should have led us to victory. Instead, we missed our free throws and didn't get defensive stops when we needed them the most. At this point, we were 1 game away from elimination. It's not over until the fat lady sings, and for us, she had stepped up to the microphone and started practicing her scales. We had one more opportunity to advance—we had to beat Australia.

It was do-or-die time for us. If we defeat Australia, we would move on to the next round; if we lost, we were mathematically eliminated from advancing. In watching film of our opponent, I didn't like the match-up. Australia was big, athletic, and fast. If we had been playing better basketball, I would have shrugged my shoulders at Australia's strengths and liked our chances. However, we had been struggling and would have to play darn-near perfectly to beat them. Add to this, a few of our key players were hampered by injury and I knew this contest would be an uphill battle. Our team leader Andrei Kirilenko was having problems with his fingers, our next best all-round player, Victor Khryapa, was still recovering from a severe ankle injury, and our center, Alexis Savrasenko, was battling a dislocated shoulder. We had a serious task in front of us. It was the first time since I had been playing with the Russian National Team that I doubted our ability to overcome some setbacks. I hoped for a stellar team performance and a trip to the next round.

From the opening minutes of the game, I felt that Australia was the better and hungrier team. They came out energetic and motivated, and set the tone for the game in the first 5 minutes. They were two steps faster than us throughout. We didn't match their intensity and had to fight an uphill battle the whole game. One thing we never did was give up. Early in the 2nd half we cut their lead to less than 10 points, but we never got any closer than 9 points the rest of the contest. I had expected that we would play better but we didn't. It had been a tough Olympics for us and this game had sealed our fate. We would be going home without an opportunity to compete for a medal. I finished the Australian game with 20 points, 6 assists, and an Olympic high for me—6 turnovers. I did try and force a few things late in the game trying to rally us back—to no avail. After the Australian defeat, knowing we were mathematically eliminated, we knew that in the final game against Argentina, we would simply be playing for pride. And honestly, that is how we played that final game against Argentina. We lost a close game and I applauded our team for playing with desire and heart.

Andrei Kirilenko played his best game of the Olympics against Argentina. He had struggled the entire Olympic tournament but he always played hard, and I respect that. Still, we finished the Olympics 1–4.

It wasn't what I had expected but that is the way the ball bounces sometimes. Moreover, I finished my last game scoring 19 points and handing out 5 assists. All in all, I played pretty well at the Olympics but, nevertheless, I went home defeated and empty handed.

With no more basketball to be played, I decided to have a little fun and hang out in Beijing. One of the last nights I was in China, I was on my way to a club when I bumped into the German Men's Basketball National Team. I had met most of the guys before, so I decided to just hang with them for the night. While having a drink in the VIP Olympic section, I bumped into Dirk Nowitzki. I had met Dirk before, but I had never spoken with him. From our conversation, I could tell that he was truly a down to earth—the "guy next door" type. You would have never known that he was a multi-millionaire and an NBA All-Star. What astonished me about Dirk was that he remembered my brother.

Dirk and Darius had met the previous summer at EuroBasket in Spain. Dirk went on to tell me that my brother was asking him all these questions about himself and Steve Nash. Darius told Dirk that he was asking him all those questions because he wanted me (J.R.) to be the best and to learn what the best do. I was sure Dirk met millions of different people every year—for him to remember my brother—put 2 and 2 together—was humbling. It showed me how genuine he was. He is a unique superstar and I am honored to have met him. Although I could have talked to Dirk for hours, I let him go back to his friends and teammates. I am sure it's nice for an NBA superstar to get away from the limelight for a while—just be a regular person unwinding and hanging with friends. Me, I wanted to enjoy my night on the town.

On the cab ride to the airport 2 days after our final defeat to Argentina, it hit me. I was an OLYMPIAN. At that moment, going 1–4 at the Olympics didn't hurt that much. Having sacrificed 4 summers in the States to play basketball for the Russian National Team was well worth it. Losing always stings, but I felt at peace with my performance during the past 5 games. I played each game with my heart. I wasn't successful as far as winning at the Olympics, but I did have good reasons to hold my head high and smile. This journey to Beijing was beyond my wildest dreams. I was nothing but a big-headed 12-year-old named Booper from

Wilkinsburg who wanted to one day play high school basketball. Now, I had just finished playing basketball at the Olympics in Beijing. My heart was smiling knowing that I had made my family and friends proud. I knew my mom and dad were proud parents. I am a by-product of all their love and hard work. I thought about my sister and brother. They loved me unconditionally. Then, my thoughts drifted to my daughter. She was my world, and I want her to always be proud of her father. None of these accolades would have been possible without the love and support of her mommy. Aireka has always been supportive of me and everything I have done to achieve my goals as a basketball player. I love her dearly. I thought about Darius and all we have been through as friends. All the arguments, all the bickering, and all the confrontations were worth the journey we had traveled together. Our friendship was stronger than it had ever been, and I love and thank him for always pushing me to be the best person and player I could be. He did this even when I didn't like it or want to hear it. But, it was the truth and the truth spoken by a genuine friend is true love.

Time magazine wrote this about me before the Olympics:

"Want more proof that the Cold War is over? Then savor a Black Russian. Yes, Russia's Olympic basketball fate is in the hands of an African-American point guard from Pittsburgh. Holden grew up in the Steel City and had a nice, though not astounding college career at Bucknell. Not exactly a hoops haven. He bounced around Europe for a while, playing pro ball in Latvia, Belgium and Greece, before catching with CSKA Moscow, the highly successful Russian club team. In 2003, Holden was named Russian Super League Player of the Year, and became a naturalized citizen of the former Evil Empire so he could play on its National Team (he hadn't met the residency requirements, but the government granted Holden an exemption). Holden hit the winning shot of last year's European championship, as Russia shocked Spain for the title. So, is Holden an Olympic talent or traitor? Let the talks begin."

I have always tried to be a humble young man. I never really got into what others thought of me but I can't lie, I always wanted to be liked. When I read this, I didn't give any thought to people calling me a traitor.

I am a basketball player—playing the game I love—no more—no less. I was fortunate enough to be given a Russian passport a few years ago. With the passport, other opportunities arose.

After hitting the game-winning shot at EuroBasket 2007 in Spain, I was given the opportunity to play basketball in the 2008 Olympics in Beijing. I was going to be on the biggest stage in the world, and with being on that stage I knew I would get the opinions and criticism of a lot of people questioning me and my character. I am a U.S.-born citizen, representing as a Russian citizen for Russian Men's Basketball at the Olympics. This is a once-in-a-lifetime opportunity and I was going to grasp and cherish every moment of it. Believe me—I made the most of my chance to display my skills in front of the entire world by finishing in the top 5 in scoring at the Olympics. My individual performance doesn't take away from our disappointing showing as a team. Make no mistake about that. Individually, I proved to the world that I can play the game of basketball at a high level—for Russia, Belgium, Greece, or the United States. I left the Olympics with my head held high knowing I performed well against the best of the best.

In spite of my personal achievements, seeing all the athletes put their hearts and souls on the line for their country was amazing. Witnessing the joy of victory and the agony of defeat; there was nothing in the world like it. There are only 3 medals to be won at each event, during the Olympic Games, and many athletes and teams would return home without anything. Just being an athlete at the Olympics made me feel successful. Being a part of a select group and a part of history leaves me searching for words. I would have never imagined or dreamed of one day being able to call myself an Olympian. I will forever be in the records as having participated in the 2008 Olympics in Beijing. I am Jon-Robert Holden—a basketball player, a son, a brother, a father, a friend, a writer, and an Olympian! All these things are great, but I am simply a child of God who pushed himself to be the best I could be. And by following my heart and pursuing my passion, I know that He blessed my steps prior to me getting here. And it's because of this I simply and humbly say, "Thank You."

Ending

As I sit in my room, here in Paris after my 8th consecutive Final Four, reflecting on a 64–54 defeat in the semi-final game, my mind races. I get a little frustrated knowing that I let Barcelona sneak a victory. Yes, they deserved to win and played a hard game, but the basketball gods let them off the hook. I missed shots I have made thousands of times, and as I sit and think, Barcelona lucked out this time. If I had hit more shots, would they still have won? I think I let this one slip away. I know that failing—coming up short—is a part of the game and I have accepted that. I don't like it, but I have accepted it. God willing, I live to fight another day, NEXT YEAR.

I sit and think about how this journey started in Latvia. I would have never thought that I would be where I am today—not in a million years. It hasn't been easy and I have had my ups and downs, but this journey has been one of a kind. Everyone says it's about the journey, not the destination. Well, when I fail, the journey is a beast; when I succeed, I smile and say, "What a journey." I guess I am a sore loser. I remember my first few nights in Latvia. I didn't think I could make it playing overseas. I would sit in my room and cry, pondering whether I was tough enough to be a successful basketball player. I couldn't contain my emotions. I had come up short so many times with the game of basketball that in my heart I felt as if I would come up short again.

Then came Belgium—a new life—a new enjoyment and a new-found love for the game and success on the court. I thought European ball couldn't get any better than that. I thought I would be there forever. As I sit here in Paris, I think, "Wow, Russia has adopted me through the good and the bad." It truly feels like a part of me hurts for them when we lose big games. I HATE losing and knowing that so many good people have supported me for so many years; I hurt for them in defeat, as well. I play for my family first, but my heart has love for all those who have supported me. I have love for those who've hated me too.

I remember playing in my first Final Four. It meant so much to me to make it that far. I felt truly blessed knowing that if I ever made it back to another Final Four game, I would bring some loved ones with me to share in the experience. As I sit here in defeat at my 8th Final Four, I sit alone. I remember sitting in the locker room after losing to Barcelona in the semi-final game, drenched in sweat, tears running down my face, thinking that I hoped to make it back some day. Sitting in my room now, having lost to Barcelona in the semi-final game, the thought that this could be my last Final Four crosses my mind.

We finished in 3rd place—arguably the 2nd best team in Europe. It's tough to lose a dogfight of a game like we did against Barcelona. We beat a tough Partizan team in overtime in the consolation game. I hit a 3-pointer with 2 seconds left in the game to win the game by 2. It's always nice to win, but I am more upset about my 3–13 shooting performance against Barcelona than I am happy about hitting a big shot to win the 3rd-place game. I shot 7–26 over the weekend—not great shooting, to say the least. I know that all the greats have struggled in big games. I just always want to be different—the exception—and this weekend knocked me right back to reality. And that reality is—I am truly blessed. Sometimes the basketball gods don't allow the ball to bounce your way. It was a good weekend. History was made. I just wish I could have won another Euroleague title.

This was the 1st Final Four in which I didn't have anyone come support me. It was different but what I needed. I didn't have any duties, responsibilities, or anything else. It felt like any other Euroleague game because I didn't have any other responsibility other than playing the game I love. No loved ones, family or friends; just me and the game. I just went out, played some ball, and relaxed. Outside of wishing I had won another championship, it was a good Final Four. I think the whole season took a lot out of me mentally. Winning means so much, and not winning always mentally frustrates and then pushes me physically to be a BEAST all summer. I love this game. Yep, the same game that I know is slowly coming to an end for me.

And as I sit and reflect, I'm left with one question—what's next for me? What challenges does life pose for me tomorrow? How long will I continue to bounce this ball? And when this ball stops, where will I find myself? Will I be simply remembered as some guy who had success overseas? Will I rely solely on my past and be one who just talks about my glory days as a professional basketball player? Not likely! J.R. Holden represents so much more than an athlete.

Tomorrow you may look up and see me as a lawyer, a doctor, business executive, teacher—or whatever I believe I can be! My story isn't about nice handles or quickness on the court, but about hard work, perseverance, and faith! I know that with God's blessings, I can accomplish anything and I mean ANYTHING!!! My story started in the outskirts of Pittsburgh—Wilkinsburg, Pennsylvania. I've gone from small-town USA to Moscow, and I believe that there is so much more to this journey I call life. I ask you this—where does your story take you? How will you put down your life's events? What do you want to be remembered as? Whatever it is that you dream to become, I encourage and challenge you to do it! Success for you is a recipe that only you know the ingredients for. So to you I say, cook up the success that only you know how to make and allow the world to see your creation!

Thank you so much for reading my story. I appreciate you doing so. And if you would like to email me about what you believe is next for you, I would love to hear from you! You can email me at tomorrow@ jrobholden.com.

Thank you again, and stay blessed.

(Continued from page 68)

himself in a mature way and that was attractive to me. This young brother had intelligent conversation and definitely seemed to be on the right path. I could tell he didn't really know how to take me, so I took the aggressive approach and gave him my number. We could catch up later. Something about him just piqued my interest and I hoped that I got that across.

Boop called me the next day and we talked on the phone for HOURS. I do mean HOURS. That conversation led to many more and we enjoyed the rest of the summer together, until it was time for him to go back to school. Fortunately Bucknell was only a few hours away, so between e-mailing and his weekend trips home, we were able to establish a strong relationship. That was the beginning of our journey together.

(Continued from page 76)

KNOW WHAT THIS MEANS?" He didn't answer, so I answered for him. "This means that all those practices, games, sprints, weights, etc—NONE OF THAT MEANS ANY-THING! After all of that, I still can beat you! And my last official basketball game was in 12th grade!"

At this moment, I was standing at least 2 steps behind the 3-point line as we checked the ball for game point! With that, I made my move. I had him moving with me when I launched a 3-pointer. Truth be told, I was way too exhausted to drive! When I released the shot, it looked perfect—high arching, ro-tation, aim—everything! I was so confident in that shot that I took my eye off the ball and glanced at J.R.'s face as I smiled. HIS EXPRESSION WAS PRICELESS! Silent—composed panic! The smile on my face grew bigger as my shot got closer and closer to the rim! It seemed like the ball was in the air for an eternity—enough for me to do a victory lap around the hardwood! But wait—my shot went in and rattled inside the rim—only to rattle out as I let out the loudest scream! NNNNNOOOOOOOOOOOOOOOOOO!!!!!!!!!!!!!!!!!!!

He got the rebound and backed me down into the paint for the game winner! He deserved it. It was indeed a thriller and the better man came out victorious. We always joke about whether or not he would have blossomed into such a well-respected professional had I made that shot! The answer is a resounding YES! His dream was to play professionally. He always respected my ability and never took it for granted. He was and remains a student of the game and has personified hard work, commit-ment, and dedication to continuous improvement. His career is concrete evidence of his work ethic. But had I made it—it would have been and always remained a great funny story to tell and share! CLASH OF THE TITANS!

(Continued from page 108)

He filled a void in my life and gave me the tools to grow into a better and stronger woman. I was very upset when my season came to an end. I knew our relationship would change because of time and distance and I was scared to lose what we had. Fortunately, J.R. and I have remained close. He is my best friend and will ALWAYS be a part of my life.

(Continued from page 124)

that gave us a 4-point victory over Iraklis. When we went to their gym 3 days later, J.R. returned the favor and hit me for a game-winning, 3-point shot at the buzzer. These types of moments made our time together very memorable.

I am very happy with how J.R. has progressed both as a player and as a young man. I remember watching one of his games and the commentators stating that he was the best point guard in all of Europe. This made me very proud. J.R. had told me about his struggles and how he had made it. These are the types of things that make him the man that he is. Basketball has provided a wonderful life for him and his family. His makeup and personality have helped build his character. Even though he couldn't beat me at shooting games, he still has turned out to be a great guy. I thank God for people like this in my life.

(Continued from page 154)

I replied "Aireka." I then said to him "So what? Are you down here on the tour bus too?"

He replied, "No, I am down here by myself." I learned that he and the other guy who followed me went to school together.

I said, "Oh, OK."

He then said, "Well, my friend told me that you didn't have a contact number so I guess I won't ask for that."

I looked in his eyes and said to him, "Oh, so you are going to believe what your friend says?"

J.R. replied "Well, can I get your contact number?"

I looked him over once again. He was attractive, clean-cut, well-spoken and at least 6-foot tall and I said, "Yes you can." He then whipped out his cell phone and proceeded to put my name and number in his phone. I stopped him and said my name is spelled "A-i-r-e-k-a."

He looked at me and said, "I've never seen Erika spelled that way before."

I said to him, "Let's just say I'm different."

We said it was nice meeting each other and went in opposite directions.

I was in New Orleans for 2 more days. My girlfriend and I went to a couple of parties and lounges and I never saw the guy in the red polo shirt in that time. We had planned to leave the Essence festival early.

I awoke early on Sunday, got dressed, and prepared to check out of the hotel and head to the airport. My phone rang. I answered and it was the guy in the red polo shirt, J.R. He asked how I was doing, and if I was enjoying myself. I told him that actually it really wasn't what I expected. I was leaving to go back home to Michigan in a couple of hours.

(Continued on page 252)

(Continued from page 251)

He replied, "I was calling to see if you wanted to go get lunch." I told him thanks for the offer but, unfortunately, I was leaving.

He said, "You know I kind of felt the same way. It's not what I expected either. I am going to call and change my plane ticket to go home early and meet you at the airport so we can have lunch."

I said, "What? Oh, OK."

He said. "I'll call you when I get to the airport."

I didn't really think that this guy that I had just met 2 days ago would actually change his plane ticket to have lunch with me. I got to the airport. My plane was departing in less than 2 hours. I thought to myself, "I'm hungry, he hasn't called, I'm not waiting any longer." I was ready to eat. I went to get my favorite food—Chinese—and started eating. Five minutes or so later, my phone rang—it was J.R. He asked where I was. I told him that I was eating in the food court. He met me there and ordered a soft drink. We talked until it was time for me to board my plane. We had a good conversation. I told him it was nice meeting and speaking to him. We hugged and I got on my plane. He asked me to call him when I landed to let him know that I had made it safely.

On my arrival home, I did call and leave him a message. He returned my call and said it was really nice meeting me. He wanted my address. I gave it to him. I received flowers from J.R. for the next 3 days, expressing how much he enjoyed the short time we had together. He wanted to get to know me better and see me again. Charming, creative, caring, and confident—this so far was what I knew of J.R. Holden.

(Continued from page 190)

We all stood clapping our hands when the Mayor spoke these words: "NOW, THEREFORE BE IT RESOLVED, on behalf of the Borough of Wilkinsburg and myself, Mayor John A. Thompson, we recognize that Jon-Robert Holden has had an enormous impact on the lives of others and his success in the game of basketball has only been surpassed by his devotion to his family. For these achievements and many others throughout his lifespan with his abundant acts in giving, I bestow my highest commendation and proclaim today July 21, 2006, to be forever known as 'Jon-Robert Holden Day.'"

(Continued from page 194)

That night I kept having faint contractions. At 4 A.M., I awoke from my sleep with the real deal. I roused my mom and said to her, "OK, I think this is it! It's hurting now!" She got dressed and I called J.R. In Russia, it was around 2 P.M. that day. J.R. said that he would get on the next flight out. He was not scheduled to land in Michigan until 6 P.M. the following afternoon.

My mother and I went to the hospital and by then I had dilated to 4 cm (within 12 hours). At this rate, 3 to 4 days looked highly unlikely. The hospital admitted me and my doctor was on call. My mother and I were in the hospital room; they hooked everything up and she called everyone to tell them that I was going into labor. J.R. was on his way from Russia, J.R.'s mom was on her way from Columbus, Ohio. My mother was right by my side coaching me and holding my hand. The pain was intense, but I refused to take any pain medication or an epidural. It would accelerate the labor, and I wanted J.R. to be able to see our daughter's birth. I went into full labor at 3 P.M. and pushed for 10 minutes. At 3:10, Miyana Jade Holden made her debut!

To hold my daughter—to see her was a joy—a blessing—a feeling that I had never experienced before. "It's so nice to finally meet you and hold you" were the first words I said to her as I kissed her. They weighed her, cleaned her, and immediately gave her back to me. I then gave her to my mother, who was awaiting her arrival just as much as J.R. and I. J.R.'s mom arrived at the hospital around 3:30 P.M. J.R. landed in Atlanta around 4 P.M., not knowing that he was already a father.

When he called, I told him of the great news. All he could say was "Really, wow!" I think he was at a loss for words. He said, "I am on my way baby, I love you, I will be there in a couple of hours."

(Continued on page 255)

254

(Continued from page 254)

When he arrived at the airport in Michigan, he came straight to the hospital to hold our blessing—our gift that he calls his "Princess." I saw the joy and amazement in his eyes unveiled—a father's boundless love for his daughter.

(Continued from page 232)

high. He loves to play with something on the line. I think the competitor in him comes alive when the odds are stacked against him. He will never shy away from a tough challenge. I think this game was a test to see if he could play at that "whole other" level.

Once he saw the ball go through the net on a move past Kobe, I know Boop realized it was simply time to just HOOP. Kobe was committed to playing hard defense against Russia's best offensive player. Kobe and J.R. are similar in their desire to compete on the defensive end. I know it had to be surreal for my boy when he talked with Kobe during a foul shot. I have no clue what they said but when I saw Kobe give him that head nod, I said my brother has made an astonishing run in his basketball career.

Thank You's

I HAVE SO MANY people to thank for my life, my career, and steady development as a man. I can't possibly put everyone in here, but just know that I thank you.

First and foremost, I have to thank God. I know my life has been and will continue to be blessed by Him. With Him, I know all things are possible, and I humbly and gratefully say thank you.

To my parents: Without all of your unconditional love, work, support, and sacrificing, I would have never made it this far in life. I love you.

To my 2 older brothers: I couldn't have been more blessed with 2 greater men to help guide me and help achieve many goals in life.

To my loving sister: My 2-years-apart twin, your love and support have gotten me through many lonely nights. Without you, the world does not know who J.R. Holden is. I love you.

To my significant other, my companion, to the most caring and understanding woman I know: I love you. You never let what you wanted get in the way of me accomplishing my goals. Your support has been priceless. I hope that one day I can support you half as well as you have supported me.

To the loving Mardese Holmes-Conyers, whom I have never seen have a bad day: Even when her days were coming to an end, she showed me that with HIM, you can fight with a smile on your face and love in your heart. I love you and we miss you.

To my 2 uncles smiling down from Heaven on me: I am still applying everything you taught me to this very day.

To my brother-in-law: Your addition to our family and support of my career has been unexplainable. You're a great man, and I thank you.

To my Belgium Family (Greta and Melissa Jochmans) who supported me 110% from the day they met me: Your hearts are golden, and I love you.

I could go on and on for another book, but I will keep it short and send my love and true thanks to: Joke Dekeersschieter, Kristen Irwin, Roger Simmons, Ray Smith, Darwin Lane, Mr. J, Coach Fleming, Patrick Flannery, Donald Friday, David Hein, David Andersen, Delisha Milton-Jones, Roland Jones, Antonio Granger, Audrey Croft, Sam "Snoop" Jones, Chris Carr, Celia Anderson, Coach Lucien, Nicole Webster, C. Eugene Uzoukwu, Darrelle (DAP) Porter, Jerry McCoullough, Will B. Hill, Samba Johnson, Heath Bailey, Dominique Fisher, Kristen Katruska, Carrie Jones, Nyree Roberts, Reno DiOrio, Mr. Plumby, Terry Conrad, Wayne Copeland, Victor Alexander, Melvin Booker, Trajan Langdon, Mike James, Tamara James, Nehemiah Brazil, Bob Beck, Jackie Smith-Carson, Tammy Sutton-Brown, Tom Pipkins, Eddie Benton, Nikos Zisis, Henry Domercant, Terrell Lyday, David Bauman, Eugene Mason, Chris Hill, Alexander Raskovic, Mire Chatman, Anne Belle, Lafayette Moran, Pops Mensah-Bonsu, Sekou Hamer, David Vanterpool, Gerald Walker, Gerald Brown, Kirby Spivey, Mike Todd Oliver, Ricky Cannon, Melita Lami, Jamilla Mourad, Maryse Shikayi-Faison, Brian Short, Stephen "Headache" Smith, Arial McDonald, The Whigham Family, The Holden Family, The Future Star Family, Coach Sakota, Coach Ivkavich, Coach Messina, Coach Pashutin, Pastor Otis Carswell, Mr. Kushchenko, Vladimir Putin, Sergei Borisovich Ivanov, Trey Brown, Keion Reynolds, Coach Ben Jobe, Mr. Vatutin, Darlene Casteel, Milton Baxter, Nana and Gran (Flint), and Pastor/stepfather Howard Williams.

To all my family, teammates, coaches, friends, fans and supporters that I have missed here: You know who you are, and I want to say thank you.

Last but not least, I couldn't have made this book a reality without the help, encouragement, hard work, and continued support on this journey from my brother, my good friend, Laroyd Boyd. Without you, brother, I don't know what this journey would have been like. So, from the bottom of my heart, I love you my friend.

Family portrait with Dad, Mom, both siblings and both Grandma's

Picture of Mom, Robyn and me at age 3 (wearing Franco Harris jersey)

Me in first Wilkinsburg midget football uniform at age 5

Michael Jackson impersonation as a kid

High School Senior honor roll ceremony at Linsly School

Graduation day at Bucknell University with college buddies Gene & Willie B.

With Future Stars coach Raj Simmons

First professional interview (Latvia)

MVP trophy at Dubai Christmas Tournament

Team-issued vehicle (Oostende Belgium)

Shooting free throw during game
(AEK in Athens Greece)

2006 semi-final game of Euroleague Final Four

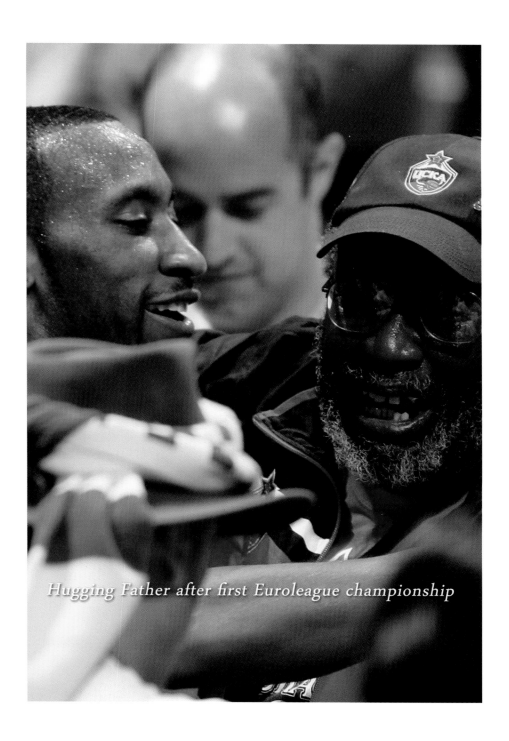

Hugging Father after first Euroleague championship

Celebration with teammates after first Euroleague championship (Prague 2006)

Prague celebration (Trajan Langdon,
David Anderson, David Vanderpool)

Surprise appreciation party organized by sister
(pictured with Mom, sister, and
mayor of Wilkinsburg)

Picture with siblings at sister's wedding

Receiving Russian Super League championship
medal from team president (Sergei Kushchenko)

2007 European championship game-winning shot (gold medal)

Signing basketball at award ceremony for Russian National Team

ProSport magazine cover in Russia

Picture for SI article with Trajan Langdon

Celebrating 2008 Euroleague championship with daughter

Family picture at sister's 30th birthday party

Traveling for 2008 Olympics

283

Being guarded by Kobe Bryant during preparation game against USA Team (2008 Olympics)

Lay-up in preparation game against USA team

Picture with WNBA star Becky Hammond during opening ceremony of 2008 Beijing Olympics

Picture with famous tennis star Lindsay Davenport during opening ceremony of 2008 Beijing Olympics

At Moscow (SVO) airport reading TD Jakes book while traveling to next game

Family trip to Disney World summer 2009

Picture from photo shoot for book premier fall 2010